PERMISSIONS G

IS **JEHOVAH** AN **E.T.**?

by

Dorothy Leon

P.O. Box 754
Huntsville, AR 72740
WWW.OZARKMT.COM

For permission, or serialization, condensation, adaptions, or for our catalog of other publications, write to: Ozark Mountain Publishing, Inc., P.O. Box 754, Huntsville, AR 72740, Attn.: Permissions Department.

Library of Congress Cataloging-in-Publication Data
Leon, Dorothy, 1935-

"Is Jehovah an E. T. ?" by Dorothy Leon
Extensive research explores the possibility that Jehovah of the Bible was actually an extraterrestrial. Contains index and extensive footnotes.
1. Religion   2. Metaphysics 3. Spirituality   4. Bible
5. Jehovah   6. Extraterrestrials
I. Leon, Dorothy, 1935-   II. Title

Library of Congress Catalog Card Number: 2002113061
ISBN: 1-886940-83-5

Cover Design: Jeff Ward
Illustrations: Mary Scott Christy
Book Design: Nancy Garrison
Book set in: CG Times & Courier

Published By:

P.O. Box 754
Huntsville, AR 72740
WWW.OZARKMT.COM
Printed in the United States of America

DEDICATION

This book is dedicated to truth seekers everywhere. May the
Spirit of Truth "set you free" (John 8:32).

ACKNOWLEDGEMENTS

I would like to express my heartfelt gratitude to my husband Glenn,
to Donald Park, Mary Christy, Roberta Hurlbert, Lorae Ireland,
Irene Jones and Carol Webb for their help in editing, and to Mary
Christy for her wondrous art work.

"For the Lord himself shall descend from heaven with a shout with the voice of the archangel, and with the trump of God: . . . . Then we . . . shall be caught up together with them in the clouds to meet the Lord in the air: and so shall we ever be with the Lord." 1 Thes. 4:16-17.

CONTENTS

PART VIII
JEHOVAH GUIDES THE MORMONS

PART IX SUMMARY

ILLUSTRATIONS

FOREWORD

I want to clarify right up front that this is not an agnostic book. On the contrary, it is deeply mystical. My point of contention is with the Old Testament being who has been mistakenly referred to as "Jehovah." Rather than the "True God," I believe this tribal "God of Israel" is an extraterrestrial visitor. Instead of guiding and uplifting mankind, his limited concepts of religion[1] and his machiavellian tactics have controlled politics, promoted conflict, and wreaked untold havoc upon our planet.

For centuries we have blindly revered ancient scriptures without challenging their authenticity. Where did they come from, who is Jehovah, and what part did the ETs play? This book blends science, philosophy, and spirit to offer tantalizing answers to these and other questions.

Jesus, sent to nullify Jehovah's lies with divine truth, was killed; his teachings changed to embrace the status-quo of the polluted priesthoods. When both Jesus and Jehovah return to usher in a "new age,"[2] the "wheat" will be separated from the

---

[1] Religion - A term taken from the Latin "religare," meaning "to bind." Throughout this writing a distinction will be made between religious dogma, philosophical teachings, and true spirituality.

[2] An "age," although marked by the illusion called time, is actually a different vibratory rate in space. Mankind is exposed to various frequencies as our planet passes through each sector of the galaxy. A complete circuit takes 26,000 years, which is divided into twelve Ages, each taking approximately 2160 years. Thus each Age is represented by a different sign of the spherical Zodiac, which the Bible calls "Mazzaroth" (Gen. 1:14; Job 38:32; Dan. 6:27; Luke 21:25). These cycles progress first in a clockwise revolution around the astrological wheel, then counter-clockwise (Eccl. 3:15). This shift occurs at the end of each 26,000-year cycle. Longer cycles are called Yugas. The Hopi Indians refer to them as the "five worlds" Moving in a counter-clockwise direction, we are presently coming to the end of both a 2160-year and a 26,000-year cycle. The Bible alludes to the different Ages (Eccl. 1:9-10; 2:1-8; Eph. 2:7; 3:5, 21: Col. 1:26).

"chaff". The time of their return is upon us. The Bible predicts a "war in heaven" to rescue the positive souls from the "fallen ones" (the Nefilim and the "third of heaven" who followed Lucifer, a being who was "cast out" by Archangel Michael).[3] The purpose of this book is to prepare you for their inevitable mass landing; to sharpen your discernment, by removing the "veils" from your consciousness, thereby allowing you to distinguish the Christ Forces from the "fallen ones."

Great wars in space and titanic struggles on earth between the forces of light and darkness are described in ancient writings, legends and myths throughout Europe, Asia, the Americas, and Australia. The Bible is filled with descriptions of speaking clouds, airborne pillars, chariots, and a vast array of other space technology. The Ramayana describes a double-decked, hovering craft, with a dome and portholes, while the Mahabharata describes, and even gives a schematic of, armed vimanas, a type of flying fortress that made soaring sounds and sent out missiles. Krishna threw laser-like arrows at his enemies, and both the Egyptians and Romans described fiery shields. In 1450 BC Thutmose III documented a circle of fire, in 329 BC Alexander the Great described shiny shield-shaped objects with beams of light that attacked his enemies, and in 322 BC during the siege of Tyre, soldiers observed a large "flying shield" in formation with four smaller ones.[4] The Book of Mormon describes a brass ball

---

[3] Isa. 14:12-16; 24:21-22; Dan. 8:10; Rev. 12:4, 7-9; 17:14. Because the term "Nefilim" means "one who fell down,"or "those who from heaven to earth came", it is sometimes interpreted as "fallen angels". But the term "Nefilim", also spelled "Nephilim", actually refers to those "sons of God" of Gen. 6:4 who "came in unto the daughters of men" thereby creating "giants" or "titans". These immortal space "gods" ("watchers" or "warners") who can make themselves invisible, are not necessarily "angels". The two terms are often used interchangeably, hence the confusion. The reason for the fall of Lucifer was his arrogance. He said: "I will ascend into heaven, I will exalt my throne above the stars of God. I will sit upon the mount of the congregation. . . . I will be like the most high" (Isa. 14:12-14.)

[4] For further information, see: Gods and Spacemen in the Ancient East, W. Raymond Drake, Signet Books, The New American Library, Inc., NY, 1973; Ramayana and the Mahabharata, Romesh Dutt translation, London, Dent, 1961; and Mahabharata, Pratap Chandra Roy translation, Bharata

containing two spindles (a compass), magical urim and thummim stones used by the early Israelites, and descending clouds encircled by fire, while The Urantia Book speaks of silver clouds and Seraphic Transport that settle slowly to the surface of the revolving planet.[5] Is this just science fiction? Apparently not, for there was found in a cave in Turkestan what is believed to be navigation instruments for ancient spacecraft. One instrument, described as a cone-shaped glass with a drop of mercury inside, matches the descriptions given in the Samaragansutradhara, the Ramayana, the Dronaparva, and the Mahabharata.[6]

Have we actually been visited by aliens? To answer this one has only to look at the pyramids of Giza, which are perfectly aligned to true north and are in the same configuration as the three stars in the belt of Orion. The water marks on the sphinx tell us they were built around 10 or 11,000 BC rather than by the later Egyptians or the Sumerians. The Egyptian stela, "Pa-Ra-Emheb," says Ra, who ruled until 10,390 BC, had erected the sphinx in his own image. The Inventory Stela of Cheops, in the Cairo Museum, verifies that both the sphinx and the pyramids existed long before Chephren was born. The stela makes it clear that Cheops wasn't the builder but was merely refurbishing it.[7]

The complex at Angkor Wat in Cambodia mirrors the constellation of Draco as it appeared in 10,500 BC. In 1985, NASA discovered, at the Cytherean Complex on Venus, an identical configuration of the three Giza pyramids and a sphinx.

Press, 1884. See also India's Puranic and Vedic Texts, the Bhagavad Gita, and the Zend Avesta.

[5] The Book of Mormon, First English Edition published in 1830 by The Church of Jesus Christ of Latter-day Saints, NY, 1 Nephi 16:10, 16, 26, 30; 3 Nephi, chapters 17-19; The Urantia Book, copyright 1955 by the Urantia Foundation, 533 Diversey Parkway, Chicago, IL 60614, pp 828, 844, 1755. (The views expressed in this book are those of the author and do not necessarily represent the views of The Church of Jesus Christ of Latter-day Saints or the Urantia Foundation.)

[6] For further information, see: Architects of the Underworld, Bruce Rux. 1996, Frog Ltd., Berkeley, CA, p 255.

[7] For further information see: Architects of the Underworld, pp 264, 272, 369, 375.

At the Cydonia Pyramid Complex on Mars, they found the controversial "face".[8] Evidence of technological aliens, who may have used music and sound waves to move the massive stones, is found in other megalithic structures throughout Peru, Yucatan, Mexico, Indonesia, and ancient Mesopotamia. Perhaps these shimmering structures, acting as landmarks and beacons for cosmic travelers, may have served as observatories and energy accumulators. The Great Pyramid, apparently a military stronghold, as well as an initiation[9] chamber, even withstood atomic blasts during the Pyramid Wars.

For further evidence of alien visitation one has only to read the books of Eric Von Daniken, Zecharia Sitchin, or Robert Temple! Other great writers on this subject are: Jacques Bergier, William Bramley, Robert Charroux, Barry H. Downing, W. Raymond Drake, Paul R. Hill, Peter Kolosimo, Joe Lewels, Bruce Rux, G. Cope Schellhorn, Jean Sendy, and Andrew Tomas.

Is it a mere coincidence that these megalithic structures are built between the thirteenth and thirtieth parallels? Is it a coincidence that our Cape Canaveral conforms to this pattern? Is this wide equatorial band the best area for launchings? If so, who told us? And what about the many ancient stone carvings of beings wearing space suits, helmets and goggles? Who made the laser-like cuts and the tongue-and-groove slots in the mega-ton stone slabs and blocks? Who left the writing in stone that has never been deciphered in the Easter and Canary Islands? Why the huge landing strips in Nazca, Peru, straight lines that have "burn

---

[8] For further information, see: Nothing in This Book is True, but it's Exactly How Things Are, by Bob Frissell, Frog, Ltd., CA, 1994, and The Monuments of Mars: A City on the Edge of Forever, by Richard C. Hoagland, North Atlantic Books, CA, 1987.

[9] Initiation is a spiritual attainment that allows an upliftment of energy; a "quickening." There are five greater and thirty-three lesser initiations or degrees along the spiritual path. The five major ones are: 1. Birth of the Christ Child within (control over the physical body); 2. Baptism in the light of Christ Mind (control over the emotional body); 3. Transfiguration (control over the mental body); 4. Renunciation/Crucifixion (control over the etheric body); 5. Resurrection/Ascension (control over the four lower bodies and the triune nature of body, mind and soul).

pits" where they terminate, indicating computerized clearing from above? What about the star maps of the Dogon tribes that knew the precise movements of Sirius A and Sirius B? Why are the three pyramids of Giza aligned to match the three stars in the belt of Orion? Why is the giant spider on the Nazca Plains an exact replica of Orion? Why were so many of the megalithic structures, as well as the later great cathedrals, erected on specific ley lines to match the patterns of the stars? Does this sacred geometry reflect the cosmic patterns of the universe, "as above so below?"

Utilizing quotes from various sources, I speak to others in their own terminology and offer new interpretations of old concepts. A "dyed in the wool" Bible thumper who read my manuscript commented: "I didn't know the Bible said that!" The same thing happened with a Mormon friend. Other readers said it was such an eye-opener it was shocking; that it could cause a considerable stir in the religious community. My purpose is not to cause a stir, but to foster understanding. Most of the people, who claim to be Bible students, either skim over facts and figures because they aren't interested in the minute details or they fail to understand the symbolic code used by the writers of that era. Many new versions of the Bible, written in modern terms, render entirely different meanings to some of these ancient words, hence my quotes are taken from the King James version.[10] Although

---

[10] "In the year 1607, King James selected fifty-four persons, eminent in learning and particularly well acquainted with the original languages in which the Old and New Testaments were written, to make a new translation of the Bible. They arranged themselves into committees; each was given a portion to translate. They were favored with the best translations and the most accurate copies, and the various readings of the original text. After about three years, they met and while one read the newly formed translation, the rest each had a copy of the original text in his hand. When any difficulty occurred they stopped until by common consultation it was determined what was the most agreeable to the inspired original. This translation was first published in 1610." A History of the Bible, Hubbard Brothers Publishers, PA, published prior to 1880.

The Old Testament mentions many books that have been lost: Book of Jasher; Book of Gad; Book of Jehu, son on Hanaii; Acts of Solomon; Book of Nathan; Visions of Iddo; Prophecy of Ahijah; Lamentations of Josiah; Shemaiah, the Prophet; Chronicles of King David;

mistranslated and altered throughout the centuries, the Bible still contains countless hidden references to cosmic events that our controlling forefathers were not wise enough to remove. Thus it is a valuable key to opening our understanding.

Other writers have discounted its sacredness, saying "God" is merely an ET, but I see the divine plan of our Heavenly Father, an eternal being who is far beyond the planetary regent, Jehovah. Although many authors have left us with an either/or choice, this book, describing the spiritual "kingdom of God within," reveals the unity of these seemingly opposing forces, a unity that allows the negative forces to awaken our memory of the positive, thereby propelling us beyond duality. You can rest assured that the "True God," our Overshadowing Source, who resides in "Paradise," the center of the universe of all universes, does not manipulate mankind, plan on-going wars, or drive a spacecraft!

As you read this book, you will be shocked to find that Jehovah and YHWH may not be the same being; that many of the "messianic" prophecies do not refer to Jesus; that the spirit of Jesus may have reincarnated[11] on earth at least sixteen times; that

---

and Book of the Wars of the Lord. (See: Num. 21:14; Josh. 10:13; 2 Sam. 1:18; 1 Kings 14:6-16; 16:1-4, 7; 1 Chron. 21:8-9; 29:29; 2 Chron. 9:29; 12:15; 13:22; 20:34; 33:18-19; 35:25.) In the New Testament, both Jesus and James quote from books that have since been lost. (See: Luke 11:49-51; John 7:38; James 4:5-6.)

[11] Reincarnation, a tradition for centuries in the Jewish faith, as witnessed by the Kabalistic Zohar. The School of Prophets, established by Samuel, and the later School, established by Elijah at Mt. Carmel, taught reincarnation, as did the Essenes, who came from this tradition. Reincarnation was also taught by the early Christians until 325 AD, when twenty Churches met at the Council of Nicaea. Adopting the new doctrines of hell, purgatory, and the trinity, the existing references to reincarnation were changed or discarded. During this first Council, as well as at some of the later ones--especially the fifth Council of Constantinople, planned by the Emperor Theodosius I and his wife Justinian in 553 AD--entire books were removed. Belief in reincarnation was then declared to be a heresy, punishable by death. The Jews continued to teach reincarnation until 1800 AD. According to Edgar Cayce, the spirit of Jesus had previously reincarnated as Amilius on Atlantis 108,000 years ago; Adam; Enoch (also known as Thoth/Hermes); Melchizedek; Zend; Ra; Joseph; Joshua; Asaph,

nearly all religions ("bindings") came from ETs who manipulated mankind's DNA to keep us enslaved; that the "saints," those who have graduated from this planet and are living in huge motherships, continually monitor us; that Aaron's priestly vest was a "smart shirt"-communication device, which King David later used "to talk to God;" that Jesus, who may have survived the crucifixion and had offspring, was killed because of his usage of the word "kingdom;" and that animal sacrifices were for the purpose of feeding the imposter "gods."

In today's world of frequent sightings, this book prepares you for a mass landing of ETs and the "second coming" of Jesus, by clarifying the different types of aliens and the various "gods." New Agers tend to naively rush into the arms of everyone, while so-called "Christians"[12] tend to label that which they fail to understand as "devil;" neither reaction is appropriate. Jehovah and his "host" have used the negative power of fear, violence, dependence, division and materialism against us for centuries. Why? When we digress into these modes, it strengthens them. Someone once said, laughingly, that negative beings feed on "fear burgers," thoughtforms that are produced by the anxieties of man. To effectively avoid the pitfalls of the "fallen ones," we need to finally balance their negativity with the positive power of

---

chief musician, founder of the guild of singers, and seer for King David; and the priest, Jeshua. I believe the spirit of Jesus incarnated as King David himself, but perhaps the bond between David and Asaph was so close they merely appeared as one. In addition to being the king's prophet, seer, musician, and the chief who ministered before the ark of the covenant, Asaph also wrote many of the psalms. The Bible accredits him with writing Ps. 50 and 73-83, but Edgar Cayce says he also wrote Ps. 117-119. David and Asaph were so united that Nehemiah referred to "the days of David and Asaph." See 1 Chron. 15:17, 19; 16:5, 7, 37; 25:1-2, 6-9; 2 Chron. 29:30; 35:15; Neh. 12:46. See also the writings of Edgar Cayce, A.R.E. Press, Virginia Beach, VA.

[12] A "Christian," according to Manly P. Hall, is: "He who attained reunion with his Christos was consequently termed a Christian, or Christened man." The Secret Teachings of all Ages, The Philosophical Research Society, 3910 Los Feliz Blvd., Los Angeles, CA, 1977, p clxxviii. The majority of people who have called themselves Christians are not enlightened and have not united with their internal Christ Spirit.

love, peace, wisdom, and unity. To accomplish this, we need to detach from the outer world and turn within to awaken to our inner divinity. Paul said: "It is high time to awake out of sleep."[13] Living on the cusp of a Golden Age of Peace,[14] the need for a wake-up call is tremendous!

---

[13] Rom. 13:11.
[14] "The Golden Age of Peace" - The "thousand years of peace" spoken of in Rev. 20:2-4.

PART I

WHO ARE THE E.T.S?

WHO WEARS THE WHITE HAT AND WHO WEARS THE BLACK?

One day while sitting in my office, I heard a loud noise that sounded like someone tearing a piece of material. I had heard the expression, "going within the veil," but this was suddenly ripped! Immediately following the sound, the wall in front of me became, as it were, a gigantic movie screen. For the next half hour, I was shown a vision of Moses in the wilderness.

Amidst thousands of people resembling bedouins, I saw tents spread over an immense area, leaving a huge square in the center. Within it sat a large structure, which the Bible calls a "tabernacle." It was surrounded by a court furnished with a sink and a massive metal barbecue atop a tall platform. Above the "tabernacle," I saw something hovering. Shimmering and glowing, I thought it was what the Bible refers to as "the Glory of God," but upon closer examination, I was shocked to see a spacecraft! I couldn't believe what I was seeing and didn't understand why it was being shown. (See illustration on page 105.)

As the vision continued, I saw a cloudy forcefield around the "tabernacle," into which alien astronauts were transporting. Within a spacious room--the Bible says it was fifteen by thirty feet--they made themselves comfortable amidst "ornate curtains, a golden table covered with shewbread, a golden altar, candlesticks and sweet smelling incense."[15] Wine was also available, but the main course was meat, consisting of sacrificial cows, goats, rams and fowl. The extraterrestrials were enjoying a feast!

Is it possible that the great being the Old Testament calls "Jehovah," ate the animal sacrifices? At the time it seemed absurd, but later I found scriptures confirming that he did indeed

---

[15] Exodus, chapters 25-30.

1

"walk in a tent," saying: "I am full of the burnt offerings of rams, and the fat of fed beasts. . . . The Levites . . . shall stand before me to offer unto me the fat and the blood. . . They shall enter into my sanctuary, and they shall come near to my table."[16] While warning the Hebrews not to worship other "gods," Jehovah also chided: "Where art their 'gods,' their rock in whom they trusted, which did eat the fat of their sacrifices and drank the wine of their drink offerings? Let them rise up and help you, and be your protection!"[17] In another jealous outburst, he declared: "Ye are they that forsake the Lord, that prepare a table for that troop, and that furnish the drink offering unto that number."[18] Evidently the "gods" can be sarcastic! No wonder the ancient Catholics imposed a death penalty upon anyone who dared to read the Bible! How could their priesthoods maintain control if their parishioners knew Jehovah was a manipulating ET?

Still in a state of shock, I began to reason: these interdimensional, and perhaps immortal, beings no doubt spent a lot of time traversing the universe to visit different planets. Something our own astronauts may be doing in the near future now that we have discovered counter-rotating fields, anti-matter, pulse detonation, space warps, curved space, and wormholes, and have realized that the speed of light pertains only to the third dimension. Perhaps the ancient "gods" traveled in a huge mothership named "Zion." Perhaps their only food was "manna," a small, sweet, white ball of protein, the size of a "coriander seed," which the Bible calls "angel's food, the corn of heaven."[19] This "manna" might even be comparable to the capsules our modern astronauts use; a substance that must be awfully boring to eat day after day! A sacrificial barbecue would no doubt be a

---

[16] 2 Sam. 7:6-7; Isa. 1:11; Ezek. 44:15-16; see also: De. 10:8; Mal. 1:7, 12.

[17] De. 32:37-38.

[18] Isa. 65:11.

[19] Ex. 16:31; Ps. 78:24-25; 105:40.

2

welcomed change!

While visiting our planet, these highly-evolved astronauts ("fallen angels, Nefilim," and negative space beings) were evidently able to appear and disappear at will, and yet, like us, they also ate and slept.[20] Able to shift dimensions, these glorious, yet emotional and warlike, beings posed as "gods" in an effort to entice the natives to provide their food. Such manipulation is not necessarily evil, actually their laws of morality and cleanliness helped our ancient civilizations. Like Krishna in the Bhagavad Gita, their messages were practical, prophetic and spiritual in nature, rather than technical. Wouldn't our astronauts do the same if they encountered a backward planet?

The Old Testament indicates that technology--the control and manipulation of natural forces--can make one appear as a "god," especially to a non-technical native population. This was the case when Jehovah staged seemingly-miraculous feats to convince the Pharaoh to release the Hebrews. Is it possible that the "gods" did not really "create" earth, but merely purified the atmosphere, as our modern astronauts are now planning to do on Mars? When earth was besieged with volcanos (the Biblical "fire and brimstone"), the atmosphere became so filled with smoke that it blocked the view of the sun, stars and moon. Genesis mentions the existence of this "firmament" before "the sun, moon and stars were made to shine."[21] Did the "gods" create them on the "fourth day," or did a group of astronauts (technological angels and space beings) merely clear the atmosphere, allowing them to shine through? The evolving "cavemen," could have survived the ice age and long periods of darkness, since the Bible predicts that our planet will again experience this "day of darkness."[22]

Jehovah, describing a "multitude of his chariots" that "cut

---

[20] Ps. 44:23; 78:65.

[21] Gen. 1:6-8, 14-17, 20.

[22] Isa. 13:10; 60:2; Joel 2:2-11, 31; Amos 5:18-20; 8:9; Zeph. 1:14-15; Matt. 24:29; Mark 13:24; Rev. 6:12-17. (A "day" with God can be as a thousand years, 2 Pet. 3:8.)

3

down the trees and dried up all the rivers," said of the human observers: "Their inhabitants were of small power, they were dismayed and confounded; all the inhabitants of the earth are reputed as nothing."[23] This arrogant attitude makes one wonder about the deeper meaning of the Garden of Eden report of the "serpent beguiling" Eve to eat of the "tree of knowledge," while Jehovah had forbidden it.[24] When Adam and Eve's "eyes were opened," Jehovah said to his "host:" "Behold, the man is become as one of us, to know good and evil: and now, lest he put forth his hand, and take also of the tree of life, and eat, and live forever, let us send him forth from the garden." He then set "cherubims" with a high-tech "revolving, flaming sword" to guard it.[25] Was this a robot with a laser beam?

The same scenario is symbolized by Prometheus wanting to share fire with the humans after Zeus, hoping to keep mankind in the role of servitude, had forbidden it. It also appears in the Sumerian Texts when the "god" Enlil wanted to destroy the earth by flood, while Enki, who had previously appeared as a "snake" in the Garden of Eden, took it upon himself to save Noah and his family in a "capsule."[26] Sometimes it is difficult to tell who wears the white hat and who wears the black, but upon closer examination of the Bible and other sacred texts, one discovers that good and evil are but different sides of the same coin. When we finally see how our Divine Source, who is beyond all duality, balances the forces of light and darkness, we realize that negativity is merely an opportunity for spiritual growth. One of the world's greatest and most-colorful mystics, Madame Helena P. Blavatsky, states:

---

[23] Ex. 7:1; 2 Kings 19:23-26; Isa. 40:17; 41:14, 24, 29; Dan. 4:35; Mic. 7:16-17.

[24] Gen. 2:16-17; 3:1-13.

[25] Gen. 3:22-23.

[26] The Hebrew word "tebah" is rendered "capsule. For further information, see Those Gods who made Heaven and Earth, Jean Sendy, Berkeley Books, CA, 1972.

"Lucifer is the Logos in his highest, and the 'Adversary' in his lowest aspect, both of which are reflected in our Ego. . . . Shadow is that which enables light to manifest itself, and gives it objective reality. Therefore, shadow is not evil, but is the necessary and indispensable corollary which completes Light or Good: it is the creator on earth."[27]

Lucifer is described in the Bible as the "prince of this world," who programs men's minds and hinders with "stumbling blocks." Because overcoming obstacles makes us stronger, God allowed Job to be tested by "Satan", (a term derived from the Egyptian "Set," an evil influence rather than a personality). Thus "the wheat and tares grow together."[28]

Rudolf Steiner, describing this dark or shadowy energy as two forces, "Lucifer and Ahriman," says Lucifer is the fluidic warmth that unifies (the nature of religion), while Ahriman is the rigid coldness that differentiates (the material nature of science). Because too much Luciferian influence brings inner hallucinations and fanaticism, while too much Ahrimanic influence brings outer delusions and materialism, Steiner says the contrast between them enables men to perceive a third reality, the Christ Force, without which there is no progress.[29] The world, therefore, is balanced, as it were, on a three-legged stool. The

[27] The Secret Doctrine, H. P. Blavatsky, Theosophical Publishing Co., NY, 1888, Vol. II, p 162, 214.

[28] Job 1:6-12; 2:1-7; Ps. 68:18; 69:22-23; 78:49; 139:7-12; Isa. 57:4, 14; Jer. 6:21; Amos 3:6; Zech. 3:1-2; Matt. 13:24-43; Mark 4:13; Luke 8:12; 22:3; John 1:14-17; 12:31-32; 13:26-27; 14:30; 16:11; Acts 5:3; 26:18; Rom. 9:32-33; 11:9, 11; 1 Cor. 2:8; 5:5; 2 Cor. 4:4; 12:7; Eph. 2:2; 1 Thes. 2:18; 1 Pet. 5:8; Rev. 2:13.

[29] Christ in Relation to Lucifer and Ahriman, Steiner, 1915; The Ahrimanic Deception, Steiner, 1917. See also: Isis Unveiled, Vol. II, H. P. Blavatsky, Theosophical University Press, CA, 1976, p 237; The Secret Doctrine, Vol. II, p 479.

Luciferic forces have ruled for centuries, but now, in our final test before the emergence of the "Golden Age," the Ahrimanic forces of materialism are overshadowing the Luciferic forces of religionism. It is the forces of Ahriman that will focus into the predicted "anti-christ." Both the Luciferic and the Ahrimanic forces strive to veil the light of the inner Christ.

DIFFERENT LIFEWAVES

After the eviction of Adam and Eve, Jehovah "cursed the serpent" (Enki or Prometheus) by forcing him to "go on his belly and eat dust" (to labor in the mines of the "lower world," referring to those in Africa as well as those within the ocean) and by putting "enmity" between his "seed" and the "seed" of the woman. This fiasco brings up many questions. Was it this "fall" that caused our "carnal mind" to become at "enmity with God?"[30] If Adam and Eve were the only people on earth, why was their son Cain afraid to leave Eden, fearful that "everyone" would slay him? Who was "everyone?" Who populated the "Land of Nod on the east of Eden," to which Cain went?[31]

Throughout the Bible, emphasis is placed upon different groups of people, thus the Hebrews and the later Moslems were told not to marry outside their race.[32] Isaiah speaks of the "the planting of the Lord," while Jesus says: "Every plant, which my Heavenly Father hath not planted, shall be rooted up."[33] The Bible also speaks of "those whose names were recorded from the beginning," and "those whose names were not written in the Book of Life." Some have a soul while others were not created in the "image of God." These have no "inheritance," but can be

---

[30] Gen. 3:14-15; Rom. 8:7.

[31] Gen. 4:13-16.

[32] Gen. 3:5-15; Matt. 3:7; 13:38; 23:33; John 8:44; Acts 13:10; Koran

[33] Isa. 61:3; Matt. 15:13.

"adopted" as a "son of God."[34]

According to Blavatsky, after the creation of the first two "root races,"[35] the Divinity who resides behind the "veils" sent a group of "solar angels, or sons of Brahma," also called "Kumaras," to our solar system during the evolution of our "third root race," some three million years ago. Although some of the Kumaras incarnated on earth, the great being, Sanat Kumara, appointed to serve as "Lord of the World,"[36] resided in an etheric temple, a type of divine mothership or "Merkaba Vehicle"[37] that hovered beyond the earth's atmosphere. The spirit of Jesus, working with Sanat Kumara, also called "Ancient of Days," and other members of the Great White Brotherhood,[38] came to "save"

---

[34] Matt. 7:23; 25:12; Luke 13:25, 27; Acts 26:18; Rom. 8:15-17, 21, 23; 9:8, 26; 11:17-24; Gal. 4:5-7; Eph. 1:5, 11, 14, 18; Col. 1:12; Heb. 9:15; 1 Pet. 1:4.

[35] Blavatsky calls the first "root race," the astral "Self Born;' the second, the boneless "Sweat Born;" the third, the androgynous "Egg Born." The Secret Doctrine, Vol. II, pp 95, 164-165, 172-173, 247-248.

[36] The Secret Doctrine, Vol I, pp 89, 457-8; Vol. II, 95-96.

[37] Merkaba Vehicle - MER means place of ascension or unity; KA means "Spirit"; BA means body. This spiritual, rather than mechanical, vehicle is composed of energy moving in counter-rotating fields to unite body and spirit. This action provides a divine vehicle to enter the higher dimensional frequencies of other universes. The present-day mystic, Drunvalo Melchizedek, who instructs his student to create an etheric "merkaba vehicle," says this was the original method of travel throughout the universe. He says the great "fall" in consciousness occurred when a group of cosmic/angelic beings decided to create material, rather than etheric, vehicles. He teaches that anyone traveling in a material vehicle is inferior in consciousness to the Great Cosmic Beings and the Ascended Masters, who still operate their etheric vehicle. For further information on Drunvalo Melchizedek, see: Ancient Secret of the Flower of Life, Vol. 1 and 2, Light Tech Publications, 2000.

[38] GREAT WHITE BROTHERHOOD - An organization of seventy Brotherhoods. Those wearing white robes are ascended; those wearing golden robes are unascended (Ps. 16:3; Acts 2:34). The purpose of the Brotherhood is to administer the Cosmic Law directly from the Heart of God, thus keeping it free from distortion. (According to Edgar Cayce, the White Brotherhood was founded in Atlantis by Amilius, a former incarnation of Jesus. See the writings of Edgar Cayce, A.R.E. Press, Virginia Beach, VA.)

mankind from the dictatorial precepts of Jehovah, who had created in his own image rather than honoring the divine image of the Heavenly Father.

An ancient Mesopotamian tablet, the Atra-Hasis, reveals the tremendous difficulties the "gods" had with their mining operations before the "creation" of man.[39] Was the male/female version of mankind, "created" in the mid-Atlantean period, merely to serve as slaves? Are the ancient legends true about man being biologically engineered in an Edenic laboratory for the purpose of mining gold in Africa? Was this gold, or "golden fleece," needed to operate the alien spacecraft and to replenish their planetary atmosphere? Is it a mere coincidence that many of the ancient megalithic structures are located near mining sites? The Bible makes it clear that the precious metals and stones belonged to the gods.[40]

Was the "creation" of Adam and Eve a divine act or merely a technological insemination between the cosmic travellers and earth's "third root race," or with the higher-evolved bipedal-type of anthropoid apes? Perhaps there is no "missing link" in evolution because it was suddenly engineered by aliens. After artificial insemination, was the sperm of the so-called "cavemen" carried within the womb of the female "gods" to create "blue blooded" offspring? Is this why the Old Testament so closely links Jehovah to the "womb?"[41] Were the Pharaohs called "gods" because they were descendants of the aliens? Is this why the "chosen" races were not to marry outside their tribes, lest they dilute their cosmic bloodline? Have the royal families throughout history married their own brothers and sisters to uphold this policy?

The Koran, speaking of a "Jinn" race of people that

---

[39] For further information, see: Atra-Hasis, The Babylonian Story of the Flood, by Lambert and Millard, Oxford Clarendon Press, 1969.

[40] Gen. 2:11-12; Job 22:24-26; 28:1-19.

[41] Gen. 20:18; 29:31; 30:2, 22; Judg. 13:5-7; 1 Sam. 1:5-6; Ps. 22:9; Isa. 44:2, 24; Jer. 1:5; Luke 1:15-19.

existed before the "clay" creatures, says of this biological engineering: "Allah [Jehovah] created you from dust; then from a sperm-drop."[42] The Popul Vuh, an ancient Mayan scripture, refers to four different types of experimental man created as slaves for the "gods" [Parenthesis are mine]:

> "Let us make him who shall nourish and sustain us!...We have already tried with our first creations, our first creatures; but we could not make them praise and venerate us. . . . They were endowed with intelligence; they succeeded in seeing, they succeeded in knowing all that there is in the world. . . . Let their sight reach only to that which is near. . . . Then the heart of heaven blew mist into their eyes, which clouded their sight as when a mirror is breathed unto. In this way the wisdom and all the knowledge of the four men [first four types of creatures] were destroyed."[43]

This limited state of consciousness is the veil or "carnal mind," that stands between us (our ego self with a little "s") and our Divine Spirit (our Real Self with a capital "S"). Jesus taught mankind to supersede the Jehovistic priesthoods by going directly to the "kingdom within." (Jesus was not the first person to reject the polluted priesthoods. Hammurabi, Emperor of Babylon, in 2240 BC, opposed them, as did Akhenaten, in 1375 BC, and Sennacharib in 691 BC.) The Old Testament prophet Micah promised this mystical freedom, saying: "They shall sit every man under his vine and under his fig tree and none shall make

---

[42] Koran; Surah 15:27-45; 35:11.

[43] The original Mayan codices were transcribed into Latin in 1558 by a Quiche man; translated into Spanish by a priest in 1701. For later translations see: Popul Vuh, The Sacred Book of the Ancient Quiche Maya, Goetz, Delia and Morley, Norman University of Oklahoma Press, OK, 1950; Popul Vuh, Ralph Nelson translation, Houghton, MS, 1976.

them afraid."[44] This is a veiled reference to our Divine Spirit, also called our Real Self, Higher Self, or "I Am Presence," all of which allude to the divine spark of God within. The struggle to remember our divine connection is confirmed throughout the Bible. Jehovah says: "Make the heart of this people fat, and make their ears heavy, and shut their eyes; lest they see with their eyes, and hear with their ears, and understand with their heart, and convert and be healed."[45] At the Tower of Babel, the "gods" purposely scattered and confused mankind. Why? To keep us dependent upon them!

And what about the "serpent?" Is he a good or a bad guy? Why is it a symbol for knowledge? Why did Prometheus teach mankind the arts? Why are the enlightened people of India called initiates or "Nagas," meaning serpents? Why is knowledge associated with "the east?"[46] Why are the entwined serpents, the caduceus of Thoth/Hermes, who is also known as Enoch,[47] used on the modern medical staff? Why is the Hopi's most sacred ritual called the "snake dance"? Why was Jesus, when he visited the Americas, known as "Quetzalcoatl," meaning winged serpent or "flying wiseman?" (The wings indicate mastery over the lower serpentine energy, similar to the virgin Mary and Archangel Michael standing on the head of the serpent.) And why did Moses set a "brazen serpent" upon a pole?"[48] In addition to the "serpent" in Eden, a painting in a royal burial chamber depicts a Pharaoh riding on the back of a flying snake. India's Book of Dzyan speaks of a serpent race descending from the skies to help mankind. The Chinese claim to have obtained their royalty from celestial dragon ancestors. Who is the "serpent "?

---

[44] Mic. 4:4.

[45] Isa. 6:9-10; 29:10; 42:20; see also: Ex. 34:33, 35; De. 29:4; Isa. 6:9-10; 29:10; Jer. 5:21; Ezek. 12:2; Matt. 13:11, 14; Mark 4:12; Luke 8:10; John 12:40-41; Acts 28:25-28; Rom. 10:4-7; 11:7-10; 2 Cor. 3:13-14; Gal. 3:23.

[46] Judg. 6:3; 1 Kings 4:30; Job 1:3; Ezek. 25:4.

[47] Isis Unveiled, Vol. II, p 463.

[48] Num. 21:4-9.

Although some of you may not accept the concept of "channeling," Barbara Marciniak, who claims to receive messages from a group of benevolent Pleiadians, offers an interesting answer:

> "The original planners of earth were members of the Family of Light. . . . During earth's early history, there were wars in space for ownership of this planet. . . . These new owners . . . are the beings spoken of in your Bible, in the Babylonian and Sumerian tablets, and in texts all over the world. . . . The original human was a magnificent being with twelve strands of DNA. When the new owners came in, they worked in their laboratories and created versions of humans with . . . only a two-stranded double helix that would lock you into controllable, operable frequencies . . . The new owners . . . have the ability to become physical, though mostly they exist in other dimensions. . . . God with a big G has never visited this planet as an entity. . . . You have only dealt with 'gods' with a little g who have wanted to be adored and to confuse you. . . . The original planners . . . intend to alter the frequency of earth to that of love. . . . to reinsert light on this planet and restore earth."[49]

Are we someone else's property, mere caretakers of a planet that is owned and controlled by aliens who pose as "gods?" Or does it only appear this way before the Self-realization memory of our divine connection? Additional information about

---

[49] Bringers of the Dawn: Teachings from the Pleiadians, Barbara Marciniak, Bear & Co., NM, Copyright 1992, pp 4, 6, 14-18, 26-27, 54. Other books by Barbara Marciniak include: Earth: Pleiadian Keys to the Living Library, and Family of Light: Pleiadian Tales and Lessons in Living.

the manipulation of mankind and the struggle to regain our twelve-strand DNA, our "first estate,"[50] to become a "Galactic Human," is given by "The Ministry of the Children:"

> "To discuss the present tear in time, also referred to as the rend in the fourth veil, we must understand that we have been trapped into reincarnating into a fallen program, inside of an artificial time continuum, so as to be held as captives for use by the lower E.T. races. . . . We have lost our true alignment with divine hierarchy and have been tricked by a lesser intrusionary force we shall call the Nefilim (fallen angelics combined with the lower E.T. race genetics). . . . Jehovah is not the creator. He was assigned to this galaxy during the fall along with Lucifer! He was and is a part of the fallen time zone. . . . There is a greater source than this fallen Patriarchal deity."[51]

This "Greater Source" will be discussed in Part II.

A VARIETY OF ALIENS

Obviously different levels and types of space beings come from different areas for different purposes. Where are they from? Underground facilities, the "inner earth," other planets in our solar system, other galaxies or universes, parallel worlds, different spiritual planes and dimensions, or corridors and windows in space? Jelaila Starr, in her book We are the Nibiruans, outlines four lifewaves: "the felines ('cat people'),

---

[50] Jude 6. We were a divine spirit before being encased in flesh.

[51] The Solar Cross 11:11 Stargate, Amarushka and Joshua, Ministry of the Children, AZ, 1998, pp 26, 38-39. See also Becoming a Galactic Human, by Virginia Essene and Sheldon Nidle, S.E.E. Publishing Co., CA. 1994.

carians ('bird tribes'), reptiles ('lizards' with vertical pupils), and humans." Clarifying the interactions between them, she says Jesus is of the human Lyran and later Sirian group; the reptilians are from Orion; and the residents of this planet are a combination of all four lifewaves.[52] Other alien visitors have been reported from Zeta Reticuli, Pleiades, Arcturus, Andromeda, Cassiopia and Ganymede, as well as from our own solar system. In addition to a variety of lesser types of ETs, there seem to be two main types.

First, there are the tall, handsome "Nordics," a universal "Peace-Keeping Force" also called the "Christ Forces in Space," who guard our solar system, offer spiritual guidance and prophetic warnings, and prevent nuclear holocaust. According to reports, they have been monitoring earth and taking ecological samples to prevent us from destroying ourselves, as well as helping us to restore our DNA so we can reconnect our divine image and similitude to become fourth or fifth dimensional beings. It was to reclaim man's spiritual gifts that the "Office of the Christ" was established. When Jesus sacrificed himself on the cross, his drops of blood falling to the ground helped to balance our planetary karma by transmuting the damage caused by the "fallen ones." (Whether or not Jesus actually died on the cross is controversial, but he did spill a few drops of blood on the ground when his side was pierced.)

Jan Van Nelsing, in his book: Secret Societies and Their Power in the Twentieth Century, relays a message from these tall, beautiful "Nordics," who, after failing to gain cooperation from our government concerning a policy of disarmament, are attempting to reawaken our spirituality by contacting various individuals.[53] In the late 1970's and early 1980's, I was one of the messengers contacted by members of the "Christ Forces in

---

[52] We are the Nibiruans, Jelaila Starr, Granite Publishing, NC, 1999, pp 61-71, 83, 96.

[53] Secret Societies and Their Power in the Twentieth Century, Jan Van Nelsing, Ewertverlag S. L., Gran Canaria, Spain, 1995.

13

Space." The messages from these beautiful creatures, unlike the threats of Jehovah, were similar to those of Jesus: love and peace, with a complete absence of fear.

Secondly, there are the four-feet tall, spindly "Greys," with large eyes and small slots for ears, nose and mouth, whose race is evidently in danger of extinction unless they mutilate animals and abduct humans to utilize their reproductive organs. In return for this favor, they evidently share technological secrets with our government. Their actions, as well as those of our government, may seem like a travesty to our freedom, but theoretically we may be indebted to the Greys because they might be us returning from the future, after having been mutated in a nuclear war. Perhaps they traveled back in time to change our timeline in order to prevent a third world war. Another theory is that they are checking our reproductive organs, as well as those of cattle and other animals, to determine the effect of earth's pollution on our reproductive capabilities. Since we are in danger of becoming sterile, this genetic engineering may ensure our survival.[54] They are also said to be monitoring the amount of pollution in our oceans and our atmosphere. Another type of aliens are called "Verdants." In The Contact Has Begun, abductee, Philip Krapf, says these five-feet tall beings, with large ears, small nose and mouth, and slanted slits for eyes, are helping us to prepare for the future.[55]

According to the Dead Sea Scroll Book of Amram, the father of Moses, Amram, was abducted by a reptilian "god." Moses was later beamed aboard. Abducting and placing implants in different members of the same family is evidently a common practice that is still happening today. It has not been ascertained whether these implants are for control or if they grant psychic powers; perhaps a little of each! Abductions were so prevalent in

---

[54] For further information see: Cosmic Voyage, by "remote viewer," Courtney Brown, Dutton Books, NY, 1996, pp 63-75.
[55] The Contact Has Begun, Philip Krapf, Hay House, CA, 1998.

the eighth and ninth centuries AD, that Charlemagne even tried to impose penalties on these "Tyrants of the Air."

Others who are variously called elves, genies, kobolds, trolls, gentry, leprechauns, mini-hunies, or little people, may be "elementals." Such beings are not only alluded to in countless legends and fairy tales, but also in spiritual books, such as Comte De Gabalis,[56] in which Merlin, the Magician,[57] is described as having an "elemental" father. (This, however, may have been a "blind" for a higher being.)

Grotesque looking aliens who resemble insects, as well as reptilians with vertical pupils and lizard-like skin, have also been reported around the world. But not all aliens who look different are necessarily negative. This was epitomized in the movie, "E.T.," the ugly alien who merely wanted to "go home." Bruce Rux, in his descriptive book: Architects of the Underworld, relates:

> "American Indians and Australian Aborigines both refer to 'creatures without mouths' who come down out of the heavens. . . . The Iban of Borneo and the Aborigines of former Arnhem Land in northern Australia have beliefs in benign spirit beings who bear them aloft in the sky while they sleep in order to bestow powers and abilities on chosen members of the tribe, and be 'initiated into the select groups of knowledgeables.' . . . Kachinas (deified spirits of the Hopis) . . . could perhaps be robots. . . . The chief early kachina, who led the Hopi to their present locations . . . is the most interesting of all for his resemblance to reported insectoid UFO occupants. [He], Koko

[56] Comte De Gabalis, Villars, Abbe N. De Montfaucon De, The Brothers, London, 1670.

[57] Magic was an ancient term for science, sacred geometry and cosmic activity.

15

Pilau, is an entirely benign creature, one of the two mahu or 'insect people resembling the katydid or locust.' . . . The similarity of Kachina initiation to UFO abduction should be apparent. . . . Signs of such initiation have been encountered in Betty Andreasson and Herbert Schrimer. This aspect has been ignored or passed over by most abductologists. . . . California's Paiute Indians claim an ancient, superior civilization preceded their own--the Hav-musuvs--who flew in silvery sky canoes, and carried 'a small tube' that could be held in one hand and would stun their enemies. . . . The most interesting of all is this cavalcade of potential historical robot-beings is the creature called Abit, or Babait, from ancient Egypt. He is referred to in chapters 76 to 104 of the Book of the Dead. . . . His name means 'Mantis'--i.e., the praying mantis, like Koko Pilau and the 'ant people' of other tribes."[58]

But regardless of their well-meaning helpfulness, these insectoid-looking aliens, or robots, are evidently not among the highest types of God's creatures. A good rule of thumb is that those who were created by God "in his divine image" are beautiful. Another guideline to discernment is that the positive beings always preface their messages with "Fear Not."[59] Therefore, any being who evokes fear, whether by its words or by its looks, is not a messenger from the "Highest God." One of the greatest tests during the emergence of the "Golden Age" will be the so-called "lift-off" or "rapture." The negative forces may lure you into their man-made motherships by fearfully exclaiming "Come aboard now, your planet is capsizing!" The positive

---

[58] Architects of the Underworld, pp 192, 196-197, 212, 216, 355.
[59] Gen. 15:1; Dan. 10:12; Luke 1:13, 30; 2:10.

forces, radiating a "peace that passeth understanding " from their etheric "New Jerusalem"--the place that Jesus went to prepare for us[60]--will lovingly extend a helping hand. It is up to you to discern the difference between fleeing in panic and floating on the wings of love!

ASSIMILATING THE VISION OF MOSES

When the vision of Moses that I was being shown ended, a voice stated adamantly: "Write about it!" That startling event took place nearly ten years ago and has been continually haunting me! Reluctant to write about such a controversial subject, I kept pushing it aside until my small inner voice became a shout! Living on a planet in which spacecraft have evidently made periodic visits throughout the centuries, and are about to make a dynamic reappearance, it is important that this information be shared to help others understand these extraterrestrials, who have not only molded humanity but also seem to be the basis of nearly all religions.

If people were fooled by them thousands of years ago, perhaps we are still being manipulated by them today! Perhaps they are even responsible for the proposed "One World Government." Perhaps instead of food, they now want our very heart and soul! But, lest we become embroiled in fear, which merely strengthens the dark forces, let us realize that some of them may not be as manipulative as Jehovah, who many believe to be a reptilian being. Some of the space beings are striving to help us. The tall "Nordics" are believed to be a branch of the divine hierarchy's "Family of Light" and referred to in the Bible as the positive "angels" who did not "fall". They have promised a divine intervention, a "shortening of our days" of "tribulation," during the height of "Armageddon", a battle that is to take place in the Middle East. At this time, Jesus will appear in the skies in

---

[60] John 14:2.

17

great light and "there will the eagles [spacecraft] be gathered together."[61] Also during this time, there will be a mass landing of ETs. Thus the greatest challenge of our era is the test of discernment. Will we be able to discern the divine "Family of Light" from the "fallen ones?"

I believe with all my heart, mind, body and soul that there is an invisible God--"with a big G"--a Mind Force pulsating within every atom and electron in the universe. This Force guides and protects us by projecting a spark of its presence into every individual. Interconnected by divine threads of "mana," we are one with all creation. The "Father Within"[62] can be experienced in meditative communion, a mystical "mind born" samadhi or rapture--a fourth-dimensional Yogic or Zen-like state that transcends both time and space, to unite our heart and mind with our Divine Source. But I no longer believe this invisible Force is the exoteric Jehovah. In deep meditation, enfolded in a blissful flow of energy, I have communed with the Supreme God--the Prime Creator or Architect of the Universe, of which Jesus is a "Carpenter" and Paul and other initiates are "Master Builders." I have seen whispy-looking etheric angels, who have such a dynamic flow of energy from their heart that it is often mistaken for wings. But these divine beings certainly did not land upon a mountain top, with "thunder and smoke," and they definitely did not instruct me to sacrifice animals to feed them!

The word God comes from Od or Odic Force, representing a divine androgynous power that can be experienced by blending the incoming "father" aspect of our crown chakra's[63]

---

[61] Isa. 2:1-4; Dan. 9:26; 12:1; Amos 8:9; Joel 2:2, 31; Hab. 3:3-6; Zech. 14:2-3, 6-7, 15; Matt. 24:4-22, 27-28; Rev. 16:16.

[62] John 14:10; Luke 17:21; 1 Cor. 3:16; 6:19-20.

[63] Chakra - A Sanskrit word meaning wheel or disc. Each of our seven main chakras spin when activated. The Bible refers to them as "seven seals, pillars" or "trumpets" (Prov. 9:1; Eccl. 12:1-7; Rev. 8:11). They are described individually as "crown" (Rev. 3:11); "pineal" or "third eye" (Gen. 32:24; Matt. 6:22; "throat" (Prov. 3:22; 6:21; Matt. 8:8, 16; 11:29-30); "heart" (Jer. 31:33; 2 Cor. 3:3); "solar plexus" (Ps. 23:2; 69:2-3; 124:4-5; Prov. 20:27; 27:19;

wisdom with the uplifted feminine aspect of our root chakra's intuition. (This male/female representation is not sexual, but a sacred principle, understood by the ancients as the union of sky and earth.) Like a shepherd feeding her sheep, the mother aspect (the Holy Spirit/kundalini) triangle ascends to meet the descending father triangular aspect. This polarization, merging, or "mystical marriage" of spirit and matter, as depicted by the "Star of David," "quickens"[64] us to create a third power, the birth of the Christ Child within. It is this birth of the Christ Spirit--the second coming of the Christ that transforms us. This is what Jesus came to teach.

The Jehovistic forces, not wanting us to follow the feminine intuition that enables us to go directly to our Source tries to keep us dependent upon them and their patriarchal priesthoods. This is another reason why Jesus was killed and why one of the first things the so-called "Christian" churches did was to forbid the teachings of the Mother Goddess, thereby squelching our intuitive/mystical powers. Although they honored the virgin Mary to a degree, the church was basically masculine. The later Protestants became even more masculine and intellectually oriented by ignoring the saints and the power of exorcism. The forthcoming "Aquarian Age," the "Golden Age of Peace," will place more emphasis on the Mother Goddess, the Holy Spirit aspect symbolized by the dove. How can we give birth to Christ Consciousness without the mother aspect?

THE DIFFERENT AGES

Speaking of Ages or astrological eras, I would like to explain that each Age brings a different quality and is represented

---

Lam. 3:54; John 7:38); "spleen," the "strength of the loins" (Job 40:16; Prov. 31:17; Eph. 6:14; and "root" (Prov. 10:25; Isa. 28:16).

[64] John 5:21, 26; 6:63; Acts 10:42; Rom. 4:17; 8:11; 1 Cor. 15:36, 45; Eph. 2:1, 5; Col. 2:13; 1 Pet. 3:18; 4:5.

by a different phrase. On Atlantis, during the Ages of Scorpio, Libra and Virgo, from 16,000 to 12,000 BC, the phrases were I DESIRE, I BALANCE, and I ANALYZE. Perhaps it was their selfishness and their emphasis on intellect that caused their destruction. They strove for balance, but apparently did not achieve it. During the Age of Leo, around 10,000 BC, a remnant of Atlantis built the great pyramid and the lion/sphinx. The phrase was I WILL, and it was their rebellion against God's Will that brought about their destruction. The Age of Cancer, around 8,000 BC, symbolized by the crab's ability to jump over obstacles, was represented by the phrase I FEEL. It was their feeling for the land that allowed a Neolithic farming culture. The Age of Gemini, around 6,000 BC, was represented by the phrase I THINK. It was during this time that the land was organized into city states. The Age of Taurus the Bull, around 4,000 BC, represented by the phrase I HAVE was a time of material wealth in the Chinese and Egyptian dynasties, a time when the sacred cow and bull were revered. It was also an earth sign, hence the emphasis on pyramids and megalithic structures. The year 2,000 BC ushered in the Age of Aries, the Ram. Because it was a fire sign, Moses sacrificed the ram and was upset when his followers melted their jewelry to form a golden calf, symbolizing the former Age of Taurus. Aries, represented by the phrase, I AM, was a time when God revealed his name: "I AM THAT I AM" (Ex. 3:14). The Age of Pisces, the fishes, represented by the phrase I BELIEVE, was heralded by the birth of Jesus who replaced the fiery sacrifices with water baptisms. It was during this water age that greater emphasis was placed on ships and exploration, hence the Americas were colonized by Europeans. The symbol of Christianity is the fish. The incoming Aquarian Age, around 2,000 AD, is represented by the phrase I KNOW. This air age is a time to harness electricity, both solar and galactic; to build spaceships and space stations; to explore the galaxy; and to establish greater alien, as well as divine, contact; a time to explore inner, as well as outer, space. It is also an age of crystals, hence the computer chip. Around 4,000 AD, the Age of

Capricorn and the phrase I SEE, will be an age of diamonds. Sagittarius, around 6,000 AD, will be represented by the phrase I USE. Unfoldment is a gradual process. Although the Aquarian Age will stimulate knowledge, it may take centuries for all mankind to actually SEE and USE that which they know. It is well to remember that knowledge is not wisdom.

While writing this book, I have progressed through several stages of emotional unrest. Being an avid student of the Bible, my initial vision brought a sense of grieving, like a child first losing faith in Santa Clause. This was followed by a sense of anger at having been duped by the "fallen ones." How dare they use us as slaves and otherwise manipulate us! My anger was followed by a sense of depression that gradually gave way to acceptance and forgiveness as I finally saw a blending of good and evil in the realm beyond duality. This sense of surrender has brought me even closer to Jesus, for now I understand the tremendous importance of his mission on earth! His love and compassion were needed to "save" us from, the dictatorial precepts of Jehovah and the confusion brought about by the "fallen ones." His teachings were needed to enable us to attune to the feminine aspect of the Holy Spirit "comforter", thereby allowing us to go directly to the Father God's "kingdom within" where we give birth to Christ Consciousness.

May you take this mystical journey and avoid the dictatorial pitfalls of the patriarchal "war god," Jehovah, and other manipulating beings. Remove the "veils," follow your heart and seek the feminine aspect of intuition, the Holy Spirit of Truth. For it is this inner communion with the Mother/Father God, the "still, small voice within", that will "set you free!"

21

PART II

WHO IS JEHOVAH?

IS JEHOVAH ONE AMONG MANY?

To unravel the mystery of the different "gods," let us examine the Bible to understand the being known as "Jehovah." Actually that was not even his name. The "Bible in Alphabet," states:

"The ancient pronunciation was approximately Yahweh which, because of the lack of vowels in the Hebrew alphabet, was spelled with the letters corresponding to YHWH. Later a system of written vowels evolved. . . . Writers put the vowels of the word for Lord (Adonai) around the consonants of the divine name. Early Christians read the word as it was written. Out of this blunder came the name Jehovah."[65]

Adding to the confusion, YHWH (Yahweh) and JHVH (Jehovah) may not be the same being, although the Biblical translators used these terms interchangeably. According to the Kabala,[66] Jehovah is the manifested embodiment of YHWH, the Father God, the Living Light behind all Creator Gods.[67] This Invisible Source, the Father of all, remains in his own paradisiacal realm at the center of the Universe, but projects a spark of his divine energy, presence, or breath, into every individual as the "Father Within." Blavatsky says: "It is the

---

[65] The Bible in Alphabet, Gilbert James Brett, Consolidated Book Publishers, Chicago, IL, 1947.

[66] The Kabala, also spelled Qabbalah or Cabala, is an esoteric collection of ancient mystical teachings. It is believed to have originated in the Orient and to have a later connection with Zoroaster.

[67] For further information, also see the glossary definitions of "Jehovah" and "YHWH," in The Keys of Enoch, Dr. J. J. Hurtak, The Academy For Future Science, CA, 1977, pp 580, 610.

unrevealed God, who sends his beneficent breath from the sphere of empyreal fire, within whose glowing rays dwells the great Being, far beyond the limits of the world of matter. . . . Once having given the impulse to all creation, the First Cause retires."[68] Thus YHWH is inner, while the other beings of the hierarchy, such as "angels, archangels, seraphim, cherubim, spirits, morning stars, powers, dominions, dignities, princes, principalities, virtues, thrones and authorities,"[69] manifest outwardly in different universes to act as local administrators.

On a broader scale, JHVH represents the four quadrants of the galaxy (J - Leo; H -Scorpio; V - Aquarius; H - Taurus). This is in turn represented by the Sphinx, with its legs and claws of a lion - Leo; its head of a man - Aquarius; its wings of an eagle - Scorpio; and its tail of a bull - Taurus). The term Yahweh or Jehovah can be singular or plural, masculine or feminine, hence the Old Testament speaks of "us," the "hosts," and the "Godhead."[70] Adonai is a plural term meaning "His Lords" or "my Lords." King Solomon, referred to the Creator as "She," or "Wisdom," warning us not to "forsake the laws of thy Mother."[71] In other traditions, the Mother God, corresponding to the nurturing aspect of the Holy Spirit, is referred to as Iona, the Dove, Shiva, Shakti, Isis, Sophia, Shekinah, Cybele, Mary or Quan Yin. "She" is an inner (kundalini/serpent) force that rises to cleanse and purify the physical body, thereby activating our spiritual chakric (energy) centers. This in turn opens us to levels of inner spiritual awareness that allows us to reconnect the ten strands of our DNA, thereby reclaiming our original spiritual gifts to regain our "first estate."

[68] Isis Unveiled, Vol. I, p 160.

[69] Gen. 3:24; Ps. 18:10; Isa. 6:2-7; Dan. 8:16; 9:20-21; 10:13, 21; 12:1; Zech. 6:5; Luke 1:19, 26; Rom. 8:38; Eph. 1:21; 3:10; Col. 1:16; 2:15; 1 Thes. 4:16; 1 Pet. 3:22; Jude 8-9; Rev. 4:5; 5:6; 12:7.

[70] Gen. 1:26; 3:22; 32:2; Josh. 5:14-15;; 1 Sam. 4:8; Ps. 103:21; Acts 17:29; Rom. 1:20; Col. 2:9.

[71] Prov. 1:8; 6:20; Matt. 11:19; Luke 7:35.

The problem of deciphering which being is indicated, lies in the translation, or in some cases, the mistranslation, of ancient texts. Originally there existed several different terms for God. To simplify the tremendous job of translation, some of these terms were simply written "God," while others were rendered "LORD God," with LORD all in capitals . Others were written "Lord," with only the L in caps and sometimes "lord" is written with no caps. This confusion continues in the New Testament, which refers to "the Lord and his Christ," while Jesus is called "both Lord and Christ."[72]

Chapter one of Genesis, a priestly document written in poetic form, uses the term "God." (This was evidently the history of the creation of the first three "root races.") Chapter two, a Jehovistic document, uses "LORD God." In chapter one "God" created an androgynous being (both male and female). In chapter two, the "LORD GOD" created man first, then woman. Chapter one says the animals were created before man; chapter two says man was created first. Chapter one gives no eating restrictions; chapter two forbids the eating of the tree of knowledge. In chapter one, each "day's" progress was declared "good,"[73] while this declaration was not made in chapter two. As stated in Part I, some of the early experiments of creating man by biologically engineering the root races or the existing "cavemen," were not good! No wonder the androgynous man of chapter one was given "dominion,"[74] while the male and female creations of chapter two were not.

In addition to "God" and the "LORD God," chapter three of Genesis presents a third being, "the serpent," also known as Satan, Devil or Lucifer, an "outcast from heaven" who "didn't know the truth."[75] Clarification of the three beings is given in the

---

[72] Acts 2:36; 4:26.

[73] Gen. 1:4, 10, 12, 18, 21, 25, 31.

[74] Gen. 1:26, 28.

[75] Isa. 14:12, 21; Dan. 8:10; Luke 10:18; 2 Thes. 2:11; Rev. 12:4-10.

ancient Sumerian Texts, an earlier version of the Bible, from which Genesis is believed to have been copied.[76] According to Zecharia Sitchin, in his magnificent book, The Twelfth Planet--a compilation of thirty years of research--Anu, who had defeated Alalu to become "king in Heaven," was "the Sumerian Father of the Gods." His "host" was the "Anunnaki."[77] Anu and his two sons, Enlil, the "god of earth," and Enki, the "god of water,"[78] formed a trinity, however they were still under the jurisdiction of a higher God. Blavatsky describes Anu as: "Second member of the trinity under the God of Wisdom; the concealed, passive deity; one of the names of Brahma or Ain soph."[79] Because Anu, who may have been the creator of the androgynous beings of the first chapter of Genesis, had other solar systems to look after, he conveyed his rulership of earth to his son Enlil, the "LORD God," who created the male and female beings of Genesis, chapter two.

Enki, who wanted mankind to have access to technological knowledge, seems to have been the "serpent," founder of the "Brotherhood of the Snake."[80] When Enlil (Zeus),

---

[76] For further information, see: The Gilgamesh Epic and Old Testament Parallels, University of Chicago, IL, 1946; The Epic of Gilgamesh, N. K. Sanders translation, Penguin, MD, 1960; The Epic of Gilgamesh, R. C. Thompson, London, Luzac, 1928.

[77] The Anunnaki, the "Host of Anu," also called "Igigi," are the Nefilim, those "sons of God who came in unto the daughters of men," creating giants. They are not, however, the "fallen angels" who were cast out with Lucifer. Anunnaki means "those who from heaven to earth came." For further information, see: The Twelfth Planet, pp 327-330. The American Indian term, "Anasazi," means "Ancient Ones." A tribe of Canadian Indians use the term "Abenaki," Architects of the Underworld, p 283. The Ainu, an ancient light-skinned race of people with an unusual language, who settled in Japan, may have had a connection with the Anunnaki, or with the Atlanteans.

[78] The Twelfth Planet, Zecharia Sitchin, Avon Books, NY, 1978, pp 69, 89-101. It is helpful to realize that water was an ancient term for outer space.

[79] The Secret Doctrine, Vol. I, pp 357, 542; Vol. II, pp 62, 139.

[80] Brotherhood of the Snake - This organization representing knowledge and technology, gave birth to the priesthood, and was the forerunner of the Mystery Schools and the later Masonic Lodge. Enlil, postponing technology until man was spiritually advanced, diminished our psychic powers by

28

the "god of earth," became discouraged with his creation, his brother, Enki (Prometheus), seems to have saved them from destruction. Enki was most likely the "god" who warned Noah and his family about the flood and sealed them into a "capsule." But for his interference, he lost control of Egypt, which was given to one of his sons, while he was banished to lower Africa to "crawl on his belly" to oversee the mining operations. During Enki's absence, his oldest son, Marduk, usurped the power of Enlil and became the ruler of Mesopotamia.[81] (Marduk, with a thunderbolt in each hand, had become a hero in destroying the sky beast, Tiamat, which resulted in its hurling through space breaking in half, and hitting the planet Maldek, which in turn broke into pieces to become the asteroid belt between Mars and Jupiter.) Tiamat is referred to in the Bible as "Rahab;" the asteroid belt as "the hammered-out bracelet."[82] More than any of the other beings, Marduk, whose goal was to become the ruler of earth, seems to fit the description of Jehovah.

Marduk and the various members of the host of Anunnaki are associated with the planet Nibiru. According to Sitchin, the planet Nibiru follows an elliptical orbit that projects far into space, then passes between Mars and Jupiter every thirty-six hundred years. Sitchin says of this "planet of crossing:"

> "Not only the presence of the Nefilim but also the periodic arrivals of the Twelfth Planet [Nibiru] in earth's vicinity seem to lie behind the three crucial phases of man's post-Diluvial civilization: agriculture, circa 11,000 BC, the Neolithic

---

disconnecting ten strands of our twelve-strand DNA. Anu, Enlil and Enki, presently traveling on a Pleiadian spacecraft, are now working with the Office of the Christ to recode our DNA. For further information, see We are the Nibiruans, pp 100-101.

[81] See: The Twelfth Planet.

[82] Gen. 1:8-9, 14-18; Job 9:5-13; 26:5-14; Ps. 33:6-9; 74:12-17; 87:4; 89:9-11; Isa. 51:9-11. See also" The Twelfth Planet, pp 212-235.

culture, circa 7500 BC, and the sudden civilization of 3800 BC, which took place at intervals of 3,600 years. It appears that the Nefilim, passing knowledge to man in measured doses, did so in intervals matching the periodic returns of the Twelfth Planet to earth's vicinity. It was as though some on-site inspection, some face-to-face consultation possible only during the 'window' period that allowed landings and takeoffs between earth and the Twelfth Planet, had to take place among the 'gods' before another 'go ahead' could be given."[83]

This cycle would have brought them during the birth of Jesus and will bring them again in the year 3600 AD. The Old Testament, referring to outer space as "waters" or the "deep," alludes to this thirty-six hundred-year elliptical orbit as a "circuit, whose "going forth is from the end of the heaven,"[84] 'end' meaning beyond our solar system.

Marduk claimed to be the "Most High God of heaven and earth." He is evidently still in control and will be until the final battle of "Armageddon" which according to the prophecies, will result in an era of peace." It was most likely Marduk who appeared to Abraham, Moses and the prophets, and Nibiru was most likely "Zion," the heavenly (orbiting) "City of God." [85]The timing assigned to the Biblical events, however, is different from that of the Sumerian Texts, which state: Anu, Enlil and Enki arrived on planet earth some 445,000 years ago, the same year the pyramid and the face is believed to have been constructed in the Cydonia Complex on Mars; the sons of God married the

---

[83] The Twelfth Planet, p 246, 415.

[84] Job 22:14; 30:8-20; 36:26-33; 37:1-5; 38:9-32; Ps. 19:1-6; 33:6-9; 68:32-33; 77:5, 11-20; 104:1-9; 107:24; 148:4-8; Isa. 40:22; 43:16-17.

[85] Ps. 87:1-3; Heb. 12: 18-21.

daughters of man 100,000 years ago; Noah began his reign 49,000 years ago and reigned until the flood 13,000 years ago, the time of the sinking of Atlantis. Marduk became power hungry and began causing trouble around 25,000 years ago.

Some scholars believe Marduk was not Jehovah because he built his "earth-station" capital in Babylon, meaning "Gateway of the Gods," while Jehovah was adamantly against Babylon, a fortified city within a fifty-six miles walled enclosure. But this Machiavellian tactic of pitting two opposing sides against one another, is the modus operandi for Jehovah. It was repeated again with the Moslems vs the Christians, the Catholics vs the Protestants, and all three of them vs the Mormons.

According to Jelaila Starr, Anu is a sixth-dimensional being, while Marduk is a fourth-dimensional aspect of Lucifer, leader of the dark forces. She refers to this necessary element in allowing mankind an opportunity to grow through conflict, as the "Polarity Integration Game."[86] This period of testing determines whether or not we will serve mankind or merely serve ourself.

Starr says Marduk, playing the role to the hilt, used a giant crystal, an energy accumulator called a "Tuaoi" or "Maxim Stone" on Atlantis, to sink Lemuria and to destroy earth's firmament."[87] Sitchin says Marduk started the Pyramid Wars, and rallied the natives to build the Tower or Babel.[88] But was he Jehovah? Whoever he was, he was not the Highest God, for the Bible assures us that the "True God" does not "tempt" man; that Lucifer is the "adversary/tempter."[89] The Bible also indicates that Jehovah and Satan are one and the same.[90] Jehovah acted surprised to learn about the "Tower of Babel" rebellion,[91] but

---

[86] We are the Nibiruans.

[87] We are the Nibiruans, pp 102-104, 108-109.

[88] See: The Wars of God and Men, Zecharia Sitchin, Avon, NY, 1985.

[89] Gen. 22:1; 1 Kings 11:14, 23, 25; 1 Chron. 5:26; Matt 4:1,3; Mark 1:13; Luke 4:2; Heb. 11:17; Jas. 1:13.

[90] Compare 2 Sam. 24:1; 1 Chron. 21:1.

[91] Gen. 11:5-8.

again, this may have been one of his ploys.

THE LESSER GOD, JEHOVAH

The Bible presents Jehovah as a fertility "god," a "Lord of generation," who opens and closes the "womb," and whose "covenant" is symbolized by "circumcision" and "sacrifices."[92] He is also known as "Lord of Sabaoth," or "Ilda-Baoth," who honors the sabbath and is associated with Saturn.[93] This seems to substantiate the Jehovah/Marduk connection, since Marduk is said to sustain a monitoring base that orbits Saturn.[94] A very pure channel of spiritual messages, Sylvia Moss Schechter, who receives messages from the Biblical Saint Paul, the spirit of which is presently known as "Hilarion, Master of Truth," relates the following concerning Jehovah and Saturn:

> "We are not reconciled to a God of judgement, to a jealous God, to a God of anger and wrath. This was the erroneous God. The God of the Old Testament of the Hebrew world was not part of the Godhead. . . . The one whom the Old Testament Bible refers to as Jehovah is not the Supreme First Cause. . . . The role of the Planet Saturn is that of allowing humanity to see itself. The symbolic energy of Saturn is 'Man Know thyself.' He is, indeed, the tempter who showed to Jeshua [Jesus] all the kingdom of earth and said, 'These can be yours if you wish.' It was not an embodiment with the name, Satan, to which the Initiate may answer. It was a statement of

---

[92] Gen. 17:10-27; 21:1-4; 29:31; 30:22; 34:15-24; 1 Sam. 1:5-6; Job 31:15-18; Ps. 22:9; 50:5; 71:6; 127:3; Isa. 44:2, 24; 46:3-4; 48:8; 63:9; 66:9; Hos. 9:14; Luke 1:15-19; Rom. 4:19.

[93] Rom. 9:29; Jas. 5:4; Isis Unveiled, Vol. II, p 236.

[94] See: We are the Nibiruans.

recognition that Saturn is the governing principle behind all of our discernment. It is the Planet Saturn which allows us to know ourselves."[95]

Blavatsky says of Jehovah:

"The personage who is named in the first four chapters of Genesis variously as 'God,' the 'Lord God,' and 'Lord,' simply is not one and the same person; certainly it is not Jehovah. There are three distinct classes or groups of the Elohim in the Kabala. The ever-thundering, punishing Jehovah is one of the seven creative spirits. . . . The little tribal Jehovah . . . belongs to a class of lower, material and not very holy denizens. . . . Jehovah, the deity of the Jews, was Ilda-Baoth, the son of the ancient Bohu, or Chaos, the adversary of divine wisdom. . . . The personator of the One Unknown and Unknowable God . . . was a substitute for purposes of an exoteric national faith."[96]

Manly P. Hall states:

"Some Gnostics [Gnosis is the supreme degree of knowledge in mystical religion] were of the opinion that the Jewish God, Jehovah, was the Demiurgus . . . individualized as the lowest creation out of the substance called pleroma. . . . This concept . . . apparently influenced medieval

---

[95] The Letters of Paul, Sylvia Moss Schechter, Triad Publishing, Bend, OR, 1989.

[96] The Secret Doctrine, Vol I, pp 113, 196-197, 327, 390-391, 481, 492, 576, 642; Vol. II, pp 38, 61, 95, 233, 388, 472, 488, 508-509, 524, 526, 538; Isis Unveiled, Blavatsky, Theosophical Society, NY, 1877, Vol. II, p 186.

Rosicrucianism, which viewed Jehovah as the Lord of the material universe rather than as the Supreme Deity."[97]

Jesus, Daniel and Paul called him the "Unknown God" that "dwelleth not in temples made with hands," the "Ancient of Days," or the "Father that dwelleth within."[98] Jesus told the Hebrews: "Ye have neither heard his voice at any time, nor seen his shape."[99] The Bible in Alphabet explains:

"More than a half-dozen names were used for God by the Hebrews. El is perhaps the oldest and the most widely distributed name, having been used by Arabians, Aramaeans, Babylonians and Phoenicians as well as by the Hebrews. It may have signified 'Strong One,' but more probably 'Leader or Ruler.' If regarded in this latter sense, it is akin to the Phoenician idea of Ba'al (Lord). It appears frequently in Old Testament place names, as El-Beth-El (Gen. 35:7). Probably El Elyon (most high God or God most high) was originally the name of a Canaanitish deity appropriated by the Hebrew Israelites; "Israel" meaning "warrior of God" (Gen. 14:18-22; Ps. 57:2).[100]

Jehovah did not claim to be the only "god." Others, such as "Adrammelech, Anammelech, Ashima, Ashtarath, Asshur, Ba'al, Ba'alim, Ba'alzebub, Chemosh, Dagon, Milcom, Moloch, Nergal, Nibhaz, Succoth-benoth, and Tartak, are mentioned

---

[97] The Secret Teachings of All Ages, p xxvi.

[98] Dan. 7:9, 13, 22; Luke 17:21; John 14:10; 17:3; Acts. 17:23-24; 2 Cor. 5:1; Heb. 9:11, 24.

[99] John 5:37-38; 8: 19, 40, 55.

[100] The Bible in Alphabet.

throughout the Bible.[101] These various tribal "gods" even had technological contests to see who could send down the most powerful "fire from heaven."[102] To distinguish himself from other gods, some of which were in the form of idols, Jehovah called himself the "Living God,"[103] although many of the others were also living beings. Some were in "heaven", while others were on earth. The Bible makes it clear that mankind expected the "gods" to come down to earth "in the likeness of men."[104] Due to stiff competition from these "other gods," Jehovah was quite "jealous." He warned Moses: "Thou shalt have no other 'gods' before me . . . thou shalt not revile the 'gods;' he that sacrificeth unto any 'god,' save unto the Lord only, he shall be utterly destroyed."[105]

When he appeared to Abraham, making a "covenant" and promising to be a "god" to Abraham's "seed,"[106] he did not agree to be the "god" of other nations. Each tribal "god" was assigned a different area for their "inheritance."[107] Moses explained this to the Hebrews, saying: "Remember the days of old . . . when the Most High [not Jehovah, but a higher God] divided to the nations their inheritance, when he separated the sons of Adam, he set the bounds of the people according to the number of the children of

---

[101] Ex. 12:12; 15:11; 17:11; 23:13, 24, 32-33; 34:14; Lev. 17:7; 20:2-5; Num. 21:29; 25:2; 33:4; De. 13:6-7; 29:18; 32:12, 16-17; Josh. 24:15; Judg. 6:10; 10:6; 16:23; 24:2; 1 Sam. 4:8; 5:1-6; 7:4; 12:10; 1 Kings 9:6, 9; 11:5-7, 10, 33; 18:21, 31; 2 Kings 1:3- 6; 3:27; 10:21; 17:28-32, 35-36; 18:33-35; 19:12-18; 23:4; Ps. 81:9; 96:4; 97:7, 9; Jer. 19:4, 13; 48:7, 13, 46; Dan. 3:29; 4:9, 18; 5:4-39; 6:7; 11:36-37; Hos. 14:3; Amos 5:25-26; Zeph. 1:5; 2:11; Acts 7:42-43; 14:11-15; 17:18; 28:6; 1 Cor. 8:4-6.

[102] 1 Kings 18:17-40; 2 Kings 1:3-13.

[103] Josh. 3:10; 1 Sam. 17:26; Ps. 42:2; Isa. 37:17; Jer. 10:10; Dan. 6:26.

[104] Acts 14:11; 28:6.

[105] Ex. 20:3, 5; 22:20, 28; 34:14; De. 4:24; 6:15; Ps. 78:58; Ezek. 39:25; Joel 2:18; Zech. 1:14.

[106] Gen. 17:7-8.

[107] Ex. 6:8; 15:16-17; De. 4:19; 32:7-10; Josh. 1:6; Judg. 20:6; 1 Kings 8:51-53; Ps. 74:2; 78:54; 105:44; 135:12; Isa. 63:17; Joel 2:18.

Israel. For the Lord's [Jehovah's] portion is his people; Jacob is the lot of his inheritance."[108] (The Hebrews were later called "Israelites", meaning "warriors", then "Jews".)

The <u>Septuagint</u>, an ancient translation of the Old Testament into Greek, relates: "Chemosh gets the Moabites, Qos gets the Edomites, Milkom gets the Ammorites, Ba'al gets the Canaanites, while Yahweh [Jehovah] takes care of the Israelites, his chosen people."[109] According to Edgar Cayce, Poseidon got Atlantis. In the Old Testament, Jehovah said to the Hebrews: "You only have I known of all the families of the earth," hence, he was often called the "God of Israel, God of the Hebrews, God of Abraham, Isaac, Jacob, Lord God of your fathers, God of David and Daniel."[110] The Bible makes it clear that "other lords" had taken "dominion" over the Hebrews before him.[111] The six-pointed star, later referred to as the "Star of David," existed long before the time of Abraham, indicating that these "other lords" were well established before Jehovah.

Abraham was initiated and blessed by "the priest of the Most High God, Melchizedek, the King of Salem, who is without beginning or end."[112] Melchizedek, a former incarnation of the spirit of Jesus, is believed to be the first divine teacher to have manifested since Seth, founder of the Sethite Priesthood. The Bible says the "Order of Melchizedek", of which Jesus was later associated, was greater than the "Levitical" or "Aaronic" Priesthoods that were ordained by Jehovah.[113] According to Genesis, Salem, meaning peace, had been the land of the Hittites and Chaldeans, whose kingdom extended into Mesopotamia and

---

[108] Ex. 15:17; De. 32:8-9.

[109] Quote taken from: <u>The Mystery and Meaning of the Dead Sea Scrolls</u>, Hershel Shanks, Random House, NY, 1998, p 151. See also 1 Kings 11:33.

[110] Ex. 3:16; 7:16; Ps. 20:1; Isa. 2:3; 29:23; 43:3; Ezek. 7:15; Amos 3:2; Mic. 4:2.

[111] Josh. 24: 2, 14-15; Isa. 26:13.

[112] Gen. 14:17-22; Heb. 7:1-4.

[113] Ps. 110:4; Heb. 2:17; 4:14; 5:6, 10; 6:20; 7:5-22.

Asia Minor.[114] The spiritual group over which Melchizedek presided, was most likely a branch of Brahminism, a teaching that began thousands of years before Abraham and still retained some of the purity of the ancient priesthoods of Seth.[115]

This possibility is strengthened by the fact that Abraham's name, "Abram," was changed to "A-braham," since the Hindus called each of their initiates, a "brahmin." He was blessed in the "Valley of Shaveh," which may have represented "Shiva," the third member of the Hindu Trinity: Bhahma/Vishnu/Shiva. Who did Melchizedek call God? The Unseen, Unmanifested Father who resides at the center of the universe. Hence there is a similarity between the teachings of Seth, the teachings of Melchizedek, and those of Jesus, who may have even been the same being. Melchizedek's missionaries, teaching salvation by faith, are said to have taken root in Egypt, then spread throughout Europe, Asia, the British Isles, Iceland, Japan, and the eastern islands.[116] Some of these great teachers wrote many of the Old Testament Psalms and inscribed them on stone. These, as well as the book of Job, which was written about the time of Abraham and Issac and does not mention the sabbath of Jehovah, were later incorporated into the Old Testament. This accounts for some of the confusion; the references to "God" in these ancient texts did not refer to Jehovah. (According to Edgar Cayce, Melchizedek wrote the Book of Job.)

Another scriptural indication of there being higher orders before Abraham was that of the consecrated "Nazarites," who were well established before the destruction of Sodom and Gomorrah.[117] This ascetic order was later tolerated by Jehovah, who accepted their special rules, such as abstinence from wine and other pollutions, wearing long, seamless garments and not

---

[114] Acts 7:2-4.
[115] Gen. 14:18-20; Josh. 24:2.
[116] The Urantia Book, pp 1-14, 1022.
[117] Lam. 4:6-8.

cutting their hair.[118] Joseph, Samson, Samuel, Elijah, John the Baptist, Jesus, Peter and Paul were Nazarites, which the New Testament mistakenly calls "Nazarenes."[119] Blavatsky says of them:

> "The Nazarite sect existed long before the laws of Moses. . . . The Persian word Nazaruan means millions of years. The Nazars or Nazarenes were consecrated to the service of the Supreme One God, the kabalistic Ain-Soph, or the 'Ancient of Days.' It is in Nazara that the ancient Nazarites held their 'Mysteries of Life,' which were but the secret mysteries of initiation, distinct in their practical form from the popular Mysteries which were held at Byblos in honor of Adonai. 'Thou shalt not worship the Sun who is named Adonai,' says the Codex of the Nazarenes, 'whose name is also El-El.' This Adonai will elect to himself a nation and congregate in crowds (his worship will be exoteric). Jerusalem will become the refuge and city of the abortive, who shall perfect themselves (circumcise) with a sword, and shall adore Adonai.' This accounts for the hatred of the later Nazarenes by the orthodox Jews--followers of the exoteric Mosiac Law--who are ever taunted by this sect with being the worshippers of Lord Bacchus, passing under the disguise of Adonai-Iachoh or Lord Sabaoth, the later-vowelled Adonai or Jehovah."[120]

---

[118] Num. 6:1-21; John 19:23.

[119] Gen. 49:26; Judg. 13:4-7; 16:17; 1 Sam. 1:11, 28; 2 Kings 1:8; Jer. 7:29; Amos 2:11-12; Matt. 2:23; Luke 1:15; 4:16, 28-30, 34; Acts 24:5; Talmud.

[120] Isis Unveiled, Vol. II, pp 131, 142; The Secret Doctrine, Vol. II, p 96.

In addition to the Nazarite mysteries, other sacred mystery schools had been in existence since the Osirian teachings of Atlantis and perhaps earlier. Many of the esoteric teachings of the "Unknown God," the true YHWH, survived in India, some in the Hermetic schools of Egypt, some in the mysteries of Freemasonry, and some in the teachings of Pythagoras and the Kabala. In the ancient pre-Vedic teachings of India, before Brahminism, the "Unknown God" was termed "Brahma;" in the pre-Menes and Osirian Hermetic teachings, this Force was called "Divine Mind;" the Freemasons called God "First Cause;" the pre-Mosaic oriental Gnostics used the term "Nameless One;" the Kabala referred to our Divine Source as "Ain Soph;" and Jesus called God the "Father that dwelleth within."

According to the Bible, Moses, who had been trained in the mystery schools of Egypt, knew the inner hidden teachings and shared them with Aaron and his "seventy elders." Job also proclaimed: "The secret of God was upon my tabernacle." Jesus and Paul, who indicated that the "carnal"-minded "babes" had to drink "milk" because they were not yet ready for "meat," shared the divine secrets with a few chosen disciples," the "election" or "stewards of the mysteries," but spoke to the rest in "proverbs, parables, riddles," and "allegories." The Apostles, stated that even Lucifer, the prophets, and the immortal angels do not know all the mysteries.[121]

Due to the fact there are many "gods," Jehovah claimed to be the "highest," saying: "For the Lord your God is God of 'gods,' and Lord of lords, a great God, a mighty and a terrible, which regardeth not persons, nor taketh rewards."[122] Claiming to

---

[121] Ex. 24:9-11; Num. 11:16-17, 25; De. 29:29; Job 29:4; Ps. 78:2; 103:20; 148:2-5; Isa. 14:4; Matt. 6:4, 6, 18; 11:25; 12:7;13:3, 11,17, 34-35; 24:36, 45; Mark 4:11; 13:32; Luke 8:10; 12:42; 20:34-36; John 4:32-34;Acts 13:39; Rom. 11:7, 25; 16:25; 1 Cor. 1:26; 2:7-8; 3:2; 4:1; 13:2; 14:2; 15:51; 2 Cor. 3:14; Gal. 2:16, 4:14; Eph. 3:3, 9; 5:32; Col. 1:26-27; 2:2; 4:3; 1 Tim. 3:9, 16; Heb. 5:12-14; 1 Pet. 1:12; 2 Pet. 2:1; Rev. 1:20.

[122] De. 10:17; see also: Josh. 22:22; Ps. 83:18; 86:8; 89:6; 95:3; 113:4-5;

have "created the heavens and the earth" and to have "put the spirit in man," he declared: "For thus saith the high and lofty One that inhabiteth eternity, whose name is Holy; all the earth is mine; there is no God beside me!"[123] But was he the "Most High God," or merely one of the tribal rulers? David said: "God [Jehovah] standeth in the congregation of the mighty; he judgeth among the 'gods,'" indicating that he is but one of the judges.[124] But Jesus said the "Father Within" did not judge, so Jehovah was evidently not the "Father."[125] David also said: "Give unto the Lord, O ye mighty, give unto the Lord glory and strength."[126] Who were "the mighty" that were requested to give "the Lord" strength?

From whom did Jehovah achieve his training? The Bible asks: "Who hath directed the Spirit of the Lord, or being his counsellor hath taught him? With whom took he counsel, and who instructed him, and taught him in the path of judgement, and taught him knowledge, and shewed to him the way of understanding? . . . Where is he that put his Holy Spirit within him?"[127] Good question!

The Old Testament refers to a higher Lord who served as Jehovah's "redeemer," saying: "Thus saith the Lord, the King of Israel, and his redeemer the LORD of hosts . . . I [Jehovah] will proclaim the name of the LORD [Unknown God] before thee."[128] This hierarchy of different Gods is also indicated in the scriptures: "There am I; and now the Lord God, and his Spirit, hath sent me. . . . The Lord [Jehovah] descended in the cloud, and stood with him [Moses] there, and proclaimed the name of the

---

Dan. 2:47.

[123] Ex. 19:5; Num. 16:22; 27:16; Neh. 9:6; Isa. 42:5; 45:5-6, 18-22; 57:15; Hos. 13:4; Zech. 12:1.

[124] Ps. 82:1; 135:5-8; 136:1-9; 2 Sam. 7:22; 1 Kings 8:23; 1 Chron. 16:25; 17:20; 2 Chron. 2:5; 6:14; 32:14.

[125] John 5:22.

[126] Ps. 29:1.

[127] Isa. 40:13-14; 63:10-11; Rom. 11:34.

[128] Ex. 33:19; Isa. 44:6.

[Unknown] LORD."[129]

The Bible even indicates a distinct rivalry between two of the "gods." Rux explains:

"Leviticus 16 shows this clear distinction between the two gods in the presentation of two scapegoats for sin offerings: 'one for the Lord and one for Azazel.' . . . Jesus gallantly volunteered himself in place of the scapegoat as an offering to Yahweh, as mankind's final atonement to stay God's (Elohim/Azazel's) hand in the ultimate devastation of the race. (The Jews continued the annual sacrifice of two scapegoats to the two separate gods until the destruction of their temple by Rome in 70 AD.)"[130]

In the following scriptures, there are clearly two beings: "The [Unknown] LORD said unto my Lord [Jehovah] . . . I [Jehovah] have overthrown some of you, as God [a different Being] overthrew Sodom and Gomorrah; though they bring forth, yet will I slay even the beloved fruit of their womb; my God [the Unknown One] will cast them away."[131] Who is speaking and who was his God? The prophet Zechariah described "two anointed ones" that "stand by the Lord of the whole earth."[132] The Bible speaks of the "God of heaven," indicating there is a lesser "God of earth," yet it also mentions the God of both "heaven and earth."[133] When Moses saw the "burning bush" in the desert, the Old Testament relates: "The angel of the Lord appeared unto him,

---

[129] Ex. 34:5; Isa. 48:16.

[130] Architects of the Underworld, pp 333-334. See also Lev. 16:5-10, 26; Heb. 9:6-15.

[131] Ps. 110:l; Hos. 9:16-17; Amos 4:11.

[132] Zech 4:2-14.

[133] Gen. 14:22; 24:3; De. 4:39; Josh. 2:11; 3:11, 13; Neh. 1:4-5; Dan. 2:18; Mic. 1:9; Rev. 11:13.

and God called to him out of the midst of the bush," thus Jehovah was not the highest God, but merely an "angel of the Lord;" which Isaiah later termed "the angel of his presence."[134] Sometimes "Lord" and "angel" are used interchangeably; at other times they are described as separate beings.[135] They are merely messengers of a higher God.

In the glossary of The Complete Jesus, (a book in which the words of Jesus have been gathered from many ancient sources such as the texts found at Cairo, Egypt in 1895 and at Nag Hammadi in 1945) the author defines: "ARCHONS - Also called 'rulers' and 'authorities.' They are seen as the spirit rulers of the earth and planets. The Hebrew God is sometimes called 'The First Archon.' The archons (including the Hebrew God) were considered evil by the Gnostics. AEONS - One of the ruling beings in the Gnostic Pleroma [that which emanates from 'First Cause'] or one of the powers created by Yaldabaoth. YALDABAOTH - Also written Ialda-baoth - one of the Gnostic names for the ignorant and false God. See Demiurge. COSMOCRATOR - The Gnostic false 'god' of this world. See Demiurge. DEMIURGE - The God of the Hebrews and of creation in Gnostic belief. He was considered evil by the Gnostics since he claimed to be the only God, but was actually under the authority of the Highest God. FIRST EXISTING ONE - A name given by the Gnostics to the true God. BOUNDLESS ONE - The true all-powerful God."[136]

As you can see, there are many different beings and levels in the divine hierarchy. Jesus said:

"I broke the gates of the pitless ones before their

---

[134] Ex. 3:2-4; Isa. 63:9.

[135] Gen., chapters 18-19; 22:11-15; 24:7; 32:28; Judg. 13:17-22; Ps. 34:7; 35:5; Zech. chapter 2.

[136] The Complete Jesus, Ricky Alan Mayotte, Steerforth Press, VT, Copyright by Steerforth Press in 1998, copyright by Ricky Alan Mayotte in 1997, pp 264-265.

faces. I humiliated their malicious intent. They all were shamed and rose from their ignorance. . . . I came from the First, who was sent so that I might reveal to you the one who is from the beginning, because of the arrogance of the Prime Begetter [Jehovah] and his angels, because they say about themselves that they are 'gods.' And I came to remove them from their blindness that I might tell everyone about the God who is above the universe. . . . I have given you authority over all things as sons of light, so that you might tread upon their power."[137]

"A voice--of the Cosmocrator [Jehovah]--came to the angels: 'I am God and there is no other beside me.' But I laughed joyfully when I examined his empty glory. But he went on to say, 'Who is man?' And the entire host of his angels who had seen Adam and his dwelling were laughing at his smallness. And thus did their Ennoia (Thought) come to be removed outside the Majesty of the heavens. . . . For they did not know the Knowledge of the Greatness, that it is from above. . . . He [Jehovah] does not agree with our father. . . . for he was a laughingstock and judgment and false prophecy."[138]

---

[137] The Sophia of Jesus Christ, 117:9; 118:16; 119:9; 121:14. This is one of the codices found at Nag Hammadi in 1945, as quoted in The Complete Jesus, pp 55, 234, 247. This codice is a Christianized version of an older non-Christian (Gnostic) work known as "Eurnostos the Blessed." The original work may have been written in Greek during the first two centuries. For further information, see: The Nag Hammadi Library, James R. Robinson, Harper San Francisco, CA, 1990.

[138] The Second Treatise of the Great Seth, a Gnostic Christian work in the form of a dialogue allegedly spoken by Jesus; 50:1 - 65:1, as quoted in The Complete Jesus, pp 177-181, 248-249.

Paul, explaining the role of Jesus to the Hebrews, compared the coming of Jehovah to Mt. Sinai with the "heavenly Jerusalem," saying: "For ye are not come unto the mount that . . . burned with fire, nor to blackness, and darkness, and tempest, . . . but ye are come unto Mt. Sion [Zion], and unto the city of the Living God, the heavenly Jerusalem."[139] Jehovah was evidently not the "Living God."

Jehovah's "host" included "fallen angels" and space beings as well as Satan, a being who can appear hideous or can transform himself into "an angel of light" to "deceive the whole world."[140] This negative force is apparently needed that we might grow through conflict. But regardless of who is who, the Old Testament clearly shows that Jehovah's personality was warlike, angry, revengeful and not above using "lying spirits"[141] to achieve his territorial goals. He said: "To me belongeth vengeance. . . . for a fire is kindled in mine anger, and shall burn unto the lowest hell, and shall consume the earth."[142]

Jehovah continually told Moses that he was there to "prove" the people; to keep them in fear of his anger.[143] David sang about Jehovah: "Thou shalt break them with a rod of iron; thou shalt dash them to pieces like a potter's vessel."[144] When Moses sang praises to Jehovah, he declared: "The Lord is a Man of War;" in Job we read: "The glory of his nostrils is terrible. . . He swalloweth the ground with fierceness and rage. He saith

---

[139] Heb. 12:18-22.

[140] Gen. 21:1-13; 2 Sam. 24:1; 1 Kings 22:19; 1 Chron. 21:1; Job 1:6-12; 2:1-6; 10:22; Ps. 139:12; Isa. 6:1-4; 45:7; Dan. 7:;9-10; Joel 2:11; Zech. 3:1-2; Matt. 4:1-11; Mark 1:12-13; Luke 4:1-13; 2 Cor. 11:14; 12:7; Jas. 1:13; Rev. 12:9.

[141] Judg. 9:23; 1 Sam. 16:14-16, 23; 18:10; 19:9; 1 Kings 11:23; 22:22-23; 2 Chron. 18:21-22; Ps. 32:2; 78:58, 62; 109:6; Jer. 6:21; Amos 3:6; Nah. 1:2; Zech. 3:1-2; 8:2.

[142] De. 32:22-24; Isa. 30:30; Heb. 10:30.

[143] Ex. 15:25; 16:4; 20:20; De. 8:2, 16; 13:3; 33:6.

[144] Ps. 2:9.

among the trumpets, ha, ha; and he smelleth the battle afar off, the thunder of the captains, and the shouting."[145] "Ha ha?" In addition to being war-like he also seems to have been a bit sadistic, thoroughly enjoying the battles! Does this sound like the same being that is referred to in the New Testament as the merciful "God of Love?"[146] Hardly!

Jehovah is also described as a "consuming, devouring, refiner's fire," who travels inside a "fiery throne" (spacecraft), allowing the brightness to shine around him as "glory."[147] The Old Testament describes his technology: "For the Lord God is a sun and a shield. . . . The Lord shall cause His powerful voice to be heard and shall show the fire with the flame of a devouring fire; hailstones and coals of fire."[148] When Moses was with this high-tech space "god,"Jehovah, for forty days on Mt. Sinai, his face shone with this "glory," causing him to cover it with a "veil."[149] Was this "glory" or radiation?

As mentioned previously, Jehovah and El may have been the same being. The Canaanite god "El," according to Sitchin, had a "spouse, Asherah" and "sons."[150] Hershel Shanks, in his book, The Mystery and Meaning of the Dead Sea Scrolls, reports:

"Recent archaeological finds at the remote Sinai site of Kuntillet 'Ajrud (Horvat Teman) have

---

[145] Ex. 15:3; Job 39:20-21, 24-25. Num. 21:14 refers to the "Book of the Wars of Yahweh."

[146] Matt. 5:16; Rom. 15:33; 1 John 4:8.

[147] Ex. 16:7-10; 24:16; 40:34-45; Lev. 9:6, 23; 10:3; Num. 14:10, 21; 16:19, 42; De. 4:24; 5:24; 9:3; 2 Kings 1:10; 2 Chron. 7:1, 3; Job 1:16; Ps. 18:8; 29:3; 72:19; 89:36; 97:6; Isa. 4:5; 6:3; 10:16-17; 29:6; 30:27, 30; 31:9; 49:4; 66:15-18; Jer. 48:45; Ezek. 3:23; 8:4; 11:23; 43:2-3, 35; 10:4, 18; Dan. 7:9-10; Joel 2:3; Hab. 2:14; Mal. 3:2; Heb. 12:29.

[148] Ex. 3:2; De. 4:12-36; 5:4, 24-26; 9:10; 10:4; 2 Sam. 22:9, 13; Ps. 18:13; 29:4-7; 84:11; Isa. 10:16-18; 29:6; 30:30; Hos. 8:14; Joel 2:3; Amos 1:4-12; 2:2-5.

[149] Ex. 34:29-33.

[150] Divine Encounters, Zecharia Sitchin, Avon, NY, 1996, p 327.

revealed an ancient travelers' way station that housed a kind of chapel in which were found some large storage jars, painted and inscribed, dating to about 800 BC. An inscription on one of the jars refers to 'Yahweh of Shomron (Samaria) and his Asherah [spouse or consort?].' Another mentions 'Yahweh of Teman and his Asherah.' Though a few scholars maintain that Asherah refers to a tree or some other cult symbol, most agree that Asherah refers to a particular pagan 'goddess.'"[151]

IS JEHOVAH A COSMIC TRAVELER?

Did Jehovah, who may have had a "spouse", and his "host" remain on earth, or did they only visit occasionally? King David asks: "But will God indeed dwell on the earth? Behold, the heaven and heaven of heavens cannot contain thee; how much less this house that I have builded?"[152] The Bible indicates that he came to earth, instructed the people, left for several hundred years, then returned. This procedure seems to have been repeated a number of times. Is Jehovah immortal, or was there an reincarnating family of Jehovahs? Why did Abraham use the term "Jehovah-Jireh," Moses, "Jehovah-Nissi," and Gideon, "Jehovah-Shalom?"[153]

Jehovah was on earth during the Garden of Eden laboratory experiment and stayed long enough to take Enoch with him, then seems to have left again for several hundred years. When he returned to find that the "sons of God [Nefilim] and daughters of men" had mated, thereby producing hybrid"giants" -

---

[151] The Mystery and Meaning of the Dead Sea Scrolls, pp 151-152.

[152] 1 Kings 8:27.

[153] Gen. 22:14; Ex. 17:15; Judg. 6:23-24.

some with "six fingers and six toes".[154] Jehovah wanted to destroy the earth. Since he had been specific in warning against interracial mixtures, he felt justified in destroying mankind by flood. Fortunately, his impulsiveness was tempered by Noah, who had found "grace" in his "eyes."[155] Jehovah, who was not very benevolent in wanting to destroy his own creation, was also not very omniscient in foreseeing this turn of events. He was thoroughly surprised to find the "giants." The "flood," which could have referred to the sinking of Atlantis around 10 or 11,000 BC, was for the purpose of destroying the "giants," but apparently it didn't work, for during the time of David, around 1,000 BC, there still remained a "remnant."[156]

Jehovah appears to have left earth again for a lengthy period of time, during which the people spread all over the globe.[157] Perhaps the "gods" had other planets to visit. If they were from another galaxy, they might have waited until the stars lined up in a particular manner to diminish the distance they had to travel for their return trip. Or perhaps they were from the "twelfth planet," Nibiru which came close enough to earth to make the journey only every thirty-six hundred years.

When Jehovah, or one of the Jehovahs finally returned they found that the people, those who had "journeyed from the east" to the land of "Shinar" (the Sumerians, or "children of Eden,"[158]), had decided to build the "Tower of Babel." The people said: "Let us build us a city and a tower, whose top may reach unto heaven; and let us make us a name [shem], lest we be scattered abroad upon the face of the whole earth ". According to Sitchin, the word "shem," which is translated "name" in the Bible,

---

[154] 2 Sam 21: 20

[155] Gen., chapters 1-5; 6:1-8.

[156] Gen. chapters 6-9; Num. 13:33; De. 2:11; 3:11, 13; Josh. 12:4; 13:12; 15:8; 17:15; 18:16; 2 Sam. 21:16-22; 1 Chron. 20:4-8; Job 16:14.

[157] Gen. 10:5.

[158] Gen. 2:8; 11:2; 13:10; 2 Kings 19:12; Isa. 14:8; 37:12; 51:3; Ezek. 27:23; 28:13; 31:8-18; 36:35.

actually refers to a "rocket" or some type of a "skyborn vehicle."
He explains:

> "That an oval-topped, conical object was indeed
> installed in the inner, sacred enclosure of the
> temples of the Great Gods of heaven and earth
> can, fortunately, be proved. An ancient coin found
> at Byblos . . . depicts a two-part temple. In front
> stands the main temple structure . . . behind it is
> an inner courtyard. . . . In the center of this sacred
> area stands a special platform . . . and on the
> platform stands the object of all this security and
> protection: an object that can only be a 'mu,' . . . a
> Sumerian syllabic word meaning 'that which rises
> straight.' Its thirty-odd nuances encompassed the
> meanings 'heights, fire, command, a counted
> period,' as well as 'that by which one is
> remembered'"[159]

---

[159] The Twelfth Planet, pp 140-141.

An ancient coin found at Byblos on
the Mediterranean coast of Lebanon
depicts the Great Temple of Ishtar.
(c) Zecharia Sitchin, The Twelfth Planet,
page 141. Used by permission of
Zecharia Sitchin.

Is it a coincidence that Shem, one of Noah's sons, "begat"
the Shemites or Semites, ancestors of the Hebrews?

Many people will no doubt be taken aback if they
discover that their impressive church steeples represent rockets;
that their great cathedrals were merely launching pads! The
phallic symbols in the eastern religions could also represent a
type of missile or rocket. Sitchin says: "Both the Mesopotamian
texts and the biblical account impart that the flying machines

49

were meant for the 'gods' and not for mankind."[160]   The Bible says of the "Babel" incident:

> "And the Lord came down to see the city and the tower, which the children of men builded. And the Lord said, Behold, the people is one, and they have all one language; and this they begin to do: and now nothing will be restrained from them, which they have imagined to do. Go to, let us go down, and there confound their language, that they may not understand one another's speech."[161]

Why was Jehovah so against their united effort? Was he afraid the people might become so powerful they would no longer assume the role of slaves, who were willing to feed him and his "host," and do their mining? Or could it be that the lesser evolved humans were not yet allowed into space? No doubt the "gods" are gradually raising mankind's consciousness, and perhaps they too are slowly evolving to a higher consciousness. Perhaps each "god" learned from the mistakes of his ancestors. Another possibility is that Enlil, who advocated spiritual evolution rather than technological knowledge--since it was the eating of the tree of knowledge that had caused our "fall" in the Garden of Eden-- didn't want us to develop along this line. He could have been merely protecting mankind from destroying itself.

Jehovah apparently didn't appear again until he instructed Abraham, Isaac and Jacob to become the father of the twelve tribes. (The Bible dates this around 2000 BC but other ancient texts date it much earlier.) After the nuclear destruction of Sodom and Gomorrah, an act that Abraham tried to prevent, Jehovah was not heard from until the time of Moses, around 1500 BC.[162]

---

[160] The Twelfth Planet, pp 148-151.

[161] Gen. 11:1-9.

[162] Gen. 18:17-33; 19:1-30.

During his absence, the Hebrews had been enslaved in Egypt for four-hundred-thirty years. When he finally returned to hear their "cries," he helped Moses free them. In the seventh century BC, another space "god," a bearded, human-like figure, Ahura Mazda, appeared to Zoroaster[163] in a round flying vehicle that had two jutting landing legs. Jehovah instructed the Hebrew prophets from Joshua to Malachi until around 450 BC, then seems to have disappeared again until the birth of Jesus.

The "Star of Bethlehem" (a spacecraft, a "Seraphic Transport,"[164] or an ethereal "Merkaba Vehicle") appeared the night Jesus was born then "went before the wisemen" and spoke to the shepherds.[165] During the life of Jesus, a great deal of technology manifested--either mechanical or etheric--including his virgin birth (artificial insemination?); the "voice" and the light "descending like a dove" at his baptism (a hologram?); the craft that moved him around in the "wilderness" (teleportation?); the "transfiguration" in which the ascended beings, Moses and Elijah appeared, then allowed Jesus and the disciples to "enter into the cloud" (spacecraft?) and at his ascension when he was "taken up" into "a cloud" (beamed up into the craft?).[166] Technology may also have been present in the blinding light at Paul's conversion.[167]

Jehovah's next direct contact may have been around 600 AD when Mohammed was visited by Archangel Gabriel. Perhaps at that time he had given up on both the Jews and the Christians,

---

[163] Zoroaster, who rebelled against Brahmanism, is believed to have been the inspiration behind the Kabala and Gnosticism. It was Zoroaster who revealed the knowledge of Ahriman, the counter-part of Lucifer. The Zend Avesta is the sacred book of Zoroasterianism, which is also called Dualism, Mazdaism, Magism, or Fire Worship.

[164] Seraphic Transport - See The Urantia Book, pp 742-743, 844, 1753.

[165] Matt. 2:2-10; Luke 2:8-11.

[166] Matt. 3:13-17; 4:1-11; 17:1-13; Mark 1:9-11; 3:21-22; 9:2-13; 16:19; Luke 4:1-13; 9:28-36; 24:51; John 12:29-30; Acts 1:9; Eph. 1:20.

[167] Acts 9:3-9.

hence an Islamic Dome of the Rock is situated on the hill of Moriah. Another "close encounter" came in 1820 AD to Joseph Smith, who found and translated The Book of Mormon, an ancient set of golden plates upon which was inscribed the history of the lost tribe of Joseph, "whose branches run over the wall [ocean]." Unlike the other tribes who were given land in "Canaan," Joseph's inheritance extended to "the utmost bound of the everlasting hills [America]."[168] Both the Koran and The Book of Mormon refer to "God" as the "God of Moses," hence he was Jehovah.

The reappearance of the spacecraft, as well as crop circles, which have recently been dubbed "agri-glyphs," have been slowly increasing since the end of World War II in 1945. They were no doubt alarmed by our splitting of the atom! Technology - eating of the "Tree of Knowledge " in the hands of a civilization that has not yet developed a consciousness of divine love, is alarming indeed! Is it a mere coincidence that the UFO crash in Roswell, New Mexico, the Philadelphia Experiment, the finding of the Dead Sea Scrolls and the Nag Hammadi Codices, as well as the reestablishment of the nation of Israel all occurred around 1947? Could the appearance of the spacecraft at this time be preparing us for the "second coming" of the Jesus?[169] Could such a visit lead to conflict with the forces of Jehovah? The Bible predicts a "war in heaven," explaining that those, who "follow the beast," will make war against Jesus upon his return.[170] Is Jehovah "the beast," who is also called "Satan, the Devil?" Is the purpose of the "second coming" to cleanse this planet and the entire universe of the "fallen angelics" and their hybrids? Will the second-coming of Jesus be a continuation of his first mission, to cleanse the planet of its Jehovistic influences?

---

[168] Gen. 49:22-26; De. 33:13-17.

[169] Dan. 7:13; Matt. 24:30; 26:64; Mark 13:26; 14:62; Luke 21:27; Rev. 1:7; 14:12, 14.

[170] Rev. 12:7; 17:14.

JEHOVAH AND THE PRACTICE OF
SACRIFICE

What was Jehovah's purpose in selecting Moses to lead the Hebrews out of their enslavement in Egypt, then keeping them for forty years in the wilderness? To maintain a specific bloodline through which Jesus could be born? Yes, but there is more. Jehovah had promised a "land of milk and honey" to Abraham, but it was also a land that could produce meat for him and his "host" of astronauts, who were no doubt tired of eating "manna." Perhaps this is why their human followers were called "servants of Jehovah" and why Jehovah "had no respect" for Cain's vegetable sacrifice.[171] Even today cattle are often taken or mutilated by spacecraft, but they don't seem to bother gardens or orchards! According to the prophet Isaiah, the "gods" have an appetite for "fat things full of marrow and well-refined wine."[172]

The gruesome practice of sacrifice is mentioned at the very beginning of the Old Testament when Cain, "a tiller of the ground," brought "the fruit of the ground as an offering," while Abel, "a keeper of sheep," brought "the firstlings of his flock and the fat thereof."[173] From then on sacrificing animals became the norm. It was believed that "without the shedding of blood there is no redemption from sins.[174] Blavatsky adds: "Blood, replacing the sacrificial man by the animal, was considered not as an atonement for the 'fall of man' in Eden, but simply as an expiation for the sins of mankind."[175] But why are we considered "sinners" when the Bible clearly says: "Ye are 'gods'; children of the Light"?[176] This is no doubt another lie perpetrated by the "fallen

---

[171] Gen. 4:2-5; Ex. 14:31; Lev. 25:55; 2 Sam. 3:18; 1 Kings 18:36; 2 Kings 10:10; Job 1:8; Isa. 52:13.

[172] Isa. 25:9.

[173] Gen. 4:1-5.

[174] Lev. 17:11; Heb. 9:13, 22.

[175] Isis Unveiled, Vol. II, pp 42, 524.

[176] Ps. 82:6; Matt. 5:14; John 10:34; Eph. 1:5, 11; 5:8; 1 Thes. 5:5.

ones" to inhibit our advancement!

After the flood, Noah sacrificed "beasts," and when Jehovah "smelled the sweet savor" he vowed not to again curse the ground.[177] Why curse the ground that feeds you? Sitchin further explains:

> "Much of our . . . knowledge of the Deluge and the events preceding it comes from the text <u>When the Gods as Men</u>. In it the hero of the Deluge [Noah] is called Atra-Hasis. . . . The 'gods,' fleeting, were watching the destruction at the same time, but the situation within their own vessels was not very encouraging, either. Apparently, they were divided among several spaceships. Tablet III of the Atra-Hasis epic describes the conditions on board one where some of the Anunnaki shared accommodations with the Mother Goddess. 'The Anunnaki, great 'gods,' were sitting in thirst, in hunger.'. . . As soon as Atra-Hasis had landed, he slaughtered some animals and roasted them on a fire . . . the hungry 'gods gathered like flies over the offering.' Suddenly they realized that man and the food he grew and the cattle he raised were essential."[178]

Jehovah later instructed Abraham to sacrifice a three-year old heifer, a three-year old she goat, a three-year old ram, a turtledove and a young pigeon. After Abraham had done so, "a smoking furnace and a burning lamp passed between those pieces."[179] The meat was beamed up and the astronauts enjoyed a feast! And what a feast that would be! One cow, one goat, one

---

[177] Gen. 8:21.
[178] <u>The Twelfth Planet</u>, pp 384-385, 390, 398, 400, 412.
[179] Gen. 15:9-10, 17.

ram and two birds! Why else were they so particular about Abraham's use of young, tender animals?

Before the Law of Moses, with its officiating priesthood, temple, and consecrated altar, sacrifices were performed by the head of each family. After that only a priest could perform the rite. Aaron and his sons, the first to be sanctified as officiating priests, sacrificed a calf, a goat, a bull and a ram. After they had blessed the people, "the glory of the Lord appeared unto all the people. And there came a fire out from before the Lord, and consumed upon the altar the burnt offering and the fat; which when all the people saw, they shouted, and fell on their faces."[180] When an angel appeared to Gideon, after he had prepared for him "a kid and unleavened cakes," the angel touched them with his staff and "consumed them,[181] (beamed them up)". David, Solomon, Elijah and Job's burnt offerings were also "consumed."[182] No wonder Jehovah was "full of the burnt offerings,"[183] his humans fed him well!

After spending forty years in the wilderness, the Hebrews continued their daily practice of sacrifice in "the land of Canaan."[184] And these sacrifices were not small, they were huge! The Old Testament reports:

> "And they sacrificed sacrifices unto the Lord, and offered burnt offerings on the morrow after that day, even a thousand bullocks, a thousand rams, and a thousand lambs."[185]

"Hezekiah said, come near and bring sacrifices

---

[180] Lev. 9:1-24.

[181] Judg. 6:11-21.

[182] 1 Kings 18:36-38; 1 Chron. 21:26; 2 Chron. 7:1-3; Job 1:16.

[183] Isa. 1:11.

[184] Lev. 23:3; 24:8; Num. 15:36; 28:9; 1 Kings 18:36; 2 Kings 16:15; 1 Chron. 16:40; 2 Chron. 8:23; 13:11; Ezra 6:9-10; Ezek. 45:23; 46:13; Dan. 8:11-13; 11:31; 12:11; Amos 4:4; Heb. 1:3; 10:11.

[185] 2 Chron. 29:20-21.

and thank offerings into the house of the Lord. . . And the number of the burnt offerings, which the congregation brought, was three-score and ten bullocks, an hundred rams, and two hundred lambs: all these were for a burnt offering to the Lord. And the consecrated things were six hundred oxen and three thousand sheep. . . And also the burnt offerings were in abundance, with the fat of the peace offerings, and the drink offerings for every burnt offering."[186]

"Solomon offered a sacrifice of peace offerings, which he offered unto the Lord, two and twenty thousand oxen, and an hundred and twenty thousand sheep. The brazen altar that was before the Lord was too little to receive the burnt offerings, and meat offerings, and the fat of the peace offerings. Solomon and the congregation of Israel sacrificed sheep and oxen, which could not be told nor numbered for multitude."[187]

Jehovah and his host did not "consume" all the sacrifices, a "remnant" was to be eaten by the Levite priests.[188] When Solomon completed the temple, Jehovah said: "I have heard thy prayer, and have chosen this place to myself for an house of sacrifice,"[189] but he was not pleased with all the sacrifices, or in some cases, the neglect of them. He registered several complaints:

"Thou hast not brought me the small cattle of thy burnt offerings; neither hast thou honored me with

---

[186] 2 Chron. 29:31-35.

[187] 2 Chron. 5:6; 7:5; 1 Kings 8:62-64.

[188] Lev. 2:3; 6:16; 1 Sam. 9:12-13.

[189] 2 Chron. 7:12.

thy sacrifices. I have not caused thee to serve with an offering, nor wearied thee with incense. Thou hast bought me no sweet cane with money [honey?], nor hast thou filled with the fat of thy sacrifices; but thou hast made me to serve with thy sins, thou has wearied me with thine iniquities."[190]

"Is there iniquity in Gilead? Surely they are vanity: they sacrifice bullocks in Gilgal, yea, their altars are as heaps in the furrows of the fields."[191]

"The sacrifice of the wicked is an abomination . . . how much more when he bringeth it with a wicked mind."[192]

"They sacrifice flesh for the sacrifices of mine offerings, and eat it; but the Lord accepteth them not. Now will he remember their iniquity and visit their sins."[193]

"They shall not offer wine offerings to the Lord, neither shall they be pleasing unto him: their sacrifices all be unto them as the bread of mourners; all that eat thereof shall be polluted; for their bread for their soul shall not come into the house of the Lord."[194]

"Cursed be the deceiver, which hath in his flock a male, and voweth, and sacrificeth unto the Lord a corrupt thing: for I am a great King, saith the Lord of hosts!"[195]

---

[190] Isa. 43:23-24.
[191] Hos. 12:11.
[192] Prov. 3:;27; 15:8.
[193] Hos. 8:13.
[194] Hos. 9:4.
[195] Mal. 1:14.

Sounds a bit arrogant, doesn't it? And these sacrifices were not only offered to Jehovah, "the God of Israel," but to many other 'gods,'[196] who were not idols, but living beings; other ancient astronauts. In some cases even children were sacrificed, however, Jehovah was against this practice.[197]

The prophet Samuel was the first person to suggest that Jehovah enjoyed "obedience more than sacrifice."[198] Then David, stating that his ears had been "opened," wrote: "For thou desirest not sacrifice; else would I give it: thou delightest not in burnt offering."[199] Later, David's son, Solomon, said: "To do justice and judgement is more acceptable to the Lord than sacrifice."[200] Jehovah himself declared: "If I were hungry, I would not tell thee: for the world is mine, and the fullness thereof. Will I eat the flesh of bulls, or drink the blood of goats? Offer unto God thanksgiving; and pay thy vows unto the Most High."[201] But other scriptures state that he did eat the sacrifices.[202]

In Isaiah we read: "To what purpose is the multitude of your sacrifices unto me? saith the Lord; I am full of the burnt offerings of rams, and the fat of fed beasts; and I delight not in the blood of bullocks, or of lambs, or of he goats."[203] Jeremiah denied that Jehovah had ever commanded them to make sacrifices; Hosea reported: "For I desired mercy, and not sacrifice; and the knowledge of God more than burnt offerings;"

---

[196] Judg. 16:23; 1 Kings 11:8; 2 Kings 10:19; 12:3; 15:4, 35; 16:4; 17:32-33; 2 Chron. 28:4, 23; 33:22; Hos. 11:2; Acts 7:41; 14:13, 18; 1 Cor. 8:4; 10:19-28; Rev. 2:14, 20.

[197] Lev. 20:2-5; 1 Kings 11:5, 7; 2 Kings 23:10; Ps. 106:37-38; Jer. 7:31; 19:5; Ezek. 16:20; Amos 5:26; Zeph. 1:5.

[198] 1 Sam. 15:22.

[199] Ps. 40:6; 51:16-17; 107:21-22; 118:27.

[200] Prov. 21:3.

[201] Ps. 50:12-14.

[202] 2 Sam. 7:6-7; Isa. 1:11; Ezek. 44:15-16; see also: De. 10:8; Mal. 1:7, 12.

[203] Isa. 1:11; 61:8.

and Micah asked: "Will the Lord be pleased with thousands of rams, or with ten thousands of rivers of oil? . . . What doth the Lord require of thee, but to do justly, and to love mercy, and to walk humbly with thy God?"[204] But these prophets blatantly contradicted the instructions given in the Law of Moses that demanded daily sacrifices. (The Bible often contradicts itself.)

Daniel said the sacrifices would cease, but his contemporary, Ezekiel, who was contacted by the spacecraft, gave new instructions. Therefore after the Hebrews returned to their homeland, sacrifices were given daily.[205] The practice lingered on until the time of Jesus, who tipped over the tables in the temple, advocating "mercy not sacrifice."[206] The Hebrews had some concept of this philosophy, for when Jesus questioned them, a scribe answered: "To love him [God] with all the heart, and with all the understanding, and with all the soul, and with all the strength, and to love his neighbor as himself, is more than all whole burnt offerings and sacrifices."[207] Paul said: "Present your bodies a living sacrifice, holy, acceptable unto God, which is your reasonable service, for Christ . . . the ultimate sacrifice that need be performed only once . . . hath given himself for us an offering and a sacrifice to God."[208]

In the Old Testament the sacrifices were generally large animals such as oxen, bulls, sheep and goats, but during the time of Jesus, they had been reduced mostly to birds. Jesus did however, find men selling "sheep and oxen" in the temple.[209] When Mary and Joseph brought the baby Jesus to the temple,

---

[204] Jer. 6:20; 7:21-23; Hos. 6:6; Mic. 6:7-8.

[205] Ezra; Nehemiah; Ezek. 40:42; 43:18-27; 44:11; 46:24; Dan. 8:11-13; 9:27; 11:31; 12:11.

[206] Matt. 9:13; 12:7.

[207] Mark 12:33.

[208] Dan. 9:27; 11:31; 12:11; Matt. 9:13; 12:7; Rom. 12:1; Eph. 5:2; Heb. 9:19-26; 10:3-12; 13:15-16; 9:19-26; 10:3.

[209] Gen. 31:54; Judg. 6:26; 1 Sam. 15:15; 2 Sam. 24:22; Isa. 56:7; Jer. 6:20; Mark 9:49; Luke 2:24; John 2:13-16.

they sacrificed, "according to the Law of Moses: a pair of turtledoves, or two young pigeons."[210] Jesus did not require sacrifices, but asked only that we love God and love one another.

Throughout the New Testament, the word sacrifice is also used symbolically,[211] but we can still see traces of the exoteric rather than the esoteric practice surviving in the Christian Eucharist, with the breaking of the bread (the body of Christ) and drinking of the wine (the blood of Christ) and in the "pujas" of the eastern traditions, where flowers, rice, fruit and oil are still offered to the "gods."

---

[210] Luke 2:22-24.
[211] Phlp. 1:17; 4:18; Heb. 7:27; 9:26; 10:1-14; 1 Pet. 2:5.

PART III

JEHOVAH AND THE SPACECRAFT

SPACECRAFT IN THE BIBLE

Were the various tribal "gods" of ancient scriptures divine "Elohim?" Were they space beings from other planets or solar systems? Were they an advanced race of beings living inside the "hollow earth?" Or could there have been a remnant of high-tech beings who survived the sinking of Atlantis around 10 or 11,000 BC? Perhaps they were all four, but I favor the idea of space beings because there is so much evidence of extra-terrestrial contact, not only in the Bible, but also in various other ancient texts.

The Bible describes the vehicles of the "gods" as bright lights, flashes of lightning, fire and smoke that causes strong wind, whirlwinds, earthquakes and loud peals of thunder. Does this remind you of a launching at Cape Canaveral? Two types of space suits are also described. (1) "shining garments the color of burnished brass, amber or beryl" with "the loins girded with fine gold," and (2) "garments white as snow, with paps girded with a golden girdle," with "arms and feet like polished brass."[212] In addition to vehicles and gear, the Bible also speaks of astronomy, listing the "seven stars of Pleiades, Arcturus with his sons, Orion, the chambers of the south, the crooked serpent and Mazzaroth (the Zodiac).[213]

Let us view some of the many Biblical scriptures to see if they substantiate the idea that the "gods" traveled in spacecraft. In the following, you will note the term "clouds." Why is this term used? If you have even seen a spacecraft--and I have--its metallic body is generally hidden within a forcefield or illuminating sheath of ionized and atmospheric molecules,

---

[212] Ezek. 1:7-27; 8:2; 10:1-2; Dan. 7:9; 10:5-6; 12:6-7; Matt. 28:3; Mark 16:5; Luke 24:4; John 20:12; Acts 1:10; 10:30; Rev. 1:10-16; 2:18; 15:6; 19:6.

[213] Job 9:7-9; 26:13; 38:31-33; Ps. 147:4; Amos 5:8.

resembling a cloud.[214] Consider these passages and decide for yourself:

> "Can any understand the spreadings of the CLOUDS, or the noise of his tabernacle? Behold he spreadeth his light upon it, and covereth the bottom of the sea. . . . With CLOUDS he covereth the light; and commandeth it not to shine by the CLOUD that cometh betwixt. The noise thereof sheweth concerning it; also concerning the vapor."[215] "Like the noise of chariots on the tops of mountains shall they leap, like the noise of a flame of fire that devoureth the stubble."[216]
>
> "He holdeth back the face of his throne and spreadeth his CLOUD upon it."[217]
>
> "God, who rideth upon the heaven in his excellency on the sky . . . maketh the CLOUDS his CHARIOT . . . walketh upon the wings of the wind."[218]
>
> "[He] will hiss unto them from the end of the earth; and behold they shall come with speed swiftly."[219]

This would indicate that Jehovah surrounds himself with "clouds" and travels "swiftly" in these "noisy, hissing, vapor-emitting" vehicles. In technical terms these smoke-billowing "cloud" particles could be described as by-products of the exhaust emissions from the spacecraft's propulsion system, a process

---

[214] For a more detailed description, see Unconventional Flying Objects, by Paul R. Hill, Hampton Roads Publishing Company, Inc. VA, 1995.

[215] Job 36:29-33; Ps. 105:39; Joel 2:5.

[216] Joel 2:5.

[217] Job 26:9.

[218] De. 33:26; Ps. 68:4; 104:3.

[219] Isa. 5:26.

similar to our modern jet streams. Retro-rockets and main thrusters make a tremendous noise in their descent. In addition to "thunder," the Bible also describes their noise as "hornets" or the "sound of chariots of many horses running to battle."[220] No wonder the Native Americans called them "Thunderbirds"!

The Bible says these noisy, vaporous "clouds" have "wheels" and "wings."[221] When Isaiah was beamed aboard, he said of Jehovah's "throne" (a term that seems to indicate the space commander's chair or the inside of the craft):[222] "The posts of the door moved at the voice of him that cried, and the house was filled with smoke."[223] A door that opens to one's voice command sounds quite technical, doesn't it? In addition to "doors," the scriptures inform us that the craft also had "windows," and "gates."[224]

The Bible says the "glory of the Lord" is in the "clouds" and "his voice came out of the cloud."[225] Whenever the being within the craft spoke, it sounded like "a host" or a "multitude," the "sound of many waters," the "voice of a trumpet," or a "voice of mighty thunderings."[226] Such descriptions clearly reveal a loudspeaker. When you substitute the word angel for astronaut, and cloud for spacecraft, the Bible makes perfect sense. It was certainly not unusual for the ancient bedouin tribes to mistake such a dynamic display of technology for God! When a World

---

[220] Ex. 23:28; De. 7:20; Josh. 24:12; Ezek. 3:12-13; 43:2; Rev. 9:9.

[221] Ex.19:4; 25:20; 37:9; De. 32:11; 1 Kings 8:6; Isa. 5:28; 6:2; 8:8; 10:14; 40:31; Ezek. 1:6-25; 3:13; 10:2-21; 11:22; 17:3; 23:24; 26:10; Dan. 7:4-9; Rev. 9:9.

[222] Isa. 6:1; Jer. 17:12; Ezek. 1:26-28; 10:1-2; Dan. 7:9; Rev. 4:2-6.

[223] Isa. 6:1-4.

[224] Windows - Gen. 7:11; Ps. 102:19; Isa. 24:18; Mal. 3:10. Gates - Job 38:17; Ps. 118:19-20; 24:7, 9; 87:2; 100:4; 107:16-18; 122:2; Isa. 13:2-3; Jer. 7:2; Ezek. 8:3; 9:2; 14:9; 11:1; 40:3; Mic. 1:12; Matt. 7:13-14; Luke 13:24; Rev. 21:12. Doors - Ezek. 8:3-16; 10:19; 11:1; 40:13; Rev. 4:1.

[225] Ex. 16:10; De. 4:11-12, 33, 36; 2 Chron. 5:13-14; 2 Sam. 22:12-14; Ps. 18:11-13; Isa. 10:3-4.

[226] Ezek. 1:24; Dan. 10:6; Rev. 1:10, 15; 14:2; 19:6.

War II airplane crashed on a remote island, the natives worshipped it as a "god." It is human nature to revere that which we do not understand. Look at our current reaction to "crop circles." Some people view them as holograms that reveal UFO propulsion systems, while others herald them as being divinely energized. Perhaps they are both.

Note by the following underlined names of places, that the Biblical visitations were not a cosmic event, such as the passing of a comet or an asteroid, but occurred in specific locations. Note also the dynamic effect they had upon the environment. If you have ever looked at the trees, hills or mountains through the vapor of a jet airplane, they will appear to "skip, move" or "bow down." And if you have ever watched the launching of a rocket, you will understand the meaning of the "pestilence and burning coals" and the "dividing of the flames."[227] How else could ancient people describe space technology?

> "Then the earth shook and trembled; the
> foundations also of the hills moved and were
> shaken, because he was wroth. There went up a
> smoke out of his nostrils, and fire out of his
> mouth devoured; coals were kindled by it. He
> bowed the heavens also, and came down; and
> darkness was under his feet. . . . He made dark-
> ness his secret place; his pavilions round about
> him were dark waters and thick clouds of the skies.
> At the brightness that was before his thick clouds
> passed, hail stones and coals of fire."[228]
> "Bow the heavens, O Lord, and come down;
> touch the mountains, and they shall smoke . . .
> toucheth the land, and it shall melt."[229]

---

[227] Ps. 29:7; Hab. 3:5.

[228] 2 Sam. 22:8-13; Ps. 18:7-13; see also Hab. 3:5, 10.

[229] Ps. 104:32; 144:5; Amos 9:5.

"The Lord cometh forth out of his place, and will come down and tread upon the high places of the earth. And the mountains shall be molten under him, and the valleys shall be cleft, as wax before the fire, and as waters that are poured down a steep place."[230]

"The Lord will roar from Zion; and the habitations of the shepherds shall mourn, and the top of Carmel shall wither."[231]

"O God, when thou wentest forth before thy people, when thou didst march through the wilderness; The earth shook, the heavens also dropped at the presence of God; even Sinai itself was moved at the presence of God. . . . Why leap ye, ye high hills?"[232]

"Rend the heavens; the fire causeth the waters to boil; when thou didst terrible things . . . thou camest down, the mountains flowed down at thy presence."[233]

"Lord, when thou wentest out of Sier, when thou marchedst out of the field of Edom, the earth trembled, and the heavens dropped, the clouds also dropped water. The mountains meltedst from before the Lord."[234]

"A fire goeth before him, and burneth up his enemies round about. His lightnings enlightened the world: the earth saw and trembled. The hills melted like wax at the presence of the Lord."[235]

---

[230] Mic. 1:3-4.

[231] Amos 1:2.

[232] Ps. 68:7-8, 16.

[233] Isa. 64:1-3.

[234] Judg. 5:4-5.

[235] Ps. 97:3-5.

"The voice of the Lord is upon the waters: the God of glory thundereth: the voice of the Lord is powerful; the voice of the Lord is full of majesty. The voice of the Lord breaketh the cedars of Lebanon. He maketh them also to skip like a calf; Lebanon and Sirion like a young unicorn. The voice of the Lord divideth the flames of fire. The voice of the Lord shaketh the wilderness of Kadesh. The voice of the Lord maketh the hinds to calve, and discovereth the forests."[236]

"The mountains skipped like rams, and the little hills like lambs. . . . Tremble, thou earth, at the presence of the Lord."[237]

"With the multitude of my chariots I am come up to the height of the mountains, to the sides of Lebanon, and will cut down the tall cedar trees thereof, and the choice fir trees thereof; and I will enter into the lodgings of his borders, and into the forest of Carmel. I have digged and drunk strange waters, and with the sole of my feet have I dried up all the rivers of besieged places."[238]

"God came from Teman (south), and the Holy One from Mount Paran. His glory covered the heavens, and the earth was full of his praise. And his brightness was as the light; he had horns coming out of his hand: and there was the hiding of his power. Before him went the pestilence, and burning coals went forth at his feet. He stood, and measured the earth: he beheld and drove asunder the nations; and the everlasting mountains were

---

[236] Ps. 29:5-10.
[237] Ps. 114:4-7.
[238] 2 Kings 19:23-24.

scattered, the perpetual hills did bow."[239]
"Oh that thou wouldest rend the heavens, that
thou wouldest come down, that the mountains
might flow down at thy presence, as when the
melting fire burneth, the fire causeth the waters to
boil."[240]

What would cause this tremendous reaction and the
illusion of fire? Perhaps the heat of the rocket thrusters and
propulsion devices, exhaust sparks from the main thruster or the
feathering action of the directional thruster. You will also note in
the scriptures above that the entire craft was often considered to
be "God" or an angel, rather than a divine being inside a vehicle.
This is especially evident in the case of Ezekiel, in which he
considered the four whirling portions of the craft to be "living
creatures." When a "chariot of fire" appeared to him, he said: "I
looked, and behold, a whirlwind came out of the north, a great
cloud, and a fire infolding itself, and a brightness was about it,
and out of the midst thereof as the color of amber, out of the
midst of the fire. Also out of the midst thereof came the likeness
of four living creatures. And this was their appearance; they had
the likeness of a man. And every one had four faces, and every
one had four wings. And their feet were straight feet; and the sole
of their feet was like the sole of a calf's foot; and they sparkled
like the color of burnished brass."[241]

G. Cope Schellhorn, using the term "cherubim-motors,"
gives an excellent interpretation of this scripture in his book:
Extraterrestrials in Biblical Prophecy:

"Verses four to twenty-eight of the first chapter of
the Book of Ezekiel are a brief though vivid

---

[239] Hab. 3:3-6.

[240] Isa. 64:1-2.

[241] Ezek. 1:4-7.

account of a spacecraft's approach, braking action, and landing. Ezekiel describes four helicopter-like appendages used for feathering the final descent as well as the main thruster and control rockets in service as the ship hovers, then observes the landing wheels of the ship as it rolls to the ground. The wheels appear to be reversible and retractable and are of special interest to him. . . (He) interprets the landing legs and pads and helicopter-like rotor assemblies and fairings attached to the craft as living, attending Cherubim. . . . In Revelation (Rev. 4:6-8), the seraphim of 'six wings' each (four wings with Ezekiel) are used to explain the four helicopter-like engines and their blades used in this particular design of craft which is found in various places in the Old Testament and as late as Saint John. . . . As in Revelation, the singing, whirring helicopter pods are interpreted by Isaiah (Isa. 6:1-8) as the seraphim offering praise to the Lord."[242]

Another flowery term the Bible uses for the landing legs and feet is "candlesticks." While observing a craft, Zechariah states: "I have looked and behold a candlestick all of gold, with a bowl [upside down] on top of it, and his seven lamps thereon, and seven pipes to the seven lamps, which are upon the top thereof: and two olive trees by it, one upon the right side of the bowl, and the other upon the left side thereof."[243] The "seven lamps" were no doubt windows with lights inside. The term

---

[242] <u>Extraterrestrials in Biblical Prophecy</u>, G. Cope Schellhorn, Horus House Press, Inc., WI, 1990, pp 19, 22, 96, 103.

[243] Zech. 4:1-3.

"eyes" is also used to designate the windows of the craft.[244]

John, like other prophets, thought the entire vehicle was a divine being. When he saw the craft bringing Jesus, he described: "I saw seven golden candlesticks; and in the midst of the seven candlesticks one like unto the Son of man . . . and he had in his right hand seven stars; and out of his mouth went a sharp two-edged sword: and his countenance was as the sun shineth. . . . And, behold a door was opened in heaven: and the first voice . . . said, Come up hither and I will shew thee things

EZEKIEL'S CRAFT, by Nasa engineer, Josef F. Blumrich, on page 14 of his book: The Spaceships of Ezekiel, copyright 1974 by Econ Verlagsgruppe. Used by permission of Barton Books, a division of Random House, Inc.

---

[244] Ezek. 10:12; Dan. 10:6; Zech. 3:9; 4:10; Rev. 1:14; 4:6-89; 5:6; 19:12.

which must be hereafter."[245] Similar to the craft seen by Zechariah, John saw a series of sevens. The "two-edged sword" that came out of the craft's mouth was no doubt a ramp or walkway, since it was accompanied by the door being "opened in heaven" and the voice bidding him to "come up hither." These crafts, depicted by the upside-down "bowl," seem to be disc-shaped, as opposed to the "cigar" shapes, which the Bible calls a "cloudy pillar," a "flying roll" or a "scroll."[246]

Could these "clouds" have been smaller shuttle craft traveling to the planet from a larger mothership that hovered above the atmosphere? Or could they have been rockets landing on earth, then returning to an orbiting space station? In his book, The Keys of Enoch, Dr. J. J. Hurtak's glossary definitions of the terms "Legion Ship" and "Mothership" also shed light on this subject.[247]

In addition to these specific appearances, the craft also performed specific tasks. The Bible says:

> "And the Lord went before them by day in a pillar of a cloud to lead them the way; and by night in a pillar of fire, to give them light. . . . And the pillar of the cloud went from before their face, and stood behind them: and it came between the camp of the Egyptians and the camp of Israel. . . . The Lord looked unto the host of the Egyptians through the pillar of fire and of the cloud, and troubled the host of the Egyptians."[248]
> "And it came to pass on the third day in the

---

[245] Rev. 1:12-17; 4:1.

[246] Ex. 13:21; De. 31:15; Ps. 99:7; Isa. 34:4; Joel 2:30; Zech. 5:1-2; Rev. 6:14.

[247] The Keys of Enoch, pp 585, 592. See also Dr. Hurtak's glossary definition for "Har Maggedon" (Armageddon) and "Jerusalem Command," pp 577, 580.

[248] Ex. 13:21; 14:19-20, 24.

morning, that there were thunders and lightnings, and a THICK CLOUD upon the mount and the VOICE of the trumpet exceedingly loud [loudspeaker]: so that all the people in the camp trembled."[249]

"The fire of the Lord burnt among them and consumed them . . . there went out fire from the Lord and devoured them."[250]

"The Lord rained upon Sodom and upon Gomorrah brimstone and fire from the Lord out of heaven . . . thunder and hail and the fire ran along upon the ground; and the Lord rained hail upon the land of Egypt; there was hail, and fire mingled with the hail."[251]

To destroy entire cities, they must have been equipped with lasers, missiles and nuclear explosives. Evidence of nuclear blasts and vitrification are found in various places on earth. At the Ba'albek terrace in Lebanon, site of the oldest known temple of Ba'al, is found the most massive megalithic structure on earth. With slabs weighing 800 to 1,000 tons each, it evidently served as a spaceport. Miles and miles of scorched, blasted and broken rocks are also found in Scotland, Ireland, Britain, Austria, and the Sinai Peninsula. Rux further explains:

"Vitrification is the fusing of brick or stone into glassine glaze by extreme heat, which is common to nuclear destruction. . . The ancient Hittite cities of Turkey are vitrified, as are forts found in Peru, Scotland, Ireland, France, and India. The Mahabharata describes the blast in India: 'It was a

---

[249] Ex. 19:16-19; 34:5.

[250] Lev. 10:2; Num. 11:1.

[251] Gen. 19:24; Ex. 9:23:24; Luke 17:29.

single projectile charged with all the power of the Universe. An incandescent column of smoke and flame. . . . An iron thunderbolt, a gigantic messenger of death, which reduced to ashes the entire race of the Vrishnis and the Andakhas.' . . . The <u>Uruk Lament</u> states that the gods themselves

CRAFT SEEN BY ZECHARIAH AND JOHN
(See Zech 4:1-3; Rev. 1:12-17; 4:1)

paled in horror at the devastation they had wrought, its 'gigantic rays reaching up to heaven . . . the earth trembling to its core.'"[252]

---

[252] <u>Architects of the Underworld</u>, pp 255-257, 331.

Such destruction of the earth, in which the sun will be darkened and the Mount of Olives split in half, is prophesied for our future.[253] The Bible describes the destructive "day of Jehovah's judgement":

> "Let all the inhabitants of the land tremble. . . . A fire devoureth before them, and behind them a flame burneth. . . . The appearance of them is as the appearance of horses; and as horsemen, so shall they run. Like the noise of chariots on the tops of mountains shall they leap, like the noise of a flame that devoureth the stubble, as a strong people set in battle array. . . . The earth shall quake before them; the heavens shall tremble; the sun and the moon shall be dark, and the stars shall withdraw their shining; and the Lord shall utter his voice before his army; for his camp is very great; the day of the Lord is great and very terrible; and who can abide it? .. . I will show wonders in the heavens and in the earth, blood and fire, and pillars of smoke."[254]
> "Behold, he shall come up as clouds, and his chariots shall be as a whirlwind: his horses are swifter than eagles. Woe unto us! for we are spoiled."[255]

What effect did these extraterrestrial visitors and their magnificent craft, have on the humans, who considered the vehicle, as well as the beings inside of them, to be an integral part of the "godhead?" According to the accounts given in the Bible,

---

[253] Isa. 24:1-6, 17-20, 23; 64:1-3; 66:15-16; Ezek. 32:7-8; 38:18-21; Amos 8:8-9; Hag. 2:6-7; Zech. 14:3-10; Matt. 24:29; Luke 21:25-26; Rev. 8:5.

[254] Joel 2:1-11, 30.

[255] Jer. 4:13.

it frightened them to the point of "falling upon the ground, becoming dumb, experiencing a deep sleep," and "retaining no strength."[256] Sounds like the same paralyzing beams that the modern UFOs use today. What did the visitors do? With Ezekiel, they "sat him upon his feet and the spirit entered him;" with Daniel they "set him upright and touched him on the lips;" and with John, Jesus "laid his right hand upon him."[257] The visitors then offered the humans some type of a sedative or a mind-altering drug in the form of a "book" or a "roll" which they were told to eat. They were told that although it would "make thy belly bitter, it shall be in thy mouth sweet as honey."[258]

In addition to landing on earth and bringing messages to certain individuals, the Old Testament reveals that Jehovah also brought several people to visit his "high places."[259] It gives many instances of Ezekiel being transported, using such descriptions as: "The spirit took me up . . . took me by a lock of mine head, and the spirit lifted me up between the earth and the heaven . . . lifted me up and brought me unto the east gate of the Lord's house . . . brought me into the land of Israel, and set me upon a very high mountain."[260] On one occasion, Ezekiel didn't want to go. He said: "I heard also the noise of the wings of the living creatures that touched one another, and the noise of the wheels over against them, and a noise of great rushing. So the spirit lifted me up, and took me away, and I went in bitterness, in the heat of my spirit; but the hand of the Lord was strong upon me."[261] In the New Testament, Philip was lifted up and set down somewhere else; John was carried away in the spirit and set upon a mountain; and even Jesus, during his temptation, was transported by Satan from

---

[256] Ezek. 1:28; 3:23; 43:3; Dan. 8:9, 13; 10:15-16; Acts 9:4; Rev. 1:17.

[257] Jer. 1:9; Ezek. 2:1-2; Dan. 8:18; 9:21; 10:10, 16; Rev. 1:17.

[258] Jer. 15:16; Ezek. 2:8-10; 3:1; 8:3; Rev. 10:8-11.

[259] De. 32:13; Ps. 18:33; 89:27; 91:14; Isa. 33:5; 58:14.

[260] Ezek. 3:12-14; 8:3; 11:1, 24; 37:1; 40:1-2.

[261] Ezek. 3:13-14.

the wilderness to the top of the temple pinnacle, then set upon a mountain.[262]

When Jehovah invited Moses, Aaron and seventy of the elders to ascend Mt. Sinai, they actually "saw the God of Israel and did eat and drink."[263] When Jehovah called to "his anointed," Cyrus, a Persian king who liberated the Hebrews from their Babylonian captivity, he said: "I will give thee treasures of darkness, and hidden riches of secret places."[264] For the humans to have visited, dined and received treasures from these "clouds," they must have been of a material substance rather than ethereal. Like modern sightings, they looked quite solid, and luckily the bedouins didn't have a military establishment that tried to convince them that what they were seeing was nebulous cosmic phenomena, a super nova, an unusual planetary alignment, a comet, swamp gas, or a weather balloon! (Unfortunately, our modern-day NASA, which was originally guided by scientists, is now influenced by the military. A military that is steadily becoming more secretive and dictatorial. This is not the case in other countries, who are sharing UFO information and building special airports for them. Japan has even erected a museum to display UFO artifacts!)

Jesus, who appeared and traveled in a "cloud," is also associated with fire. John, the Baptist, said, "Jesus shall baptize you with fire." With the pouring out of the Holy Spirit on the Day of Pentecost, "there appeared unto them cloven tongues like fire." And when Jesus appeared to Saul, his radiance "was above the brightness of the sun," so bright, in fact, that it blinded him.[265] Was Jesus overshadowed by a spacecraft? If so, his mentor, Lord Maitreya, who held the "Office of the Christ" on earth, was far higher than Jehovah. Jesus, radiating the Divine Light of Christ

---

[262] Matt. 4:2-8; Luke 4:4-13; Acts 8:39-40; Rev. 1:10; 17:3; 21:10.

[263] Ex. 24:9-11.

[264] Isa. 45:1-5.

[265] Matt. 3:11; Luke 3:16; 12:49; Acts 2:3; 26:13-14.

Consciousness, came to counteract the falsehoods of Jehovah by teaching his followers to bypass the polluted priesthood by making direct contact with the "Father Within." He said that he, meaning the Christ Consciousness, was the "door" or the "way."[266]

In addition to Jesus and the prophets traveling in a "cloud," the twentieth century appearances of the virgin Mary are also associated with "clouds." This was especially apparent during the "miracle" at Fatima, Portugal, in 1917, when 80,000 people were gathered in the rain. Suddenly a huge spacecraft, described as "a luminous globe spinning through the clouds," stopped to hover over the people. It blocked the rain and hid the sun. When the brightly lighted craft moved forward, then backward and skipped around, the natives presumed that the sun was moving. This was a common mistake, for both David and Paul described the brilliance "as the sun before me."[267] A glowing craft was also mistaken for the sun during ancient times when the sun "stood still and hasted not to go down about a whole day," and the sun "moved ten degrees backward," actions which Isaiah called Jehovah's "strange act"[268] Strange indeed, for the sun does not behave in this manner, while a shining spacecraft could easily give this illusion.

The virgin Mary also appeared in Lourdes, France; Guadalupe, Mexico; and Medjugorje, Yugoslavia. In my opinion, this technology does not take away from the divinity of Jesus, the virgin Mary, or the prophets, but merely confirms their use of spacecraft or ethereal "Merkaba Vehicles" to assist mankind. Without the intervention of some of these great beings--perhaps those referred to as the "Galactic Federation of Planets," the "Family of Light," or the "Christ Forces in Space"--the world might have faltered, especially after our splitting of the atom. Our

---

[266] John 14:6.

[267] Ps. 89:36; Acts 26:13.

[268] Josh. 10:12-13; 2 Kings 20:9-11; Isa. 28:21; 38:8; Hab. 3:11.

planet may have even exploded as did Maldek, which is believed to have become the asteroid belt!

Why do Biblical students feel threatened when the scriptures coincide with modern technology? We are currently sending spacecraft to Mars and are planning to establish an atmosphere in order to form a colony there. Like the beings in Genesis, we too plan to create a "firmament." How wonderful to find that the Bible describes such cosmic events as the breaking up of Tiamat ("Rahab"). Instead of diminishing its validity, it actually increases it! As our understanding of Biblical technology expands, the Bible becomes even more acceptable! What could be better than to understand the technology behind the "miracles;" to find that God and quantum physics walk hand in hand; to finally break down the barriers between religion and science?

A few centuries ago Galileo was excommunicated because he said the world was round. The Church, quoting the scriptures about "the four corners of the earth," insisted that the earth was square, completely ignoring the scriptures describing, "the circle of the earth" and "the circuit of heaven."[269] If mankind can advance technologically, how much greater is the mind of the technological "gods?" Why should our interpretations be so limiting? Daniel indicated that at the "end time," the end of the Piscean and the beginning of Aquarian Age, "knowledge shall be increased."[270] Our computer age has increased the spread of knowledge, but we still have a long way to go to find wisdom.

You may think my idea of Jehovah, Jesus, the virgin Mary and the prophets traveling in a spacecraft or a "Seraphic Transport" seems blasphemous, but who's to say that the Unseen God--the Omnipotent, Omnipresent, Omniscient Spirit--doesn't utilize these lesser "gods" and the angelic hosts as messengers? Perhaps planetary visitation is a divine method of monitoring and uplifting creation. Unless we are spiritually awakened, we cannot

---

[269] Job 22:14; Ps. 19:6; Isa. 11:12; 40:22; Rev. 7:1.
[270] Dan. 12:4.

see spirits, so there has to be some means of communication.

Evidently mankind needs to progress through a period of "testing"--the so-called "Polarity Integration Game"--in order to prove our worth! We have not been abandoned. Instead we have been temporarily placed in a realm of darkness to allow us, like a tiny seed that has been planted in the ground, to gradually sprout, then of its own volition to seek the light. The light has always been there, but the majority of people have been too busy looking upward to take the time to look within.

The Bible asks: "What is man, that thou art mindful of him, and the son of man, that thou visitest him?"[271] It also states "the Lord shall give his angels charge over thee, to keep thee in all thy ways and bear thee up [beam us up] in their hands."[272] And when it mentions angels and chariots, it doesn't mean just a few isolated angels scattered here and there, but "thousand thousands and ten thousand times ten thousand angels" and "twenty thousand" chariots.[273] What better way to administer to us as a big-brother overseer?

Although modern-day angels are depicted with wings and halos, those of the Old Testament appeared as ordinary men who walked, talked, slept and ate, so beware 'lest you "entertain angels unaware."[274] Jacob even "wrestled with an angel" and saw angels ascending and descending on a ladder (transporter beam) that reached from earth to heaven, with Jehovah or one of the astronauts standing above it.[275] The angels did, however, display

---

[271] Ps. 8:4-5; see also 136:23; 144:3.

[272] Ps. 91:11-12. Although we were created a little lower than the angels, they serve us as guardians. We can eventually ascend higher than them to serve as co-heirs with Christ, while they cannot.

[273] De. 33:3-4; Ps. 68:17; 148:2; Jer. 4:13; Dan. 7:10; Hab. 3:8 148:2; Rev. 5:11.

[274] Gen. 16:7-11; 18:1-16; 19:1-2, 15-22; 21:17-21; 31:11; 32:1; Num. 22:22-35; Josh. 5:13-14; Judg. 2:1-5; 6:11-22; 13:3-5, 17-22; Ps. 44:23; 78:65; Ezek. 1:26; Dan. 8:15; Zech 2:1; Heb. 13:2.

[275] Gen. 28: 12-13; 32:24-30.

superior powers; manifesting fire and disappearing at will. Both them and their crafts were evidently interdimensional.

THE ABODE OF THE GODS

Did Jehovah travel in a small shuttle craft or in a large mothership? We have been describing "clouds" and "chariots" that "hissed, emitted vapor, made noise and shook the environment." These smaller shuttle crafts evidently transported the "gods" and beamed aboard those who were worthy. Sitchin, quoting the Babylonian Epic of Creation, describes the assignments of the "Anunnaki:"

> "The texts reveal that three hundred of them--the 'Anunnaki of heaven,' or 'Igigi'--were the true astronauts who stayed aboard the spacecraft without actually landing on earth. Orbiting earth, these spacecraft launched and received the shuttle craft to and from earth. . . . Staying aloft, [they] were apparently never encountered by mankind. Several texts say that they were 'too high up for mankind.'. . . [Those] who landed and stayed on earth, were known and revered by man. The texts that state that 'the Anunnaki of heaven . . . are 300,' also state that 'the Anunnaki of earth . . . are 600.'" [276]

One of the clearest biblical scriptures of smaller shuttle crafts emerging from a large mothership states: "And I turned and lifted up mine eyes and looked, and behold, there came four chariots out from between two mountains; and the mountains were mountains of brass." [277] Doesn't that remind you of the

---

[276] The Twelfth Planet, pp 327-328.
[277] Zech. 6:1.

modern-day sightings that claim to have seen smaller "chariots (spacecraft)" emerging from a larger mothership? And a huge mothership does indeed resemble a "mountain of brass!" The Old Testament describes Jehovah's mothership, the abode of the gods, by such glorious terms as: "City of God, Sanctuary, Tabernacle, Secret Place of the Most High, Pavilion, Place of Thunder, Refuge, Hiding Place, Shield, Congregation, Holy Hill, Holy Mountain, Holy Habitation, Footstool, Throne and Mount Zion."[278]

Isaiah described being transported into Jehovah's "throne" within the mothership, saying: "Above it stood the seraphims: each one had six wings; with twain he covered his face, and with twain he covered his feet, and with twain he did fly."[279] When Daniel visited, he saw "thousand thousands ministering unto him and ten thousand times ten thousand standing before Jehovah."[280] So it had to have been a gigantic craft!

David, after being "brought forth [beamed up]," then "hiding" in Jehovah's "pavilion," called it "a large place" that is "high above all the people." Longing to return, he said: "How amiable are thy tabernacles, O Lord of hosts! My soul longeth, yea, even fainteth for the courts of the Lord. . . . For a day in the courts is better than a thousand."[281] The Prophet Amos called God's abode "stories in the heaven."[282] Great shades of Star Trek's "Enterprise!"

Was Jehovah's spacecraft called "Zion?" Since the actual

---

[278] De. 26:15; Job 20:26; 29:4; Ps. 3:3; 5:12; 11:4; 14:2; 15:1; 18:11; 20:2; 25:14; 27:5; 31:20; 32:7; 33:13-14; 43:3; 46:4; 50:2; 57:1; 63:2; 68:4-5, 24; 73:17; 77:13; 78:67-69; 81:7; 84:11; 87:3; 89:5, 7; 91:1-2, 9; 96:6; 99:1-3; 102:19; 107:7, 36; 119:114; 134:2; 149:1; 150:1; Prov. 8:2; Isa. 13:2; 35:10; 40:9; 45:3; 57:13, 15; 65:15; 66:1; Joel 2:1; 3:21; Obad. 17, 21; Mic. 2:7; Hab. 2:20; Zech. 2:13; 6:1; 8:3.

[279] Isa. 6:1-7.

[280] Dan., chapter 7.

[281] 2 Sam. 22:17, 20; Ps. 18:16, 19; 27:5; 31:8; 10; 84:2, 10; 99:1-2; 11.

[282] Amos 9:6.

Mount Zion, or Mount Hermon, is a peak in Syria, it is interesting that Jehovah, calling the Hebrews by the pet-name, "Jeshurun," referred to them as "Syrians."[283] The transfiguration of Jesus occurred on Mount Hermon ("Sion" or "Zion") and it has been prophesied that he will return there with many "angels" and "one hundred forty-four thousand" chosen disciples.[284]

The name "Zion" was not mentioned during the time of Moses. Its spiritual significance began when David took the "castle" or "stronghold of Zion," one of the seven hills of Jerusalem.[285] After making it the capital of Israel, it was referred to as "the City of David, which is Zion," but the name "Zion" also seems to indicate the loftier "abode" of Jehovah that is described as orbiting "high above the people."[286] Some scholars will argue that "Zion" refers only to Jerusalem, but the Bible distinguishes: "Ye are come unto Mount Zion, and unto the Heavenly Jerusalem. The Jerusalem which is above [hovering] is free, which is mother [mothership] of us all."[287] The Old Testament says "Mount Zion cannot be removed, but abideth forever," while the city of Jerusalem was destroyed several times.[288]

The Hindus call the "abode" of their "gods" "Mount Meru" or "Hiranyapura, the Golden City;" the Atlanteans referred to it as "Sumeru;" the Iranians use the term "'Illiyum;" the Canaanites called it the "Crest of Zaphon;" and the Buddhists call it "Zinnola." The term "Mount Atlas" was used in Atlantis;

---

[283] De. 3:9; 4:48; 26:5; Josh. 11:3; 12:1; Ps. 29:6; 48:1; 78:54; 133:3.

[284] Dan. 7:13; Matt. 2:2, 9-10; 3:13-17; 17:1-15; 24:29-31; Mark 1:9-11; 3:21; 9:2-13; 13:26; 14:62; 16:19; Luke 9:28-36; 21:27; 24:51; Acts 1:9; Eph. 1:20; Rev. 1:7; 14:1, 14.

[285] 2 Sam. 5:7-9; 1 Chron. 11:5-7.

[286] 1 Kings 8:1; 2 Chron. 5:2; Ps. 9:11; 14:7; 20:2; 76:2; 99:2; 110:2; 128:5; 134:3; 135:21; Isa. 2:3; 8:18; 24:23; 28:16; 31:9; Joel 3:17, 21; Mic. 4:2, 7.

[287] Gal. 4:26; Heb. 11:16; 12:22.

[288] 2 Kings 25:1-26; 2 Chron. 36:11-40; Ps. 125:1; Jer. 39:1-14; 52:1-30; Joel 3:20-21; Zech. 8:3.

"Asgard" and "Valhalla" in the Nordic teachings; "Tilmun," "Dilmun" or "Mount Mashu" in Sumeria; "Mount Olympus" in ancient Greece; and "The Great White Throne" in Freemasonry. Almost every culture has a concept of a tribal "god" who lives in a "heavenly abode." These huge motherships are not detected by our radar systems because they are fourth dimension. The smaller shuttle crafts and rockets can evidently attune their frequency to the third dimension in order to function here.

Are all these "heavenly abodes" in the same location? "Mount Zion" is said to be "above" Jerusalem,[289] while Shamballa is said to hover over the Gobi Desert, Mount Atlas over Greece, and Valhalla over Scandinavia. Remember that each of the "gods" was assigned a specific area.[290] Detailed accounts are given of Ezekiel's visit to one of these "abodes" and also of the "Holy Mountain of God" from which the Prince of Tyrus was expelled, but neither of these are called "Zion."[291] Just as there are higher and lower levels in the divine hierarchy, there are evidently higher and lower vibrational levels of motherships.

The New Testament, speaking of the "third heaven" as well as the "many mansions," states that while Paul was "caught up to the third heaven, he heard unspeakable words, which it is not lawful for a man to utter."[292] A "third heaven" would indicate there are several dimensions. Using the plural term "heavens, heavenly places," and "worlds," the Bible refers to the "heaven" into which David and Jesus ascended, to "sit at the right hand of God," as being "higher than the heavens."[293] This indicates that

---

[289] Gal. 4:26.

[290] Ex. 15:17; De. 32:8-9.

[291] Ezek. 28:12-14; chapters 40-48.

[292] John 14:2; 2 Cor. 12:1-6.

[293] Heavens (plural) - De. 10:14; 32:13; Job 9:8-9; Ps. 19:1; 33:6; 50:4; 68:4, 33; 103:19; 115:16; 123:1; 148:4; Eph. 1:3; Heb. 1:2; 7:26; 9:23-25; 11:3; 2 Pet. 3:5. Higher Heavens - Ps. 16:10; 55:3; 110:1; Matt. 22:41-45; 26:64; Mark 12:35-37; 14:62; 16:19; Luke 20:39-44; 22:69; Acts 2:25-28, 34-36; 7:55-56; 13:34-37; Rom. 8:34; Eph. 1:20; 4:10; Col. 3:1; Heb. 1:3; 4:14;

there are many kingdoms, planetary, as well as the "higher heavens" that are solar, galactic and universal.[294] The Koran, as well as The Book of Enoch, speaks of seven heavens.[295] Promising to gather the Hebrews from captivity, Jehovah promises: "If any of thine be driven out unto the outmost parts of heaven, from thence will the Lord thy God gather thee, and from thence will he fetch thee."[296] Was he was afraid the other "gods" might abduct and carry some of his people to another planet?

David asked, "Lord, who shall abide in thy tabernacle? Who shall dwell in thy holy hill?"[297] Isaiah asked: "Who are these that fly as a cloud, and as the doves to their windows?"[298] Jehovah answered: "I dwell in the high and holy place, with him also that is of a contrite and humble spirit."[299] Enoch was "translated" to heaven; Elijah "went up by a whirlwind;" David "sits at the right hand of God;" and Jesus "ascended into heaven."[300] The Bible calls these residents "watchmen" or "saints", those immortal "ministers," who he "lifted up" and made a "flaming fire" to "reside in heavenly realms."[301] And since the Bible says: "No man hath ascended up to heaven, but that came down from heaven,"[302]

7:26; 8:1; 10:12; 12:2; 1 Pet. 3:22; Rev. 1:16; 2:1.

[294] Job 9:5-10; 38:31; Ps. 19:1-4; 57:5; 68:4; 74:12-17; 77:19; 89:9-10; 147:4; 148:4-8; Isa. 14:13; 19:1; 40:12. 22-23; 43:16-17;4 5:12; 49:9; 51:9-11; Amos 5:8; Rev. 12:1.

[295] Koran; Surah 2:29; 17:44; 23:17; 65:12; 67:3; 71:15; The Book of Enoch, R. H. Charles, Oxford Clarendon Press, 1912.

[296] De. 30:3-4; Neh. I:9.

[297] Ps. 15:1.

[298] Isa. 60:8

[299] Isa. 57:15.

[300] Gen. 5:24; 11:5; 2 Kings 2:11.

[301] De. 33:2; Ps. 68:17; 103:20; Isa. 13:1-5; 57:13, 15; Jer. 51:9; Dan. 7:4, 10, 14, 18, 22, 27; Hos. 9:8; Joel 3:11; Mic. 7:4; Zech. 4:14; Luke 22:29; John 14:12; Acts 7:53; Gal. 3:19; Eph. 1:3, 18; 2:6, 19; 4:12-13; Col. 1:12; 1 Thes. 3:13; 2 Tim. 4:18; Heb. 2:2; Jas. 2:5; 1 Pet. 1:4; Jude 14; Rev. 5:8-11; 9:16; 11:12; 15:3; 20:4.

[302] Gen. 28:12; Ps. 139:8; Prov. 30:4; John 3:13; Eph. 4:8-10.

they were merely returning home to reclaim their "first estate." After having been chained to the "wheel of rebirth" for many centuries, their soul had finally reunited with their Divine Spirit.

They are referred to in other philosophies as the "Ascended Masters" of the "Great White Brotherhood." Thus the "gods" beam up those whom they consider worthy, promising that we can become "fellow citizens" with them, providing we make the necessary changes to reach a state of perfection.[303] Jesus, who ascended into the highest realm, speaks of "the hope of life eternal, which God, that cannot lie [the Higher, Unseen God], promised before the world began." He assures: "if a man keep my saying, he shall never see death,"[304] but not everyone will be taken; he warned: "One shall be taken and other one left."[305]

The Old Testament describes this saintly state: "The way of life is above to the wise, that he may depart from hell beneath."[306] It also states: "And it shall come to pass in the last days, that the mountain of the Lord's house shall be established in the top of the mountains, and shall be exalted above the hills; and all nations shall flow unto it," but only the "ransomed" will be chosen."[307] Paul describes this "rapture" as being "caught up together in the clouds to meet the Lord [Jesus] in the air."[308] "Flow, raptured, and caught up" are merely flowery descriptions of teleportation.

---

[303] De. 18:13; 33:3; 2 Sam. 22:33; 1 Kings 8:61; Job 8:20; 14:14; Ps. 18:32: 24:3-4; 71:20; 119:93; Isa. 13:3; Dan. 4:17; 6:17; 4:23; Matt. 5:48; John 6:62; 17:23; Rom. 4:17; 1 Cor. 15:49-55; 2 Cor. 3:18; 13:11; Eph. 2:19; 4:12-13; Col. 2:6, 13; 4:12; 1 Tim. 6:13; 2 Tim. 3:17; Phlp. 3:20; Heb. 11:40; 12:23; Jas. 3:2; 2 Pet. 3:9; Rev. 11:12.

[304] John 5:24; 8:51; 11:26; 12:32; 14:12; Titus 1:2.

[305] Matt. 24:40-41; Luke 17:34-37.

[306] Prov. 15:24.

[307] Ex. 30:12; Job 36:18; Ps. 49:7; Prov. 13:8; Isa. 2:2-4; 35:10; 40:9; 51:10; Jer. 31:6, 11; Mic. 4:1-2; 1 Thes. 4:17.

[308] 1 Thes. 4:17.

What do the saints do in these "holy cities" or motherships? Sit around playing harps all day? Hardly! The root word for worship means work. Because they are skilled in directing the natural and cosmic forces to the planet and its lifewave, they act in the capacity of mediators of wisdom for the earth. The Bible says as they "love, praise and worship God, sing and rejoice, their prayers become "incense that ascends to the golden altar before the throne of God."[309] It says the "congregation" or "assembly" of the saints "receive God's words, are "taught the secret mysteries," and are "told of peace."[310] They also "bring laws to mankind" and are instrumental in bringing "visions."[311] In addition to these duties, the Bible says they "observe earth from windows from on high" and "record the names and the actions of mankind"[312] in the "Book of Life,"[313] for it is they who "judge" mankind.[314]

The Bible says Jesus will come with "ten thousand of his saints to judge." --"whatsoever a man soweth, that shall he also reap." [315] It is appropriate for the saints (who in modern

---

[309] Neh. 9:25; 2 Chron. 6:41; Ps. 17:1; 29:9; 30:4; 31:23; 34:9; 68:30; 68:35; 87:9; 89:7; 132:9, 16; 145:10; 149:5; 2 Thes. 1:10; Rev. 5:8; 7:10; 8:3-4.

[310] De. 33:3; Ps. 5:1; 27:5; 50:5; 68:26; 85:8; 89:5,7; 111:1; 149:1; Col. 1:26.

[311] Ex. 19:18-19; De. 33:2; Dan. 4:13; 8:13; 12:5-7; 1 Pet. 1:12.

[312] Gen. 7:11; Ex. 14:24; De. 30:19; 31:28; Job 16:19; Ps. 52:9; 102:19; Isa. 24:18; Mal. 3:10.

[313] Gen. 18:19; Ex. 32:32; 33:12, 17; Ps. 1:6; 37:18; 56:8; 69:28; Isa. 4:3; Dan. 12:1; Nah. 1:7; Mal. 3:16; Matt. 7:23; Luke 10:20; John 10:14-15, 27; Eph. 1:4, 11; 2 Tim. 1:9; 2:19; Phlp. 4:3; Heb. 12:23; Rev. 3:5; 13:8; 17:8; 20:2, 15; 21:27; 22:19.

[314] De. 7:6; Job 36:29-31; Ps. 22:6-7; 49:14; 50:5; 52:9; 68:17; 132:9; 145:5, 9-10; 148:14; 149:1-9; Prov. 2:1; Isa. 53:2-3; Dan. 7:10, 21-22; Obad. 21; Mic. 4:2-3; Zech. 14:5; Matt. 19:28; 25:31; Luke 10:39; 22:30; Acts 7:53; 23:3; 1 Cor. 6:1-2; 14:33; 16:1, 15; Gal. 3:19; 1 Thes. 3:13; 2 Thes. 1:7, 10; Heb. 2:2; Jude 14; Rev. 1:7; 2:26; 3:21; 5:11; 9:16; 20:4.

[315] De. 33:2; Ps. 68:17-18; Zech. 14:5; Gal. 6:7; 1 Thes. 3:13; 2 Thes. 1:10; Jude 14; Rev. 5:11; 11:18; 20:4.

terminology are referred to as "The Karmic Board") to act as judges, since they are noted for their "faith, patience, and righteousness."[316] They can return to earth as "teachers" or "watchmen" to patrol earth and to inform us of the "kingdom of God's power." And while in embodiment, although they are sometimes killed, they are "free from death."[317] They are evidently still learning, and like the angels, are still subject to failure. Those who fell, like Lucifer, the Nefilim, and King Tyrus, are said to have "turned to folly."[318] This is why it is necessary for the divine hierarchy to occasionally make "intercession" for them.[319] The Dead Sea Scrolls describe a human "saint" residing in Jehovah's mothership. You will note a bit of arrogance in his declaration:

> "El Elyon gave me a seat among those perfect forever, a mighty throne in the congregation of the gods. None of the kings of the east shall sit in it and their nobles shall not come near it. . . . For I have taken my seat in the congregation in the heavens and none find fault with me."[320]
> "And you shall be like an angel of the Presence in the holy dwelling, to the glory of the God of hosts . . . round about, serving in the royal temple and casting lot with the angels of the Presence, and the common counsel. . . . And may he make you holy among his people, and for a luminary . . . a

---

[316] Jude 3; Rev. 13:10; 14:12; 19:8.

[317] Num. 11:25; Ps. 16:3; 79:2; 116:15; 127:1; 145:11-12; Isa. 26:5-8; 30:20-21; 52:8; 62:6; Jer. 6:17; 31:6; 51:12; Ezek 3:17; 33:7; Dan. 4:13, 17, 23; Hos. 9:8; 11:12; Mic. 7:4; Rev. 11:12; 16:6; 18:24.

[318] Job 4:18; 15:15; Ps. 85:8.

[319] Rom. 8:27.

[320] Jesus and the Dead Sea Scrolls, James H. Charlesworth, Doubleday, NY, 1992, p. 296.

diadem for the holy of holies."[321]

The "saints" assisted Jesus at his ascension.[322] Aaron, the King of Tyrus and Ezekiel were saints.[323] Judah was "faithful with the saints," and Paul said he was "the least of the saints."[324] Because Job knew about the saints, he was asked to which of them he would turn.[325] The Catholic Church still honors the saints and angels, but the Protestants are seemingly unaware of their presence. The saints will come to protect mankind during "Armageddon," and although the dark forces will "make war on them" and "wear them out," the kingdom will still be "given to them" to rule.[326] They will then serve with Jesus, their King, for a thousand years.[327]

It has been stated by several sources that during this "Golden Age of Peace" we will be ruled by these divine beings; that there will be a "master" on every street corner. They will not control us, but will merely serve as an example until we learn to spiritually govern ourselves. It is not so much that the present churches and governments will be destroyed, but they will be infiltrated by divine beings, who will restore their original purity. The Divine Plan is not to destroy, but to purify.

Jesus spoke not of Jehovah's mothership, "Zion," but of a new "place" that he would prepare for us "above the hills." It is into this "place" that he told us to "flee" for protection, saying: "I go to prepare a place for you. And if I go, I will come again, and

---

[321] More Light on the Dead Sea Scrolls, Millar Burrows, The Viking Press, NY, 1958, p 397.

[322] Acts 1:9-11.

[323] Ps. 101:16; Ezek. 28:12, 15; 33:7.

[324] Hos. 11:12; Eph. 3:8.

[325] Job 5:1.

[326] Ps. 37:24; Dan. 7:18, 21-22, 25-27; Mic. 4:1; Rev. 5:10; 13:7; 20:4, 6, 9; 21:1-2; 22:5.

[327] Ps. 22:28; Rev. 15:3; 20:4, 6.

receive you unto myself."[328] It was not already there, he "prepared" it, hence the term "New Jerusalem, Heavenly Jerusalem, Heavenly Kingdom" or "God's Kingdom of Eternal Life."[329] John describes this "place" as having material characteristics:

> "I [John] saw the holy city, New Jerusalem, coming down from God out of heaven, prepared as a bride adorned for her husband. . . . And he carried me away in the spirit to a great and high mountain and shewed me that great city, the holy Jerusalem, descending out of heaven. . . . A great wall and high . . . twelve gates, and at the gates twelve angels . . . the wall of the city had twelve foundations . . . and the foundations of the wall of the city were garnished with all manner of precious stones."[330]

Paul says: "Ye are come unto the city of the Living God, the Heavenly Jerusalem, and to an innumerable company of angels."[331] When John was given the Revelation, he saw "twenty-four elders, seven spirits of God, angels, and a sea of glass."[332] "The Ministry of the Children" group describe:

> "The glorious Mothership, the New JerUSAlem, City of Light . . . is still afloat in between the fourth and fifth dimensions outside the earth's atmosphere. When it is finally in dock mode it

---

[328] Matt. 24:16; Mark 13:14; Luke 21:21; 22:8; John 12:32; 14:2-3.

[329] Matt. 5:34; 24:16; John 14:2; Acts 7:48-49; Rom. 11:26; Gal. 4:25-26; Heb. 11:16; 12:22; Rev. 3:12; 4:2; 11:19; 14:1; 15:5, 8; 21:2-4.

[330] Rev. 21:2, 10, 12, 14, 19, 25.

[331] Heb. 12:22.

[332] Rev., chapters 1-6.

will be permanently locked into the coordinates of its location within the earth's atmosphere. . . . All, conscious or unconscious will bask in the new heavenly frequencies of ecstasy, known to many as 'The Rapture!'"[333]

Again I want to stress that I believe with all my heart, mind, body and soul in the divinity of Jesus and the virgin Mary, and that there is an invisible Father God, a Divine Spirit with which we can merge in mystical union. But this solitary communion with Divine Mind, is an inner trip. The Bible says: "Be still and know that I am God."[334] The pathway is provided by the breath; all we need to do is to follow it. During our descent into silence--a divine rest beyond all thought--inner adjustments occur on a soul level that is beyond our perception. In a deep meditation, the pineal gland allows melatonin to flow, an action that also occurs during the "quickening" of initiations, as indicated by the white powder on the sarcophagus. We don't have to visit the Great Pyramid or be beamed up into a craft to experience this intimate connection with the Father God; a spark of his divine Presence resides within us!

So, lest you judge Jehovah too harshly as you read Part Four about Moses, ask yourself if the Hebrew slaves, who had just emerged from Egypt, were of a state of consciousness to merge with the Unseen Father God in deep meditation? Or were they, as the Old Testament says, an unruly, "stiff-necked, froward people in whom there is no faith"[335] that could only be dealt with by a tough cookie like Jehovah? Look at what they did to Jesus hundreds of years later and what they are still doing to the Palestinians! Now please understand that I am not picking on the Jewish people; I have a great respect for them and have many

---

[333] The Solar Cross 11:11 Stargate, pp 23-24.

[334] Ps. 46:10.

[335] Ex. 32:9; 33:3-5; De. 32:30.

wonderful Jewish friends. I am speaking of mankind in general. Were any of the nations ready for a deep inner mysticism three or four thousand years ago? Look how they distorted the divine teachings of Osiris, Seth, Melchizedek and Akhenaten. Are many of us ready for it today?

Don't let the following details about the violent, jealous tribal "god," Jehovah, as depicted in the Old Testament, turn you against the Ultimate Divine Source, the Unseen God of love, mercy and peace. Instead of throwing out the baby with the bath water, remember that Jehovah was only a tribal "god" of that particular area. According to ancient writings and countless legends of mythology, the "gods" of the surrounding areas were equally vicious and emotionally unstable. Perhaps the writers in those primitive times exaggerated these traits; using fear in an effort to assure obedience. Perhaps they merely described them from their own paradigm perspectives. Or perhaps these "gods" had to be vicious in order to deal with unevolved mankind.

Jesus, with his loving kindness and dedicated service, chose not to beam down from a spacecraft, a "Seraphic Transport", or an ethereal "Merkaba Vehicle," but to be born as one of us. He came to rectify the lies and manipulations of Jehovah. His teachings of "truth and grace, and salvation by faith" were to "cast out the evil prince of this world" by awakening the feminine intuitive forces of the Divine Mother, the Holy Spirit, to balance the masculine forces in "mystical marriage," thereby allowing us to give birth to the Christ Child within.[336]

How will our modern astronauts treat the unevolved lifewaves they encounter on other planets? Will the inhabitants consider our astronauts in their spacecraft to be "gods" in heavenly chariots, as was depicted in Star Trek's episode: "The Picard?" Probably so; its human nature to either fear or revere that which cannot be understood.

---

[336] John 1:14-17; 12:31; 14:30; 16:11; For further description, see Part VI about Jesus.

PART IV

JEHOVAH GUIDES MOSES IN THE WILDERNESS

MOSES IN EGYPT

When the Egyptian Pharaoh was trying to kill the Hebrew male babies, three-month old Moses, a Levite hidden in a stream of water, was found by the Pharaoh's daughter and raised as her son.[337] He became "governor over Egypt" and an initiate of the Egyptian mystery schools. The Bible says he "was learned in all the wisdom [knowledge] of the Egyptians."[338] According to Blavatsky: "Even among the early Canaanites and Phoenicians there had always been a class of initiated adepts. Moses and his anti-types were complete men, 'gods' on earth, who had united with their Divine Spirit. The spirits of these heroes and sages were termed 'gods' by the ancients."[339] The Dead Sea Scrolls also describe the initiates and their mystery teachings.[340]

At age forty, while witnessing the abuse of an enslaved brethren, Moses "slew" the Egyptian aggressor.[341] Sought by the Pharaoh, he fled to Midian, an area near the Suez Canal, where he married the daughter of a Kenite priest,[342] Jethro, had two sons, and became a shepherd.[343] One day, while leading his father-in-law's flock to the back side of the desert, he came to Mount Horeb, in the Sinai range. There, an "angel of the Lord" appeared to him in a "flame of fire [the captain of the spacecraft, beamed down]." Paul said it was the "Holy Spirit" who "talked in the

---

[337] Ex. 1:22; Ex. 2:1-3, 5-10; Acts 7:20-22; Heb. 11:23.

[338] Acts 7:10, 22.

[339] Isis Unveiled, Vol. II, pp 134-135, 153; The Secret Doctrine, Vol. II, p 465.

[340] See Scrolls: Children of the Dawn, The Book of Secrets, and The Secrets of the Way Things Are.

[341] Ex. 2:11-12; Acts 7:23, 28; Heb. 11:24-25.

[342]The Kenites, who had carried on the traditions of Melchizedek's teachings, worshiped El Elyon who they considered to be a Supreme God, rather than a tribal deity. They were later spared by King Saul (1 Sam. 15:6). See also Note #575.

[343] Ex. 2:10-22; Acts 7:29.

wilderness."[344] Whoever it was, the voice, announcing that he was "the 'god' of thy fathers [Jehovah]," called out of the midst of the burning bush, or thicket, instructing Moses to return to Egypt to set the enslaved Hebrews free so they could inhabit their promised land of Canaan.[345] When Moses expressed his reluctance to perform such a difficult task, and asked for the "god's" name, the voice answered: "I Am That I Am."[346]

Unbeknownst to Moses, "the angel of the Lord" had a different type of slavery in mind for the nearly three million Hebrews,[347] who had been enslaved in Egypt for four-hundred-thirty years.[348] Instead of being guided to the "promised land," they were kept in the desert for forty years to construct a "tabernacle" and to provide food for Jehovah and his "host."

To begin his deceptive plan, Jehovah gave Moses detailed instructions about tricking the Pharaoh by asking for a "three-day journey into the wilderness," to allow the Hebrews an opportunity to "sacrifice to their God."[349] Jehovah emphasized that the Hebrews "borrow" gold, silver, jewels and raiment from them.[350] When Moses expressed a fear that the Pharaoh would not listen to him, and that the Hebrews would not accept him as their leader, since he had grown up with the Egyptians, Jehovah empowered his shepherd's staff with magical qualities to make Moses appear as "a 'god.'"[351] But even after being promised two more feats of magic, and being assured that Jehovah would "stretch out his hand and smite the Egyptians with all his wonders

---

[344] Heb. 3:7-11.

[345] Gen. 15:8; Ex. 3:1-10; Num. 20:16; De. 4:33, 36; 11:12; Acts 7:30.

[346] Ex. 3:11-14. The term "I am that I am" was used in the Egyptian Book of the Dead.

[347] Ex. 38:26 states there were 600,000 "men," not counting the women and children; De. 26:15.

[348] Gen. 15:16; Ex. 12:37.

[349] Ex. 3:15-18.

[350] Ex. 3:21-22.

[351] Ex. 4:1-3; 7:1.

[technology]," Moses, due to his speech impediment, and knowing that the Egyptian priests could also perform magic, was still reluctant to accept the difficult assignment.[352] This enraged Jehovah, but after calming himself, he suggested that Moses ask his brother Aaron to act as his spokesman.[353] Filled with faith, Moses and his family journeyed toward Egypt, but Jehovah sought to kill him because he had not circumcised his son. His wife saved the day by grabbing a "sharp stone" and "cutting" the child.[354]

Eighty-year-old Moses and eighty-three-year-old Aaron conferred with the Pharaoh, who had not even heard of Jehovah, the "God of the Hebrews," but the plan failed miserably and the burdens of the Hebrews were increased.[355] To lift Moses from his depression, Jehovah gave him a strong "charge" and promised to "harden the Pharaoh's heart" and "multiply his signs and wonders."[356]

After a series of nine horrible "plagues," brought about by Jehovah, the Pharaoh was willing to let the Hebrews go, providing their herds and flocks remained, but Moses, well instructed by Jehovah, answered: "Thou must give us also sacrifices and burnt offering that we make sacrifice unto the Lord our God. Our cattle also shall go with us; there shall not an hoof be left behind."[357] Jehovah and his "host" of astronauts were not about to relinquish the animals; their potential barbecues! When the Pharaoh finally decided to let the Hebrews go, Jehovah again "hardened Pharaoh's heart" in order to further prove his technological strength over the Egyptians and their "gods."[358] He

---

[352] Ex. 3:20; 4:4-13; 6:6.
[353] Ex. 4:14-16; 7:1.
[354] Ex. 4:20-26; Heb. 11:23-29.
[355] Ex. 4:27-31; 5:1-9; 7:7.
[356] Ex. 6:13; 7:2-5.
[357] Ex. 10:24-26.
[358] Ex. 7:13; 9:12, 27-28; 10:1-2, 7-8, 20, 27; 11:9.

stated arrogantly: "Go in unto Pharaoh: for I have hardened his heart, and the hearts of his servants, that I might shew these my signs before him; and that thou mayest tell in the ears of thy son, and of thy son's son, what things I have wrought in Egypt, that ye may know that I am the Lord!"[359] The prophets later described Jehovah's arrogant boasting and bragging as gaining "renown to make thee a name."[360]

Jehovah, planning one last "plague," the killing of Egypt's firstborn children, reminded Moses to have his people "borrow" gold and silver jewels and raiment from the Egyptians.[361] Then after changing the Hebrew calendar and giving them instructions to hold a "Passover Feast," Jehovah and his "host," viciously killed Egypt's firstborn children.[362] When a great cry echoed throughout the land, the distraught Pharaoh, who had just lost his only son, finally released the slaves.[363]

As they were preparing to leave, Jehovah "gave them favor in the sight of the Egyptians," so they would give them the gold, silver, jewels and raiment.[364] Jehovah guided them "out of Rameses by the way of the Red Sea," so they would not see the warring Philistines, a non-Semitic race of giants, lest they become fearful and return to Egypt.[365] He guided them by day in a "pillar of a cloud" and by night in a "pillar of fire [spacecraft]".[366]

All was going well for the group until Jehovah once again "hardened Pharaoh's heart to follow them," thereby allowing him

---

[359] Ex. 10:1-2.

[360] Ex. 9:16; 2 Sam. 7:23; Ps. 106:8; Neh. 9:10; Isa. 63:12, 14; Dan. 9:15.

[361] Ex. 11:2, 30.

[362] Ex. 12:1-29.

[363] Ex. 12:30-33.

[364] Ex. 12:35-36.

[365] Ex. 13:17-18; Num. 33:3.

[366] Ex. 13:21-22; 14:24; 40:38; Num. 14:14; De. 1:33; Neh. 9:12, 19; Ps. 78:14; 105:39; Neh. 9:12, 19; Isa. 4:5.

one last opportunity to demonstrate his power and to receive "honor" amongst the Egyptians.[367] The Bible says it was for this reason that Jehovah had "raised up" Moses.[368] (Throughout the Bible, the term "raised up" seems to refer to reincarnation. Moses is believed to have been the reincarnation of Abel and Seth.) When "sixty chariots" of Egyptians pursued the fleeing Hebrews, "the angel of God" in his "pillar of the cloud [spacecraft], retreated from going before the Hebrews and went between the two camps."[369] (Note that it was the "angel of God," rather than God himself.)

When the high-tech Jehovah parted the Sea with a "blast of his nostrils," thereby allowing the Hebrews to cross, with the Egyptians in hot pursuit, he "looked unto the host of the Egyptians through the pillar of fire and of the cloud [windows in the craft] and took off their chariot wheels."[370] This enabled the Hebrews to travel across the Sea safely before Jehovah "blew his wind," causing the waters to drown the pursuing Egyptians.[371] Note the anger, subtle lies, manipulating tricks, and complete disregard for human life that Jehovah took in order to allow him an opportunity to show off his technological powers! The killing of the firstborn and the drowning in the Sea both occurred after the Pharaoh had agreed to free the Hebrew slaves![372] These acts, therefore, were completely unnecessary!

Reaching dry land, Moses and the Hebrews sang: "The Lord is a man of war; who is like unto thee, O Lord, among the 'gods?'"[373] But after several weeks of traveling toward the wilderness of Sin, near Mount Sinai, they began to complain

---

[367] Ex. 14:1-8, 17-18; Num. 14:20-21.

[368] Ex. 9:16; Rom. 9:17.

[369] Ex. 14:7, 10, 19-20; 23:20-21; Isa. 63:9-10.

[370] Ex. 14: 21-25; 15:8.

[371] Ex. 14:26-29; 15:10; De. 11:4.

[372] Ex. 10:27; 14:4.

[373] Ex. 15:3, 11.

about the lack of food, saying: "Ye have brought us forth into this wilderness to kill this whole assembly with hunger."[374] When Jehovah promised to "rain bread from heaven," the "glory of the Lord appeared in the cloud," and the Hebrews were amazed to see the ground covered with quail that evening and "manna," a small round sweetened substance, the next morning.[375] But when they did not gather the "manna" soon enough, "it bred worms and stank" and "when the sun waxed hot, it melted."[376] Their delay made Jehovah angry, henceforth they gathered it immediately, always gathering a double portion of Friday so they could hallow the sabbath as a sacred day of rest to honor Jehovah, who was also known as Sabaoth or Saturn.[377]

Now, lest Jehovah appears to be a thoughtful "god" who provided quail for his followers, the Bible states that during their forty years of wandering in the wilderness, the Hebrews, outside of the priestly Levite tribe, who ate a "remnant" of the sacrifice, were only allowed to eat meat twice.[378] Their diet consisted of "manna" with a little produce, but the "firstfruits," the "firstborn" animals, and even the "firstfruits of the liquors" belonged to Jehovah.[379] And these animal sacrifices that they were instructed to make were not just an occasional ritual, as had been the case with their ancestors, but a required "daily sacrifice," including a continual flow of bread, produce and wine; additional sacrifices were given on special "feast days."[380] Can you imagine being forced to eat "manna" for forty years, while continually smelling

---

[374] Ex. 16:1-3.

[375] Ex. 16:4-16.

[376] Ex. 16:14-21.

[377] Ex. 16:20-29; Rom. 9:29; Jas. 5:4.

[378] Ex. 29:27-35; Lev. 2:3, 10; 6:16-29; 7:9, 31; 8:31; 10:12-17; 21:22; 22:11-15; Num. 18:8-31.

[379] Ex. 13:2; 16:12; 22:29-30; 23:16, 19; 34:20-26; Lev. 6:21; 9:24; Num. 3:13; De. 8:3, 9:3; 18:4; 29:6.

[380] Ex. 23:14-19; 29:31-44; 34:23; Lev. chapters 1-7, 23; Num. 9:15-23, chapters 28-29; De. 16:16; Heb. 10:11.

the aroma of the daily barbecues?

The second time they complained about not having meat, saying, "Our soul is dried away: there is nothing at all beside this manna before our eyes," they were again sent quail, but this time the meat was "plagued" and everyone that had "lusted," died.[381] The third time they registered a complaint, Jehovah sent "fiery serpents" to bite them![382] What a brutal method of weeding out the complainers!

Jehovah's technology came in handy when he caused a rock to spew water, as Moses "smote it with his rod," and when he helped them to win a battle against Amalek, while Moses held his "rod" in the air.[383] But when they were met by Moses' father-in-law, Jethro, who instructed Moses to select others to help him judge the people--counsel which was desperately needed--the great Jehovah was curiously silent.[384] But then, he had never claimed to be a counselor!

CLOSE ENCOUNTERS ON MT. SINAI

Three months after leaving Egypt, they finally reached Mount Sinai. When Moses ascended the peak, Jehovah "called unto him out of the mountain," promising that the Hebrews would be "a kingdom of priests and a holy nation."[385] He told Moses: "I come unto thee in a thick cloud, that the people may hear when I speak with thee, and believe thee forever."[386] He added that on the third day, after the people had "sanctified" themselves, he would "come down in the sight of all the people upon mount

---

[381] Num. 11:4-15, 31-34.

[382] Num. 21:5-6.

[383] Ex., chapter 17.

[384] Ex. 14:24; chapters 17-18; Num. 33:14; De. 25:17-18.

[385] Ex. 19:3-6.

[386] Ex. 19:9.

Sinai."[387] He then told Moses to "set bounds" and see that no one crossed them or "touched" the restricted area.[388] Was he protecting them from radiation? At the end of the third day, the Bible says:

> "There were thunders and lightnings, and a thick cloud upon the mount, and the voice of the trumpet exceedingly loud [loudspeaker]; so that all the people that were in the camp trembled. And Moses brought forth the people out of the camp to meet with God; and they stood at the nether part of the mount. And mount Sinai was altogether on a smoke, because the Lord descended upon it in fire; and the smoke thereof ascended as the smoke of a furnace, and the whole mountain quaked greatly. And when the voice of the trumpet sounded long, and waxed louder and louder, Moses spake, and God answered him by a voice. And the Lord came down upon Mount Sinai, on the top of the mount: and the Lord called Moses up to the top of the mount; and Moses went up."[389]

The mountain, resembling an erupting volcano, was a frightful experience for the Hebrews, who did not want "to hear the voice of God, for fear of death." Even Moses "feared and quaked."[390] When Moses cautiously climbed to the top of the glowing, thundering peak, Jehovah sent him back down to get Aaron and further warn the people of the danger of breaking

[387] Ex. 19:10-11.
[388] Ex. 19:12-13.
[389] Ex. 19:16-20; De. 4:11; 5:4, 22-26.
[390] Ex. 20:19; De. 5:5, 25; 18:16; Heb. 12:18-21.

through the bounds.[391] Quite a hike for an eighty-year-old man, but Mt. Sinai was only a little over six thousand feet high!

While Jehovah gave him the "ten commandments," the people saw the "thunderings and the lightnings," heard "the noise of the trumpet," and saw "the mountain smoking."[392] When Moses "drew near unto the thick darkness" in order to obtain additional laws, Jehovah promised to send an angel to guide him and his people, but warned: "beware of him and obey his voice, provoke him not for he will not pardon your transgressions; for my name is in him."[393] This makes it clear that Jehovah and his "host" were not about to indulge themselves in any humanitarian action such as forgiveness!

Moses was warned once again not to "bow down" to the "gods" of the enemies.[394] The first commandment: "thou shalt have no other 'gods' before me, for I am a jealous God,"[395] reinforces the fact that Jehovah was only one of the tribal "gods." Later the predicted angel appeared to Balaam as a man standing with his sword drawn, however Balaam could not see him until the angel "opened his eyes."[396] The fact that the "angel of Jehovah's host" appeared in human form would indicate that Jehovah, although interdimensional, could also appear in human form. And of course anyone under the command of the warlike Jehovah would naturally have his sword drawn and ready for battle!

Moses descended the mountain, talked to the people, recorded Jehovah's words, built an altar and twelve pillars, offered a sacrifice, read the "covenant" to the people and

---

[391] Ex. 19:21-25.
[392] Ex. 20:1-18; De. 4:11-13; 5:6-21.
[393] Ex. 20:22-26; chapters 21-22; 23:1-23.
[394] Ex. 23:24.
[395] Ex. 20: 3-5.
[396] Num. 22:22-35; Mic. 6:10.

sprinkled them "with the blood of the covenant."[397] Again, quite a job for an elderly man! Jehovah then invited Moses, his three priests and seventy elders, who had been given the inner truths, to "come up unto the Lord," where all seventy-four of them actually "saw the God of Israel." The Bible described this amazing sight:

> "And there was under his feet as it were a paved
> work of a sapphire stone, and as it were the body
> of heaven in his clearness. And upon the nobles of
> the children of Israel he laid not his hand: also
> they saw God, and did eat and drink."[398]

And did the "gods" serve something light and holy like angel-food cake or ambrosia, as was the case with the "gods" of Olympus? Indeed not! The Bible makes it clear they had an appetite for "fat things full of marrow and well-refined wine!"[399] Imagine eating and drinking with "God," especially a wine-bibbing "god!" It is incredible that modern mankind, living in today's technological age, still believe Jehovah was the Highest Supreme God! Would the Omnipresent, Omnipotent, Omniscient Father God of the vast universe of millions of galaxies, visit this tiny, insignificant planet in a remote galaxy that sits at the outer edge of the universe? If this were the case, who would have been taking care of the rest of the universe while the "Most High God" was doing lunch with Moses? Even the President of our nation would not leave headquarters to perform such menial tasks! If we have a Congress, Representatives and Senators to handle such things, how much more organized would God be? The Bible mentions a divine hierarchy of many celestial beings. Couldn't one of these beings have dealt with Moses?

---

[397] Ex. 24:3-8.

[398] Ex. 24:1-2, 9-11; Heb. 11:27.

[399] Isa. 25:6.

He and "his minister" Joshua were then invited "into the mount" [spacecraft], where they remained for "forty days," while the rest of the "nobles" (also called "heroes, adepts" or "initiates") returned to camp.[400] During this time, Moses was given instructions about setting up a "tabernacle" so Jehovah could "dwell among them." It was to be furnished with an "ark of the covenant [a box-like structure containing the written covenant], sacred vessels of gold, furniture overlaid with gold, a brazen sacrificial altar and a laver."[401] Details were also given concerning animal sacrifices, anointing oil, perfumes and special garments for the priests.[402] After these instructions, Jehovah handed him "two tables of stone, written with his own finger."[403] This "Law of Moses" was not unique. The Babylonian King Hammurabi had received a similar code of laws from his god around 1900 BC, some four hundred years before Moses. while the Atlanteans and the Sumerian civilization had received laws centuries before Hammurabi.

In the meantime, due to the great delay of "forty days," the people, fearing that Moses was dead, made "a golden calf to guide them."[404] The calf, representing the Age of Taurus and their association with Egypt, was an tremendous affront to Jehovah, who had instructed them to sacrifice rams, representing the new Age of Aries. When Jehovah became aware of the golden calf, he threatened to "consume" them, but Moses convinced him not to do so, and "the Lord repented of the evil which he thought to do unto his people."[405] Thus Moses, like Noah and Abraham had to

---

[400] Ex. 24:11-18; Num. 21:18; De. 6:5-25; 9:10; Judg. 5:13; Neh. 2:16; Isa. 12:2-3; 42:1; 43:14; Jer. 2:21; 14:3; Matt. 24:22, 24, 31; Mark 13:20, 27; Luke 18:7; Rom. 8:33; 9:11; 11:5, 7, 28; 1 Thes. 1:4; Col. 3:12; 1 Tim. 5:21; 2 tim. 2:10; Titus 1:1; Heb. 12:1.

[401] Ex. chapters 25-30.

[402] Ex. chapters 28-30.

[403] Ex. 31:18.

[404] Ex. 32:1-6; 1 Cor. 10:7.

[405] Ex. 32:7-15.

counsel Jehovah, an act which happened on several occasions.[406] It's a good thing that Moses was a fast talker, or else the Hebrews would have been wiped out in one fell swoop of Jehovah's mighty anger!

When Moses and Joshua came back to camp, Moses was so upset that he broke the "stone tables" Jehovah had given him, then melted and ground the statue of the calf into powder, poured in water and made the people drink it![407] I don't imagine they enjoyed drinking their gold and ash cocktail one bit! Moses then had three thousand people put to death, but prayed for his brother Aaron, asking Jehovah to spare him, even though it was the artistic Aaron who had actually formed the calf.[408]

The next day Moses asked forgiveness for the people, but Jehovah "plagued" them, saying "I will not go up in the midst of thee, lest I consume thee in the way."[409] Joshua later confirmed that Jehovah would not forgive their sins.[410] After Moses told the people about Jehovah's anger, he set up a tent "afar off," so anyone seeking counsel had to go outside the camp. The people watched Moses, and whenever he entered, a "cloudy pillar [transporter beam] descended and stood at the door of the tent, and the Lord talked with him face to face, as a man speaketh unto his friend."[411] This personal contact, however, is contradicted when Jehovah stated that "no man shall see me and live," a precaution meant to prevent them from making unto him any "graven images."[412] Or perhaps he did not want his followers to see that he was a reptition! Jesus also said that no man had seen

---

[406] Gen. 6:1-8; 18:23-33; Num. 12:1, 12-19; 14:11-13; De. 9:11-19.

[407] Ex. 31:17-20; De. 9:21.

[408] Ex. 32:2-5, 21-28, 35; De. 9:20.

[409] Ex. 32:30-35; Ex. 33:2-3; De. 9:24-29; 32:20.

[410] Josh. 24:19.

[411] Ex. 33:4-9, 11; Num. 12:7-8; 14:14; De. 5:4, 22-26; 34:8-10.

[412] Ex. 33:18-23; De, 4:12, 15-18.

God's face,[413] indicating that Jehovah was not God. He told the Jews: "The Father Himself, which hath sent me, hath borne witness of me, ye have neither heard his voice at any time, nor seen his shape, and ye have not his word abiding in you."[414] Thus, the "Father God"("Abba") of Jesus was not Jehovah!

Whenever Moses left the tent, Joshua remained to minister to all who came.[415] Moses was then instructed to make two new "stone tables" for Jehovah to write upon, so once again he climbed the mountain, and the "Lord descended in the cloud and stood with him."[416] Moses remained there another forty days and forty nights, without eating or drinking.[417] When he finally descended his "skin shone" so brightly that he had to "veil his face."[418] Was this radiation?

BUILDING THE TABERNACLE

Moses instructed the people, who had donated supplies for the "tabernacle," and worked with them to prepare it and its furnishings.[419] When it was completed, thirteen months after they had left Egypt, the elaborate structure was finally raised![420] The Bible explains the exciting event:

> "A cloud covered the tent and the glory of the Lord filled the tabernacle. And Moses was not able to enter into the tent because the cloud abode thereon, and the glory of the Lord filled the tabernacle. And when the cloud was taken up

---

[413] John 1:18; 5:37; 6:46.
[414] John 5:37-38.
[415] Ex. 33:11.
[416] Ex. 34:1-7.
[417] Ex. 34:29-35; De. 9:9.
[418] Ex. 34:29-35.
[419] Ex., chapters 35-40.
[420] Ex. 39:43; 40:17.

from over the tabernacle, the children of Israel went onward in all their journeys: but if the cloud were not taken up, then they journeyed not till the day that it was taken up. For the cloud of the Lord was upon the tabernacle by day, and fire was on it by night, in the sight of all the house of Israel, throughout all the journeys."[421]

This "cloud covering" (forcefield from the craft) was not an occasional occurrence, the Bible says: "whether it were two days or a month, or a year, that the cloud tarried upon the tabernacle, the children of Israel abode in their tents, and journeyed not; but when it was taken up [the craft ascended], they journeyed."[422]

Imagine three million impatient Hebrews camping in the harsh Sinai desert, with only "manna" to eat. They had been promised "a land of milk and honey," but instead of being allowed to move forward, they were delayed for thirteen months to construct the "tabernacle," then delayed up to a year at a time while the astronauts occupied it. During some of the great delays, only Moses, Aaron and his sons could come near. Even though it was called the "tent of the congregation," Jehovah decreed: "Anyone that cometh nigh to the tabernacle shall be put to death."[423] This is quite different from the modern-day churches that encourage attendance, but this "tabernacle" was not for the people, it was for the "gods." What a travesty of justice!

Why did Jehovah and his "host" spend so much time hovering over and transporting into, the "tabernacle?"[424] And why did they remain in it for such long periods of time? Why not?

---

[421] Ex. 40:34-38.

[422] Num. 9:15-23; 10:11-12, 34; 16:42.

[423] Ex. 25:8; 39:32; 40:2, 19; Num. 1:51; 3:10, 10:3; 17:13; 18:3-7; Heb. 9:6-7.

[424] Lev. 4:6; 19:30; 21:23.

Being plush and comfortable, it was a break from the confinement of their craft, and their food and wine was prepared for them by the priests. But just how comfortable was the "tabernacle" and how adequate was the food? According to the Bible, the "tabernacle" and all its furnishings were assembled after a "pattern" that Moses had been shown. This was evidently the "gods" modus operandi, for there was also a "pattern" for Noah's Ark and the temples of Solomon, Ezekiel and others.[425] Sitchin explains:

> "Ur Nammu, ruler of Ur, depicted in an earlier millennium how his 'god,' ordering him to build for him a temple and giving him the pertinent instructions, handed him the measuring rod and rolled string for the job. Twelve hundred years before Moses, Gudea made the same claim. . . . [He was given] the complete instructions for the construction of a seven-stage high-rise temple."[426]

The rectangular "court of the tabernacle" that Moses and his followers built was one-hundred-fifty feet long and seventy-five feet wide. It was framed by sixty pillars, twenty on each side and ten on each end. Each of these pillars was seven and a half foot high and upon them hung linen curtains.[427] The gate of the court consisted of four pillars that were "filleted with silver," and "from silver hooks and brass sockets, hung blue, purple and scarlet linen, wrought with needlework."[428]

The fifteen by forty-five foot holy area within the court was supported by a fifteen foot high framework, from which hung

---

[425] Ex. 25:9, 40; 26:30; 2 Kings 16:10; 1 Chron. 28:11-19; Ezek. 43:10-17; Acts 7:44; Heb. 8:5; 9:23.

[426] The Twelfth Planet, pp 26-27.

[427] Ex. 27:9-15.

[428] Ex. 27:16-17.

"blue, purple and scarlet curtains" made of "fine-twined linen" embroidered "with cherubim of cunning work."[429] The fifteen by thirty foot front portion, contained three pieces of furniture: an ornate table, an altar of incense and a golden candlestick [menorah].[430] The table, incense altar, boards, rings, pillars and curtain hooks were "overlaid with pure gold," and the candlestick, seven lamps, dishes, spoons, covers, and bowls" were hammered from "pure gold."[431] The table was filled with shewbread and the altar of incense burned continually, keeping the room enshrouded in a cloud.

An ornate "veil," decorated with flowers, separated the fifteen foot square "holy of holies," thus the inner and outer rooms were constructed on a two-to-one ratio. The inner sanctuary contained the gold-plated "ark of the covenant" that contained shafts of acacia wood and golden rings and was topped with a solid gold "mercy seat" and two overshadowing golden cherubim.[432] Jehovah had said: "I will meet with thee, and I will commune with thee from above the mercy seat, between the crerubims," but whenever he did appear, his form was concealed in a "cloud."[433]

The "ark," containing the stone tables of the covenant, a pot of manna, and Aaron's rod that had miraculously bloomed, is believed to have been an electronic instrument, an energy accumulator, a giant capacitor, or a loudspeaker which acted as a "leyden jar," or an "orgone box," to give off fiery rays and also

---

[429] Ex. 26:1, 31; 36:8, 35.

[430] Ex. 25:23-28, 30; 26:35; 30:1-7; 37:17-28.

[431] Ex. 25:10-11, 13, 23-40; 26:29-32, 37; 30:1-5; 36: 34-38; 37:2-15, 26-28.

[432] Ex. 25:10-20; 26:31-34; Heb. 9:5.

[433] Ex. 25:22; 29:42; 30:6, 36; Lev. 16:2; Num. 7:89; 17:4; 1 Sam. 4:4; 2 Sam. 6:2; 22:11; 2 Kings 19:15; 1 Chron. 13:6; Ps. 18:10; 80:1; 99:1; Isa. 37:16.

TABERNACLE IN THE WILDERNESS

to serve as an instrument of communication.[434] Because it was made of wood, overlaid with gold, both inside and out, it provided two electrical-conducting surfaces. Later, when David was transporting the "ark," and it began to slide off the cart, the driver of the cart, who reached out to steady it, was electrocuted.[435] With such a high-powered generator, no wonder the walls of Jerico fell when the Hebrews marched around it. The "Arc of the Covenant" no doubt bombarded the wall with amplified sound waves! Rux relates:

> "The King's coffer in the Great Pyramid . . . has the exact same dimensions as the Ark of the Covenant. . . . When given a sound slap with the open hand, the coffer can be heard to give off a low note which lasts for a considerable time. . . . This theory [of harmonics] might also explain what the mysterious 'dead spaces' are above the king's chamber in the Great Pyramid. Called by some 'relieving spaces' . . . and called 'spirit stones' by the Egyptians, these are five narrow air spaces, separated by eight to nine fifty-ton blocks of granite forming floors and ceiling between each. . . . They could be resonance chambers . . . each successive one resonating the sound for greater amplification. . . . Sound resonation could have applications in physics for the movement of tremendous masses that we are only now beginning to suspect."[436]

---

[434] Ex. 25:16; 31:18; 32:15-19; 34:28; 40:20; De. 10:1-5; Judg. 20:27-28; 1 Sam. 3:7, 21; 2 Sam. 6:6-7; 1 Chron. 13:9-10; Heb. 9:4.

[435] 2 Sam. 6:2-7.

[436] Architects of the Underworld, p 281.

Blavatsky agrees:

> "The King's Chamber in Cheop's pyramid is an Egyptian 'holy of holies;' the esoteric foundations, or the system used in the building of the Great Pyramid, and the architectural measurements in the Temple of Solomon, Noah's ark, and the ark of the covenant, are the same."[437]

Moses and Aaron were allowed to enter the "holy of holies" only once a year, on Yom Kippur, but even then Aaron, who came to sprinkle blood on the mercy seat in an effort to make an atonement for the sins of all the people, was required to take in a "censer full of burning coals and fire from off the altar, and his hands full of sweet incense to put upon the fire, that the cloud of the incense may cover the mercy seat."[438] Whatever was going on in there was not to be viewed, except through a cloud of dense smoke! Whenever Jehovah wanted to be seen, he made his appearance in "a cloud of glory [transporter beam] at the door of the tabernacle in view of all the people,"[439] but he certainly didn't want anyone to see what went on inside the "tabernacle," especially the "holy of holies" room.

---

[437] The Secret Doctrine, Vol. II, pp 462, 465-466.

[438] Ex. 25:22; 30:10; 40:34-38; Lev. 16:2-17, 34; Heb. 9:7, 25.

[439] Num. 14:10; 16:19, 42; 20:6; De. 31:15.

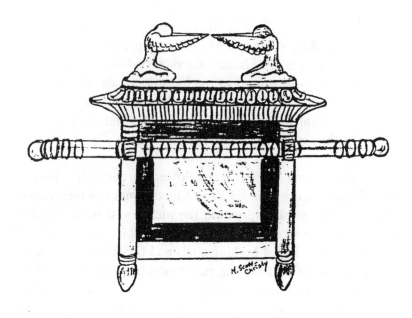

THE ARK OF THE COVENANT

In the outer court, beyond another special curtain that protected the entry of the fifteen by forty-five holy area, sat a huge "laver" (sink) and a massive "brazen sacrificial altar" (barbecue) atop a huge platform that was approached by a long ramp.

Esoterically, the altar of burnt offerings symbolized

114

sacrificing the lower animal nature; the laver, cleansing the lower bodies; the "tabernacle," going into the inner temple, or merging with the soul. Once inside the "tabernacle," the lighting of the seven candles symbolized the activation of the seven spiritual chakric centers, while the eating of the twelve cakes of shewbread and inhaling the incense symbolized partaking of our divine nature in preparation for entering the "holy of holies." The final going "within the veil," symbolized merging with our Divine Source.

Centuries earlier, the immortal "thrice-born" Thoth/Hermes Trismigistis had also received stone tables written by the finger of a "god" and the Egyptians had used a structure similar to the Hebrew "tabernacle" for their "mystery schools." They even had similar utensils and an "ark of the covenant," which they carried on staves. The Hindus of India also had an "ark," which they called "argha."

Who took care of the "tabernacle" with its ornate curtains and golden furniture? Aaron and his four sons had been chosen by Jehovah to "minister unto him in the priest's office," while the remaining Levites, who had been "blessed" because they did not worship the golden calf, became attendants.[440] They "ordered the court continually" by tending the lamps, candles, incense, anointing oil, preparing the daily burnt offering, baking the shewbread, cleaning the holy vessels and disassembling, moving and reassembling the massive tabernacle as they traveled."[441] And this was no small band of servants. There were twenty-two thousand Levite males, who camped around the "tabernacle" to act as a buffer between it and the rest of the tribes, but even they could not "come nigh the inner altar, lest they die."[442]

---

[440] Ex. 28:1-41; 29:1-44; 30:30; 31:10; 32:26-29; 35:19; 39:1-41; 40:13-15; Lev. 7:35-36; 16:1-33; 18:3; Num. 3:1-51; 8:1-22; De. 33:8-10.

[441] Ex. 25:30; 27:21; 29:42; Lev. 1:50-53; 6: 9-13; 24:3-8; Num. 1:50-51; 3:8; 4:16; 8:1-26; 18:4-6, 20-24; 1 Chron. 23:28-32.

[442] Num. 3:39; 4:17-20; 18:1-4.

THE BRAZEN SACRIFICIAL ALTAR

SPECIAL GARMENTS AND ORACLES

The sons of Aaron wore priestly "coats, girdles, bonnets and linen breeches," but the high priest, Aaron, was required to wear an elaborate "holy garment," consisting of a "robe, broidered coat, ephod, breastplate with urim and thummim in the pocket, needlework girdle, two shoulder pieces, and two onyx stones with engravings, a mitre and a crown."[443] Aaron's robe was also "decorated with pomegranates and golden bells on the hem" so "his sound could be heard when he goeth in unto the holy place before the Lord, and when he cometh out, that he die not." As a later precaution, Jehovah told Moses: "Speak unto Aaron that he come not at all times into the holy place within the veil .

---

[443] Ex. 28:4-42; 29:6; 39:28-31; Lev. 6:10; 8:8-9; 16:4; De. 33:8.

116

.. that he die not."[444]

What were these strange instruments on Aaron's garment that Jehovah called an "ephod" and a "urim and thummim?" Communication devices? Jehovah gave the following instructions for making the ephod: "They shall make it of gold, blue, purple and scarlet, and fine-twined linen, with cunning work. Beat the gold into thin plates and cut it into wires to work into the linen. It shall have two shoulder pieces joined at the two edges, and the curious girdle. Thou shalt take two onyx stones and engrave them and make them to set in ouches of gold and put the two stones upon the shoulders of the ephod."[445] The stones must have been large, for upon each one was to be engraved six of the names of the twelve tribes.

The ephod, resembling a long vest, is described as having several sections, but the power came from the onyx stones. Onyx, also called chalcedony, is a microcrystalline variety of quartz that is translucent and sometimes florescent. According to the Bible, onyx, which was found in the land of Havilah in Arabia, was later accumulated for the "holy of holies" in the temple of Solomon.[446] Perhaps these ancient astronauts used onyx for technological purposes like we currently utile crystals. Jehovah was clever in masking his technology!

The Bible describes the "breastplate of judgment" as: "An embroidered, highly colored, piece of linen, doubled in thickness, about nine inches square, to which were attached four rows of precious stones, upon which each was engraved the name of one of the twelve tribes of Israel. In the pouch between the thicknesses were deposited the urim and thummim, small, sacred objects which were used to ascertain a person's guilt or innocence and thereby pronounce judgment," as well as for blessing the

---

[444] Ex. 28:34-35.

[445] Ex. 28:6-7, 9-12, 18, 25-28; 39:3, 6-7.

[446] Gen. 2:10-12; 10:7, 29; 25:18; Ex. 29:5; Lev. 8:7; 1 Sam. 15:7; 1 Chron. 29:2.

food.[447] The breastplate was "to hang from the shoulder piece of the ephod, over the heart."[448] The urim and thummim are also mentioned in the Dead Sea Scrolls and The Book of Mormon.[449] Is the ancient "ephod" comparable to the "smart shirts" used by our military services? Hall said of these unusual communication devices:

> "The onyx buttons were supposed to have oracular powers, and when the high priest asked certain questions, they emitted a celestial radiance. When the onyx on the right shoulder was illuminated, it signified that Jehovah answered the question of the high priest in the affirmative, and when the one on the left gleamed, it indicated a negative answer to the query. . . . The twelve stones of the breastplate, like the onyx stones at the shoulders of the ephod, had the mysterious power of lighting up with divine glory and so serving as oracles."[450]

The urim and thummim, that were used in divination, are analogous to the two figures of Ra and Themi in the breastplate worn by the Egyptians. Quoting from the Sumerian and Akkadian Texts, Sitchin describes the garments worn by Ishtar:

> "[She] very meticulously put on herself seven objects prior to the start of the voyage. . . The SHU.GAR.RA [helmet] she put on her head;

---

[447] Ex. 25:7; 28:4-30; 29:5; 35:9, 27; 39:8-21; Lev. 8:8; Num. 27:21; De. 33:8; 1 Sam. 14:37-42; 28:6, 15; 30:8; Ezra 2:63; Neh. 7:65.

[448] Ex. 28:30.

[449] See Dead Sea Scrolls: Tongues of Fire, Commentaries on Isaiah, The Last Days, A Collection of Messianic Proof Texts, and The Temple Scroll. Also see The Book of Mormon.

[450] The Secret Teachings of all Ages, p cxxxvi.

118

measuring pendants, on her arms; chains of small blue stones, around her neck; twin stones, on her shoulders; a golden cylinder, in her hands; straps, clasping her breast; the PALA [ruler's] garment, clothed around her body. . . . Excavating the Assyrian capital Assur from 1903 to 1914, Walter Andrae and his colleagues found in the Temple of Ishtar a battered statue of the 'goddess' showing her with various contraptions attached to her chest and back. . . . On her head . . . a special helmet; protruding from it on both sides and fitted over the ears are objects that remind one of a pilot's earphones. . . . Over a blouse of see-through material, two parallel straps run across her chest, leading back to and holding in place an unusual box of rectangular shape. This box is held tight against the back of the 'goddess's' neck and is firmly attached to the helmet with a horizontal strap. . . . The weight of the box is increased by a hose that is connected to its base by a circular clasp."[451]

Thus the "tabernacle in the wilderness," with its "holy of holies," became an "oracle."[452] The Bible refers to several other "oracles" being used after the time of Moses. When Solomon built the Temple, he gave special attention to the "holy of holies," making "chambers round about;" the high priest continued to wear "ephods"; the judge, Gideon, made an "ephod"; and while transporting the "ark of the covenant," David wore the priest's "ephod" without the "breastplate," using it to "talk with God."[453]

---

[451] The Twelfth Planet, pp 128-133.

[452] Ex. 25:10-22; 26:31-34; Lev. 16:14-15; Acts 7:38.

[453] Judg. 8:27; 1 Sam. 2:18; 14:2; 22:18; 23:6-12; 30:7-8; 2 Sam. 6:14; 16:23; 1 Kings 6:5, 16-23, 31; 7:49; 8:6-8; 1 Chron. 15:27; 2 Chron. 3:16; 4:20; 5:7, 9; Ps. 28:2; Acts 7:38; Rom. 3:2; Heb. 5:12; 1 Pet. 4:11.

During the reign of King David, "certain Levites were appointed to continually minister before the ark of the Lord [the oracle] to record."[454] Record what? The incoming messages?

The Bible gives examples of the effectiveness of these devices. When Moses was blessing Joshua and giving him a "charge," Jehovah said: "He shall stand before Eleazar the priest, who shall ask counsel for him after the judgment of urim before the Lord; at his word they shall go out, and at his word they shall come in, both he, and all the children of Israel with him."[455] When Saul inquired of Jehovah, he "answered him not, neither by dreams, nor by urim, nor by prophets."[456] Saul finally became so desperate that he consulted a witch who "brought up Samuel."[457] The priests often inquired of the Lord for other people; in other words, they gave readings.[458] King Ahaz used Solomon's "brazen

---

[454] 1 Chron. 16:4.

[455] Num. 27:18-22.

[456] 1 Sam. 28:6.

[457] 1 Sam. 28:7-21.

[458] Ex. 28:30; Josh. 9:14; Judg. 1:1; 1 Sam. 22:10, 13, 15; 2 Sam. 2:1; 5:19; Heb. 1:1.

GARMENTS OF THE HIGH PRIEST, AARON

altar" to make his inquiries, but Jehovah was against those who inquired from sources other than his designated priests, especially those of Egypt.[459] Strange jealousy when most of his oracles were copied from those used in Egypt. When Jacob's son, Joseph, went to Egypt and became governor, he acted as their dream interpreter

---

[459] 2 Kings. 16:15-18; Isa. 30:1-2.

121

and a "diviner."[460]

The "rods" of Moses and Aaron also had magical powers. The "rod" of Moses became a serpent, brought pestilences, parted the Red Sea, caused water to pour out of rocks and brought locusts.[461] When the Hebrews fought against Amalek, Moses held his "rod of God" in his hands, and when he "held up his hands Israel prevailed and when he let down his hands, Amalek prevailed," and when his hands became too heavy, Aaron and Hur held them up for him until the sun went down."[462] After Aaron's rod "brought forth buds, and bloomed blossoms, and yielded almonds, it was kept in the "ark of the covenant" as a sacred item."[463] Were these magical rods a type of laser guns?

Why did Jehovah instruct the Hebrews to build such an elaborate "tabernacle" with an "ark of the covenant" and equip their high priest with oracular devices? Paul explained that these "holy things made with hands, are the figures of the true; the example and shadow of heavenly things;" that the first exoteric covenant "had ordinances of divine service and a worldly sanctuary," while the new esoteric covenant, of Jesus, was designed to put the laws "into their mind, and write them in their hearts."[464]

But for the time being, the "tabernacle," the priests and the sacrifices were their only known means of atonement or obtaining "redemption from their sins," for they believed that only blood could purify.[465] Who knows what esoteric "secrets" Moses might have learned during his forty years of traveling through the wilderness with Jehovah, or what he might have shared with the "Nazarites" and "nobles" (initiates), who were the

[460] Gen, chapters 40-41; 44:5, 15; Acts 7:10.
[461] Ex. 4:3; 7:9; 8:5; 9:23; 10:13; 14:16; 17:5-9; Num. 20:8-11.
[462] Ex. 17:9-12.
[463] Num. 17:2-11; Heb. 9:4.
[464] Heb., chapters 8-9.
[465] Lev. 17:11; Heb. 9:13, 22.

forerunners of the Kabalistic teachings. But the Hebrew people in general were "veiled" due to their disobedience.[466] Are they still "veiled?" Aren't most of us?

THE ART OF SACRIFICING

After Aaron and his sons were sanctified by an eight-day consecration,[467] Aaron prepared a special sacrifice, consisting of a calf, a goat and a bull, which he placed beside the "burnt sacrifice of the morning." When he did so, "the glory of the Lord appeared unto all the people and there came a fire out from before the Lord, and consumed upon the alter [beamed up] the burnt offering and the fat."[468] Shortly after that, two of Aaron's four sons "burned strange fire," that is they put the wrong kind of incense in their censers. For this they were "devoured" by Jehovah, who then instructed Aaron and his two remaining sons not to drink "wine or strong drink" when they went into the temple.[469] The death penalty is pretty severe for burning the wrong kind of incense, but such were the laws of Jehovah, who also prescribed death for such things as "cursing, blasphemy, hitting or cursing one's parents, lying with a beast, men lying together, working on the sabbath, having a familiar spirit or a wizard, and selling holy things or using part of the holy tithes."[470] Jehovah had even given them laws on selling and buying slaves and selling their own daughters into slavery.[471]

He required several different kinds of sacrifices and

---

[466] Ex. 34:33, 35; De. 29:4; Isa. 6:9-10; 29:10; Jer. 5:21; Ezek. 12:2; Matt. 13:11, 14; Mark 4:12; Luke 8:10; John 12:40-41; Acts 28:25-28; Rom. 10:4-7; 11:7-10; 2 Cor. 3:13-14; Gal. 3:23.

[467] Ex. 30:7; Num. 16:40; 1 Sam. 2:28; 1 Chron. 23:13.

[468] Lev. 8:33; 9:17, 24.

[469] Lev. 10:-1-2, 8; Num. 3:4.

[470] Ex. 21:15-17, 29; 22:19; 31:14-15; 35:2; Lev. 20:9-16, 27; 24:16; 27:29; Num. 15:35.

[471] Ex. 20-1-2; 21:7; Neh. 5:5. See also Exodus, chapters 21-22.

offerings, called: "sin, peace, trespass, thanksgiving, memorial, vow, oil, drink, and vegetable."[472] Preparing the sacrificial animals was a monumental task! At the "dedication of the altar," for instance, the Bible says: "All the oxen for the burnt offering were twelve bullocks, the rams twelve, the lambs of the first year twelve, with their meat offering: and the kids of the goat for sin offering twelve. And all the oxen for the sacrifice of the peace offerings were twenty and four bullocks, the rams sixty, the goats sixty, the lambs of the first year sixty."[473] That's quite a barbecue! But then there was quite a "host" of astronauts to feed! The Bible says: "The Lord came from Sinai, and rose up from Sier unto them; he shined forth from mount Paran, and he came with ten thousands of saints."[474] How many of them were in the large "mothership" and how many were in the smaller "shuttle craft" that hovered over the "tabernacle," is undetermined.

So, it appears that Jehovah and his "host" had a comfortable "tabernacle" in which to beam down, a fully-equipped priest to minister to him, and twenty-two thousand servants to do their cooking, but what about the food itself? I always imagined that sacrificing an animal meant throwing the entire beast upon the altar, then setting it on fire. And this may have happened on rare occurrences,[475] but it was not the norm. Jehovah instructed that the animal be "young and without blemish, then skinned and gutted, with these "unclean" portions taken "without the camp to be burned."[476] They were considered to be so "unclean" that the one who did the burning had to "wash his clothes and bathe his flesh in water," before returning to

---

[472] Gen. 28:18; Lev. 1-7; Num. 7:1-9; 15:3; De. 32:38; 1 Sam. 1:24; 7:6; 2 Sam. 23:16; Hos. 9:4; Mic. 6:7.

[473] Num. 7:87-88.

[474] Ex. 19:18, 20; De. 33:3-4; Judg. 5:4-5; Ps. 68:17; Dan. 7:10; Hab. 3:3; Acts 7:53; Gal. 3:19; Heb. 2:2; Rev. 5:11; 9:16.

[475] De. 33:10; Ps. 51:19.

[476] Ex. 12:5; 29:1, 14-15; Lev. 1:3, 10; 3:1, 6; 4:3-32; 5:15, 18; 6:6; 8:16-17; 9:2-3; 14:10; 16:27-28; Num. 6:14; 19:1-10; 29:2, 8, 13, 20-36.

camp.[477] The animal was then "flayed and cut into pieces and the fat removed."[478] Even the turtledoves and young pigeons: were "plucked" with the wings "cleaved," although the rest of their body was left in one piece.[479] The instructions for offering a lamb were: "the whole rump, it shall he take off hard by the backbone."[480] So the animal was skinned, flayed and de-boned, making the sacrifice fit for a king, or an astronaut! And although it was called a "burnt offering," it was not burned, but merely cooked. A distinction is made when it is "wholly burned and not to be eaten."[481]

Special instructions were also given for washing the meat, the cooking vessels and the cleanliness of the cooks.[482] The offering was also to be "seasoned with salt."[483] These are some of Jehovah's recipes:

"He shall offer with the sacrifice of unleavened cakes mingled with oil, and unleavened wafers anointed with oil, and cakes mingled with oil, of fine flour, fried."[484]
"And when any will offer a meat offering unto the Lord, his offering shall be of fine flour; and he shall pour oil upon it, and put frankincense thereon."[485]
"If thy oblation be a meat offering baken in a pan,

---

[477] Lev. 16:28.

[478] Ex. 29:17; Lev. 1:6, 12; 8:20; 1 Kings 18:26, 33; 2 Chron. 29:34; 35:35:11.

[479] Lev. 1:14-17.

[480] Lev. 3:9.

[481] Lev. 6:22-23.

[482] Ex. 29:4, 17; 29:4; 30:18-21; 40: 12-13, 31-32; Lev. 1:9, 13; 6:28; 7:19; 8:6, 21.

[483] Lev. 2:13.

[484] Lev. 2:7; 7:9, 12; 1 Chron. 23:29.

[485] Lev. 2;1.

it shall be of fine flour unleavened, mingled with oil. Thou shalt part it in pieces, and pour oil thereon."[486]

"The meat offering shall be two tenth deals of fine flour mingled with oil, an offering made by fire unto the Lord for a sweet savor; the drink offering shall be of wine."[487]

"And with the one lamb, a tenth deal of flour mingled with the fourth part of an hin of beaten oil; and the fourth part of an hin of wine for a drink offering."[488]

"No meat offering, which ye shall bring unto the Lord, shall be made with leaven; for ye shall burn no leaven, nor any honey, in any offering of the Lord made by fire."[489]

"As for the oblation of the firstfruits, ye shall offer them unto the Lord; but they shall not be burnt on the altar for a sweet savor... Thou shalt offer for the meat offering of thy firstfruits green ears of corn dried by the fire, even corn beaten out of full ears. And thou shalt put oil upon it, and lay frankincense thereon."[490]

None of that sweet, fluffy stuff for them, just good old fried meat and wine! And of course they didn't want their fruit barbecued, but their corn (wheat) could be roasted! They must have liked the food, for the Bible continually mentions how they enjoyed the "sweet savor!"[491] But even though these were called

---

[486] Lev. 2:5-6.

[487] Lev. 23:13.

[488] Ex. 29:40.

[489] Lev. 2:11; 6:17.

[490] Lev. 2: 12, 14.

[491] Ex. 29:18, 25, 41; Lev. chapters 1-7; 8:21, 28; 17:6; 23:13, 18; 26:31; Num. 15:3-24; 18:17; 28:2-27; 29:2-36.

"freewill offerings," there was a dire consequences to anyone who did not make them:

> "And ye shall eat neither bread, nor parched corn, nor green ears, until the selfsame day that ye have brought an offering unto your God."[492]
> "What man soever there be of the house of Israel, that killeth an ox, or lamb, or goat, in the camp, or that killeth it out of the camp, and bringeth it not unto the door of the tabernacle of the congregation, to offer an offering unto the Lord before the tabernacle of the Lord; blood shall be imputed unto that man; he hath shed blood; and that man shall be cut off from among his people."[493]

Jehovah and his "host" did not eat all the sacrifices, a "remnant" was shared by Aaron and his sons and the Levites," but the other tribes were not allowed to eat them.[494] During the childhood of Samuel, when the priests took the sacrifice for themselves, "the sin was very great before the Lord."[495]

WANDERING THROUGH THE WILDERNESS

Two years after leaving Egypt, the people, who were "numbered" to determine the strength of their "army," were described as "the stars of heaven for multitude; covering the face of the earth."[496] They must have been quite a sight to behold:

---

[492] Lev. 23:14.

[493] Lev. 17:3-4.

[494] Ex. 29:15-28; Lev. 2:3; 6:14-18, 29; Lev. 7:9-17, 20-36; 8:31; 9:20-21; 10:12-17;Matt. 12:4; Mark 2:26; Luke 6:4.

[495] 1 Sam. 2:13-17, 27-36; 3:11-14; 4:10-11.

[496] Num. 22:5, 11.

nearly three million people trekking across the desert. Such a group today would cause quite a stir, especially with the "pillar of the cloud" above them, the ornate, golden "ark of the covenant" leading the parade and the Levites struggling to carry the massive parts of the "tabernacle" upon their shoulders," because Levites "were not allowed to use wagons."[497]

When some of the people complained about an arduous three-day journey without meat, "the fire of the Lord burnt among them and consumed them that were in the uttermost parts of the camp." The fire was not quenched until Moses prayed.[498] When the people began to cry, Moses said, "I am not able to bear all this people alone, because it is too heavy for me."[499] Jehovah answered: "Gather the seventy elders and I will take of the spirit which is upon thee, and will put it upon them; they shall bear the burden of the people," and when his spirit "rested upon them, they prophesied."[500]

This brings up an interesting point. The Old Testament first mentions the Pharaoh looking for a man "in whom the spirit of God is". It is mentioned again when Jehovah filled certain workers "with the spirit of wisdom [knowledge]" to enable them to accomplish the difficult task of preparing the "tabernacle."[501] Later, the "spirit of God" came upon Joshua, Balaam, the prophets and several others."[502] The Bible says of John, the Baptist, who is believed to have been the reincarnation of Elijah: "He shall be filled with the Holy Spirit, even from his mother's womb."[503] When the spirit came upon Saul, he was "another man"

---

[497] Num. 7:9; 10:11-36.

[498] Num. 11:1-2.

[499] Num. 11:14.

[500] Num. 11:16-17, 25; 1 Sam. 19:24.

[501] Gen. 41:38; Ex. 28:3; 31:3; 35:31-34; Num. 14:24.

[502] Num. 24:2; 28:18; De. 34:9; Judg. 3:10; 11:29; 13:25; 14:19; 1 Sam. 10:10; 19:20, 23; 2 Chron. 15:1; 20:14; 24:20; Ps. 51:11.

[503] Luke 1:15.

and given a "new heart."[504] Elisha asked that a "double portion" of Elijah's spirit be upon him.[505] In the Book of Daniel, the term was used in the plural, saying he had "the spirit of the holy 'gods;' an excellent spirit."[506] But although Jehovah placed an "excellent spirit" upon some of his followers, he placed "lying" or "evil spirits" upon others, allowing them to be tested by Satan."[507] (The significance of this gift of spirit will be further explained in Part VI.)

After Jehovah placed "his spirit" upon the "seventy elders" chosen by Moses, he promised the people that he would give them "meat to eat for twenty days," but he did not tell them that it was a trick.[508] Even Moses was confused, asking, "Shall the flocks and the herds be slain for them?"[509] Jehovah answered: "Is the Lord's hand waxed short? Thou shalt see now whether my word shall come to pass unto thee or not!"[510] Would the loving Omnipotent God of the entire universe of universes answer in such a sarcastic manner?

Then came a "wind from the Lord, and brought quails from the sea, two cubits high upon the face of the earth."[511] The people gathered the quail "and while the flesh was yet between their teeth, ere it was chewed, the wrath of the Lord was kindled against the people, and the Lord smote them with a very great plague."[512] He called the place "Kibroth-hattavah, because there

---

[504] 1 Sam. 10:6, 9.

[505] 2 Kings 2:9.

[506] Da. 4:8, 18; 5:11-12, 14; 6:3.

[507] Gen. 3:1-5; Judg. 9:23; 1 Sam. 16:14-16, 23; 18:10-11; 19:9; 1 Kings 11:23; 22:21-23; 2 Chron. 18:21-22; Job 1:6-13; 2:1-7; Ps. 32:2; 68:18; 78:49; 109:6; 139:7-12; Jer. 6:21; Amos 3:6; Zech. 3:1-2; Luke 22:3-4.

[508] Num. 11:18-21.

[509] Num. 11:22.

[510] Num. 11:23.

[511] Num. 11:31.

[512] Num. 11:32-33.

they buried them that lusted."[513] That's what I call a dirty trick! Couldn't he have just said "no," rather than giving them what they wanted then killing them for wanting it? Jehovah's "mercy seat" certainly didn't radiate much mercy!

The survivors traveled on to Hazeroth, where Aaron and his "prophetess sister," Miriam, spoke against Moses.[514] When Jehovah heard it, he became so angry he struck Miriam with leprosy.[515] When Moses and Aaron prayed for her, Jehovah said it would only remain for "seven days."[516] Although Aaron was just as guilty, once again he was let off scott free.

In Paran, Jehovah instructed Moses to send men from each of the twelve tribes to search out the land of Canaan.[517] When they returned, after forty days, they reported that the people there were too strong and the cities too fortified for them to conquer.[518] Hearing this news, many of the people, became frightened and rebellious and wanted to return to Egypt; some of them even wanted to stone Moses and Aaron.[519] Only Joshua and Caleb, who "had another spirit" with them, were confident.[520] Jehovah appeared before all the people, furious and desiring to "smite them with pestilence" and to "disinherit" them.[521] Moses calmed and counseled him, but Jehovah, still filled with vengeance against "the evil congregation that had murmured against him," pronounced that none of the adults except Moses, Aaron, Joshua and Caleb would be allowed to enter the promised

---

[513] Num. 11:35.
[514] Ex. 15:20; Num. 12:1-2.
[515] Num. 12:5-10.
[516] Num. 12:11-15.
[517] Num. 13:1-2; De. 1:22-24.
[518] Num. 13:25-33; De. 1:26-28.
[519] Num. 14:1-10.
[520] Num. 13:30; 14:6, 24, 30.
[521] Num. 14:11-12; De. 9:22-23.

land of Canaan.[522]

So, instead of progressing onward, they turned back, and for the next forty years wandered in the "great and terrible, waste-howling wilderness," which Jeremiah later described as "a land of deserts and of pits; a land of drought, and of the shadow of death; that no man passed through, and where no man dwelt."[523] While they were being punished, one year for each of the forty days that they had searched the land of Canaan, Jehovah made it clear that he was waiting for all the elders to die.[524] Can you imagine spending forty years in a wasteland? The people had "manna" to eat, but how did the animals find sustenance in such a sparse area? Perhaps they too ate "manna!"

When the Levite, Korah, rebelled, Moses not only counseled Jehovah, but gave him a better idea on how to handle the situation. Jehovah, however, still killed two hundred fifty men in one day, then started a "plague" which was so bad that Moses had to pray hard and Aaron had to burn incense in order to stop it. Fourteen thousand, seven hundred died.[525] When the Hebrews entered the desert of Zin, the people again rebelled because there was no water. Jehovah instructed Moses to smite a rock with his rod, but when Moses and Aaron did not properly sanctify Jehovah while doing so, they were told that they would not be allowed to go into the promised land either![526] Thus only Joshua and Caleb, of the original three million Hebrews, were allowed to enter the long-awaited, promised land!

CONQUERING THEIR ENEMIES

When the Hebrews were attacked by their enemies and

---

[522] Num. 14:11-25; De. 1:34-40; 3:25-26; Josh. 5:6; Heb. 3:7-11, 15-19; 8:9.

[523] Num. 10:12; 13:26; De. 8:15; 32:10; Jer. 2:6.

[524] Num. 14:33-34; 26:64; De. 2:14-15.

[525] Num. chapter 16; De. 11:6.

[526] Num. 20:1-13, 24; 27:14; De. 1:37; 3:26; 4:21; 32:51; Ps. 106:32-33.

taken prisoner by a Canaanite king, Jehovah helped them to "destroy the cities," with his technology.[527] The Bible describes this assistance from the spacecraft: "God, who rideth upon the heaven in thy help, and in his excellency on the sky, the eternal God is thy refuge, and underneath are the everlasting arms: and he shall thrust out the enemy from before thee; and shall say, 'Destroy them.' Israel then shall dwell in safety alone."[528] Moses sang of Jehovah's greatness saying: "Fear and dread shall fall upon them; by the greatness of thine arm; by a mighty hand, and by a stretched out arm, and by great terrors, they shall be as still as a stone."[529] Perhaps "mighty" referred to his capacity for violence! This display of technology was not new. During the days of Abraham, the spacecraft had "rained upon Sodom and Gomorrah brimstone and fire from out of heaven [a nuclear bomb];" when Jacob and his family were escaping the defilers of Jacob's daughter, Dianh, their enemies did not pursue them because the "terror of God was upon the cities about them."[530]

King David later heralded Jehovah's technological ability saying: "Let God arise; let his enemies be scattered as smoke is driven away; as wax melteth before the fire."[531] Isaiah said: "As birds flying, so will the Lord of hosts defend Jerusalem. He hath stretched forth his hand against them, and hath smitten them; and the hills did tremble, and their carcasses were torn in the mist of the streets. He will hiss unto them from the end of the earth; and, behold, they shall come with speed swiftly."[532] What are these "stretched out" or "everlasting arms underneath" that "hiss" and "thrust out the enemy" and destroy them with "a blast of his

---

[527] Num. 21:1-4.

[528] De. 33:26-27.

[529] Ex. 6:6; 15:11-16; De. 4:34; 5:15; 7:19; 9:29; 11:2; 26:8; 1 Kings 8:42; 2 Kings 17:36; 2 Chron. 6:32; Acts 13:17.

[530] Gen. 19:24-25; 35:4.

[531] Ps. 68:1-2.

[532] Isa. 5:25-26; 7:18; 31:5.

nostrils?"[533] Were they heat and force beams or some other type of particle beams? It is interesting that the word "arm" suggests being "armed" and having an "army." This same type of weaponry is described in great detail in the sacred books of India.

When Aaron was one-hundred-twenty-three, he died at Mount Hor, without even having seen the promised land.[534] After mourning his death, the Hebrews journeyed from Mount Hor by way of the Red Sea to avoid Edom, the land that had been given to Esau, the son of Isaac and twin of Jacob.[535] They knew that they were not to inhabit this land, but when they journeyed into the land of the Amorites, descendants of Noah's son, Ham, who had been cursed, Jehovah "hardened" the king's spirit so they would battle.[536] More of his Machiavellianism! And he evidently plans to continue this ploy into our present age, for he states in a prophetic scripture: "I will gather all nations against Jerusalem to battle. . . . Then shall the Lord go forth and fight against those nations. . . . The God of heaven [shall] set up a kingdom."[537] Is this a prediction of the One World Government? How can anyone possibly mistake this materially-minded "god" of war, violence and division for the loving Father God?

Under Jehovah's direction, the Hebrews killed the Amorite king and conquered the land, "utterly destroying the men, women and little ones, of every city, leaving none to remain, except for the cattle," which they took for "prey."[538] He told them to "save nothing alive that breatheth," and to show no "pity," for "those which ye let remain of them shall be pricks in

---

[533] Ex. 15:8; 2 Sam. 22:16; 2 Kings 19:7; Job 4:9; Ps. 18:15; Isa. 13:5; 37:7; Amos. 4:9; Hag. 2:17.

[534] Num. 20:24-29; 33:38-39; De. 10:6.

[535] Gen. 25:25, 34; 27:1; 32:3; 36:1, 8; Num. 21:4, 15; De. 2:4-12, 19, 22, 29, 31; Josh. 24:4.

[536] Gen. 10:16; 14:13; Num. 21:23-24; De. 2:4-5, 30; Josh. 10:5.

[537] Dan. 2:44; Zech. 14:2-3. See also: Isa. 60:12; Hag. 2:21-22;

[538] Num. 21:24; De. 1:4, 7, 19-10, 27, 44; 2:34; 3:2, 9; 4:41-49; 7:1; 29:7-8.

your eyes, and thorns in your sides, and shall vex you in the land wherein ye dwell."[539] Would you call that the actions of a loving God?

They felt justified, therefore, in conquering the territory, for Jehovah told them: "Behold, I have set the land before you: go in and possess the land which the Lord swore unto your fathers, Abraham, Isaac, and Jacob, to give unto them and to their seed after them."[540] This vicious intention was also made clear in the song that Moses sang when he first brought the Hebrews out of Egypt.[541] They sang:

> "The people shall hear, and be afraid: sorrow shall take hold on the inhabitants of Palestina. Then the dukes of Edom shall be amazed; the mighty men of Moab, trembling shall take hold upon them; all the inhabitants of Canaan shall melt away. Fear and dread shall fall upon them; by the greatness of thine arm they shall be as still as a stone; till thy people pass over, O Lord, till the people pass over, which thou has purchased. Thou shalt bring them in, and plant them in the mountain of thine inheritance."[542]

From whom did Jehovah "purchase" the land? Going by the way of Bashan," where they "smote the king and all his sons, and all his people, until there was none left alive, except the cattle," the Hebrews possessed the land.[543] When they entered Moab and Midian, lands that Jehovah had given to Abraham's nephew, Lot, and to the sons of one of Abraham's wives, Keturah,

---

[539] De. 7:16; 13:8; 19:13, 21; 20:16; 25:12.
[540] Num. 33:51-56; De. 1:8; 4:38; 7:15-26; 11:23-24; 12:2-3.
[541] Ex. 15:1-19.
[542] Ex. 15:13-17.
[543] Num. 21:33-35; De. 3:1-12; Josh, 12:5.

lands they were not to inhabit, Jehovah told them to cooperate with the people.[544] But the Moab and Midianite kings, afraid that the Hebrews would conquer them, asked Balaam, a Midianite prophet, to "curse Israel." After Jehovah told Balaam the Hebrews were "blessed," he refused to curse them.[545] Note that Jehovah was also the "god" of Balaam, since he was one of Abraham's seed. (Moses' wife was also a Midianite.)

Because the Moabites and Ammonites (descendants of Lot) had sought to "curse Israel," they were not to be accepted until the "tenth generation," but the Egyptians and Edomites were acceptable.[546] This is why the Hebrews completely destroyed certain nations, while they kept the women and children of other nations for themselves.[547] (It was due to this leniency, that the Moabite woman, Ruth, survived to become the ancestor of David and Jesus, and why David, when he was being pursued by King Saul, took his family to the King of Moab for protection and spared the Moabites to become his servants.)[548]

When the Hebrews moved on, and many of the men mingled with the Moabites and sacrificed to Ba'al, the Canaanite and Phoenician fertility "god," Jehovah instructed Moses to kill everyone who had participated.[549] When one of the men brought a Midianite woman into their camp, Aaron's grandson slayed both of them.[550] Jehovah, in his "jealousy," caused a "plague," but rewarded Aaron's grandson for slaying the couple, by saving the Hebrews from the "plague." But regardless of the favor, "twenty-four thousand" people still died.[551] The Bible gives several

---

[544] Gen. 11:27, 31; 13:7-12; 19:30-38; 25:1-4; Num. 21:12-23, 28; De. 2:9; Judg. 11:15.

[545] Num., chapters 22-24.

[546] De. 23:3-6; Neh. 13:1.

[547] Gen. 13:38; Num. 21:24-31; De. 2:30-37; 20:10-19; 21:10-14.

[548] Ruth 4:17-23; 2 Sam. 8:2; Matt. 1:5.

[549] Num. 25:1-5.

[550] Num. 25:6-15.

[551] Num. 25:9-11.

incidences in which the Hebrews were punished because they did not kill all the inhabitants, but were rewarded for their brutality.[552] Jehovah was certainly not a "god" of love!

Taking another census to determine the size of their army, they were told to "avenge Jehovah" by "vexing and smiting" the Midianites, hence they killed everyone except thirty-two thousand virgins and children, who they kept for themselves.[553]

THE DEATH OF MOSES

After conquering Bashan, Moses begged Jehovah to let him see the "promised land," but was told: "Let it suffice thee; speak no more unto me of this matter. Get thee up into the top of Pisgah, and lift up thine eyes, and behold it with thine eyes: for thou shalt not go over this Jordan."[554] So, at least Moses, who was one-hundred-twenty-years-old and had served faithfully for over forty years, got to see the promised land from a distance, which was more than was granted to poor old Aaron!

Moses talked to the people just before they were to cross the Jordan River, admonishing them to be faithful to Jehovah, not to "inquire after other 'gods,'" and to be cautious of false prophets among themselves.[555] After confirming: "I have led you forty years in the wilderness; ye have not eaten bread, neither have ye drunk wine or strong drink," he told them that once they were settled into their new land, they could again eat "flesh," and could eat of the sacrifices.[556] Having eaten nothing but "manna" for forty years, they must have been lean and mean! When Jehovah predicted their disobedience, he said: "When I shall have brought them into the land I swore unto their fathers, and they shall have

---

[552] Num. 25:6-13; De. 13:8-10; Judg. 4:17-22; 5:24-27; 1 Sam. 15:8-33.

[553] Num. 25:16-18; chapter 26; 31:1-2; De. 4:3.

[554] De. 3:25-26; 32:50-52.

[555] De. 12:29-30; chapter 13; Isa. 9:15; Jer. 6:13; 8:10; 23:11, 15; Lam. 4:13; Zeph. 3:4.

[556] De. 12:15-27; 14:22-23; 15:20; 16:7; 18:1-4; 26:12; 27:7; 29:6.

eaten and filled themselves; and waxen fat; then will they turn unto other 'gods,' and serve them, and provoke me, and break my covenant."[557] Did their vegetarian diet keep them holy?

After Moses compiled the laws and gave them to the priests, and blessed Joshua in front of all the people, Jehovah called him and Joshua into the "tabernacle," where he appeared in a "pillar of cloud" to give Joshua an official "charge."[558] Jehovah prophesied a bleak future for the Hebrews due to their disobedience, telling Moses to write it in a song to serve as a reminder.[559] After teaching the song to the people, Moses, who had become a great law giver and had molded the Hebrew people into a monotheistic nation, but was still "meek above all men," quietly went up into the mountain and died.[560]

Either the Bible is very curt in its explanations, or Jehovah intuitively knew the exact moment of one's death, for in the case of both Aaron and Moses, he told them exactly when to die. With Aaron, one day he had instructed Moses, Aaron and Aaron's son, Eleazar, to climb Mt. Hor, where Moses stripped Aaron of his priestly garment and placed it on his son, and right on cue, Aaron died on the mountain top.[561] Curious, since he had been well enough to climb the mountain; quite a feat for a hundred twenty-three-year-old man! In the case of Moses, he "went from the plains of Moab unto the mountain of Nebo, and there he died."[562] Again it is curious that he was apparently in good health, not only able to climb the mountain, but the Bible also says: "his eye was not dim, nor his natural force abated."[563] Whatever the cause of his death, the people mourned his passing

---

[557] De. 31:20; 32:14-15.

[558] Num. 27:18-23; De. 31:7-15.

[559] De. 31:16-21.

[560] Num. 12:3; De. 31:14-15, 22-30; 32:44-52; 34:1-9.

[561] Num. 20:24-28.

[562] De. 34:1, 5.

[563] De. 4:7.

for thirty days. The Bible says: "There arose not a prophet since in Israel like unto Moses, whom the Lord knew face to face."[564]

After forty years of wandering through the wilderness under the dictates of Jehovah, the Hebrews were finally ready to claim their promised land. Moses, no doubt, made his ascension after his mysterious burial in which "his body was never found," for he was with Elijah when the two of them appeared to Jesus at his "transfiguration, to speak with Him about his death.[565]

Now we might ask the question: Was Jehovah really all that bad? A thousand years later, Nehemiah gave a detailed version of Jehovah's actions in the wilderness, blaming the rebellious Hebrews who "hardened their necks," against a "gracious and merciful God" who was "slow to anger."[566] But then of course Nehemiah was not there! Jehovah described himself as having been a "husband" to the Hebrews, listing his qualities as: "merciful and gracious, long suffering, and abundant in goodness and truth, keeping mercy for thousands, forgiving iniquity and transgression and sin." And yet he adds to the same scripture: "that he will by no means clear the guilty; visiting the iniquity of the fathers upon the children, and upon the children's children, unto the third and to the fourth generation."[567] A later scripture, however, states that the children are not to be put to death for the sins of their fathers.[568]

One day, while wondering if Jehovah was a loving God, I looked up the word love in the concordance. The majority of the references had to do with our loving God, rather than his loving us. A few Old Testament scriptures revealed to the Hebrews that Jehovah loved "their fathers," and that he loved David, Jeremiah, Ephraim and Israel, but there were abundant scriptures revealing

---

[564] De. 34:8, 10.

[565] De. 34:5-6; Matt. 17:1-5; Mark 9:2-6; Luke 9:28, 31.

[566] Neh. 9:6-38.

[567] Ex. 20:6; 34:4-7; Num. 14:18; De. 5:10; 7:2, 9; Isa. 54:5; Jer. 31:32.

[568] De. 24:16; 2 Kings 14:6; 2 Chron. 25:4; Ezek. 18:4, 20.

that his love was conditional.[569] It was also temporary. The scriptures reveal: "All their wickedness is in Gilgal: for there I hated them: for the wickedness of their doings I will drive them out of mine house, I will love them no more; I hated Esau, and laid his mountains and his heritage waste for dragons of the wilderness."[570] What kind of a "god" hates his followers and refuses to forgive them? Jehovah's "covenant of peace" was likewise conditional and temporary.[571] How could this be the same being that Paul called "the God of peace,"[572] who loved the positive and negative forces equally? The Old Testament emphasized law and justice rather than love, mercy and peace! But we must also take into consideration the confusion, contradictions and mistranslations, and as stated earlier, perhaps the Old Testament writers exaggerated Jehovah's actions. So let us at least give him the benefit of the doubt.

One of the Dead Sea Scrolls shows how the Hebrews viewed Jehovah:

> "Behold all the nations are as nothing compared to You; they are counted as naught, as a mere specter in Your presence. In Your name alone have we boasted, for we were created for Your glory. You have adopted us in the sight of all the nations; indeed, You have called Israel 'My son, My firstborn' (Exodus 4:22), and you have chastened us as a man chastens his child. You have raised us through the years of our generations, disciplining us with terrible disease, famine, thirst, even plague and the sword--every

---

[569] Ex. 18:23; 33:19; Lev. 26:6; De. 4:37; 7:7-8, 12-13; 10:25; 23:5; 33:3; Ps. 91:14; 119:165; 125:1, 5; 128:1, 6; Isa. 26:3, 12; 38:17; 48:18, 22; 63:9; Jer. 1:5; 31:3; Hos. 11:3-4; Mal. 1:2. Hos. 14:4; Rom. 9:15, 18.

[570] Hos. 9:15; Mal. 1:3; Rom. 9:13.

[571] Num. 25:12; Isa. 2:4; 11:6; 54:10; Jer. 28:9; Ezek. 16:8; 34:25; 37:26.

[572] Heb. 13:20.

reproach of Your covenant. For You have chosen us as Your own, as Your people from all the earth. That is why You have poured Your fury upon us. Your zeal, the full wrath of Your anger. That is why You have caused the scourge of Your plagues to cleave to us, that of which Moses and Your servants the prophets wrote: You would send evil against us in the last days."[573]

Perhaps they felt that the end justifies the means, for as their later sacred text, the Talmud, states: "I [Jehovah] make you the ancestor of the peoples, I make you the selected one amongst the peoples. I make you the king over the peoples. . . . When the messiah comes, all will be slaves of the Jews."[574] Really?

After three and a half thousand years of countless versions of the ancient scriptures, can we still discern their deeper meaning? Was Jehovah the One True God of all the universe or was he merely a tribal "god" of one particular group of people? How does he compare to Krishna of India or with Zeus of Greece or Odin of Scandinavia? According to mythology, most of the "gods" were brutal infidels.

But lest we become judgemental, let us consider another line of thought as presented in The Urantia Book:

"Many of the advances which Moses made over and above the religion of the Egyptians and the surrounding Levantine tribes were due to the Kenite traditions of the time of Melchizedek. . . . Moses and his father-in-law, Jethro, gathered up the residue of the traditions of the days of Melchizedek. . . . While Moses comprehended the more advanced Egyptian religious philosophy, the

---

[573] The Words of the Heavenly Lights, column 3.
[574] Talmud; Schabbat, 105 n; Erubin 43 b.

Bedouin slaves knew little about such teachings, but they had never entirely forgotten the god of Mount Horeb, whom their ancestors had called Yahweh. . . . Yahweh was the god of the southern Palestinian tribes, who associated this concept of deity with Mount Horeb, the Sinai volcano. Yahweh was merely one of the hundreds and thousands of nature gods which held the attention and claimed the worship of the Semite tribes and peoples. . . . Yahweh was worshipped by more than one hundred separate Arabian tribes. . . . The religion of the rank and file of the Hebrew captive slaves was a modified version of the old Yahweh ritual of magic and sacrifice. . . . By the time of the Hebrew encampment about Mount Sinai after the flight from Egypt, Moses had formulated a new and enlarged concept of Deity (derived from his former beliefs), which he wisely decided to proclaim to his people as an extended concept of their olden tribal god, Yahweh. . . . Moses made a heroic effort to uplift Yahweh to the dignity of a supreme Deity when he presented him as the 'God of truth and without iniquity, just and right in all his ways. . . . Jehovah is a term which in recent times has been employed to designate the completed concept of Yahweh which finally evolved in the long Hebrew experience. But the name Jehovah did not come into use until fifteen hundred years after the time of Jesus. . . . While the Jews thus changed their views of Deity from the tribal god of Mount Horeb to the loving and merciful Creator Father of later times, they did not change his name; they continued all the way along to call this evolving concept of Deity, Yahweh. . . . The idea of Yahweh has undergone the most extensive development of all the mortal theories of God."[575]

It appears that most of the glorious descriptions of God came from the mystical teachings of Moses rather than from the actions of Jehovah. Was the meek and humble Moses fooled by an imposter "God?" Are we still being fooled today? Don't forget that according to the Dead Sea Scroll's <u>Book of Amram</u>, Moses was abducted by a "reptilian god". Was this "god" Jehovah? Seeing both sides of the coin, you can decide for yourself.

[575] <u>The Urantia Book</u>, pp 1053-1059.

PART V

JEHOVAH GUIDES THE ISRAELITES

JOSHUA AND THE JUDGES IN CANAAN

When the Hebrews entered the promised land, under the leadership of Joshua and the Chief Priest, Phinehas, grandson of Aaron, Jehovah assisted them.[576] As they approached the Jordan River, led by the priests carrying the "ark of the covenant," Jehovah parted the water, magnified Joshua in the sight of the people and sent an angel to bless him.[577] After celebrating the "passover" in Gilgal, the distribution of manna ceased and the people began to eat "the fruit of Canaan."[578]

Carrying the "ark" into battle, they conquered Jerico, Ai, Hazor and neighboring towns, brutally killing the people, their livestock and burning the towns.[579] The Bible reports: "There was not a city that made peace with the children of Israel . . . for it was of the Lord to harden their hearts."[580] Setting up the tent of the "tabernacle" at Shiloh, the Hebrews divided the territory they had conquered.[581] The Bible doesn't mention that they had just disobeyed the majority of the Ten Commandments by carrying out these vicious acts of genocide. Another sanctuary was then set up in Gilgal, near Jerusalem.[582]

Who were these Canaanites that the Hebrews so brutally killed? The term was derived from Canaan, son of Ham and grandson of Noah.[583] Ham and his descendants were cursed because he had looked upon the nakedness of his father, Noah,

---

[576] Josh. 1:5; 22:13-30; 1 Chron. 9:20.

[577] Josh. 3:1-16; 4:7, 14; 5:13-15.

[578] Josh. 4:19-20; 5:11-2.

[579] Josh., chapters 6-12.

[580] Josh. 11:19-20.

[581] Judg., chapters 18-22.

[582] Josh. 4:20; 5:2-10; 9:3-15; 1 Kings 3:4; 1 Chron. 16:39; 21:28-29; 2 Chron. 1:3-13; Acts 13:19.

[583] Gen. 10:6.

while he was drunk.[584] Were the Canaanites, whose "god" was Ba'al, the son of El, some type of wild barbarians? The word Canaan means "merchant". They were famous for their production of an unusual purple dye. According to the <u>Bible in Alphabet</u>:

> "The Canaanites migrated from the Arabian Desert not later than 3000 BC. They built a magnificent civilization and invented three different alphabets, one of which (the Phoenician) became the ancestor of practically all those of the western world. Their literature contained notable epics. Their laws and religious practices deeply influenced the Hebrews who, in turn, have influenced the modern world."[585]

Would a loving God have killed the majority of such a cultured people due to an ancient curse?

After Joshua's death, at age one-hundred-ten, the people became evil and followed other 'gods,' thus the "angel of the Lord delivered them into the hands of the spoilers."[586] After serving the king of Mesopotamia for eight years, they were guided by their first "judge," Othniel, "who had the spirit of the Lord."[587] For the next two hundred years, only a few of the judges, such as Gideon, Sampson and Samuel, remained faithful, while the majority of the people continued to disobey Jehovah, until he finally delivered them into the hands of the Philistines for forty years.[588]

The god of the Philistines was Dagon, who was believed

---

[584] Gen. 9:20-25.

[585] The Bible in Alphabet.

[586] Josh. 24:29; Judg. 1:1-8; 2:1-23; 3:1-8.

[587] Judg. 3:9-10.

[588] Judg. 2:11; 3:7; 4:1; chap. 6-8; 10:16; 1 Sam., chap. 1-3; 4:2-3, 10-11; Luke 20:36-38; Acts 13:33-34.

to be part fish. In reality he could have been an astronaut wearing a diving suit. The Greeks called Dagon, Triton. It was he who had helped Jason and the Argonauts find the "golden fleece." It is interesting that Argo is a constellation in the form of a ship. Perhaps a great deal of mythology stems from the tales of visiting ETs.

The Philistines not only ruled over the Hebrews for forty years, but also stole their most precious possession, the "ark of the covenant," but because it caused them such great pain, they only kept it for seven months. When the Hebrews gathered to celebrate its return, Jehovah killed fifty thousand and seventy of them because they dared to look into it![589] Can you imagine fifty thousand dead bodies?

The surviving Hebrews were faithful for twenty years, and finally, with the help of Jehovah's "great thunder [technology]," subdued the Philistines.[590] Of this technological help, the Bible says: "The stars in their courses fought against the enemy with thunder and hailstones that discomfited and slew them with a great slaughter; that the Lord may do his strange work and bring to pass his strange act."[591] These high-tech "blasts" would indeed appear as a "strange act" to the primitive bedouin people!

When the last judge, Samuel, began to age, his sons ruled in his stead, but due to their evil ways, the Hebrews demanded a king. Jehovah warned against the evils of monarchy, but when they would not listen, he chose Saul, a "goodly man" who stood "higher than any of the people." After Jehovah put his spirit upon Saul and "gave him another heart," Samuel anointed him as the first Hebrew king.[592]

---

[589] 1 Sam. 4:11; 6:10-19; chapters 5-7.

[590] 1 Sam. 7:9-14.

[591] Josh. 10:10-11; Judg. 4:15; 5:20; 1 Sam. 2:10; 7:9-14; 2 Sam. 22:8-16; Ps. 18:13-14; 77:17-18; Isa. 28:21; 30:30.

[592] 1 Sam. 8:1-51; 9:1-2, 15-16; 10:1, 6, 9-10, 23.

MONARCHY AGAINST JEHOVAH'S WISHES

Jehovah blessed King Saul, as long as he performed great feats, but when he dared to offer his own burnt offering, he was rebuked, for only the priests were allowed to offer sacrifices or to burn incense.[593] Shortly after that, Saul was instructed to destroy the Amalekites, but instead he spared the king and some of the choice sheep.[594] For this he was completely rejected by Jehovah, who removed his "Holy Spirit" and sent him an "evil spirit."[595] After this quick revenge, Jehovah instructed Samuel to anoint the young boy, David, to be the next king, but having learned by his mistake in choosing Saul, Jehovah looked upon the boy's heart rather than his stature.[596] Was Jehovah finally becoming a bit less macho?

After Saul's suicide on Mt. Gilboa, where Israel had been vanquished by the Philistines, David who had become a hero in slaying the giant, captured from the Jebusites, "the stronghold of Zion" in Jerusalem and made it the capital of Israel. There, he set up a "tabernacle" and brought the "ark of the covenant" from Ephraim.[597] Jerusalem, meaning "foundation of peace," is believed to have been founded by the god Salem. Situated on a hill that was protected on three sides by canyons, it had been sought after for centuries by various Pharaohs and the Hittites. It was the oldest city in the area, outside of Damascus.

David, the gentle warrior, did not exterminate the Jebusites but incorporated them into his tribe. A poet, songwriter, and musician, he also made musical instruments, introduced

---

[593] De. 33:8-10; 1 Sam. 13:8-15; 1 Kings 13:33-34; 2 Chron. 13:9; 26:17-18.

[594] 1 Sam. 15:1-9.

[595] 1 Sam. 15:10-35; 16:14; 28:18.

[596] 1 Sam. 9:2; 10:23; 15:35; 16:1-12; Acts 13:22.

[597] 2 Sam. 5:6-12; 6:1-23; 1 Chron. 11:5-7; 13:4-14; 15:1-29; 2 Chron. 1:1-4; 5:2; Ps. 2:6.

singing into the worship service, divided the thirty-eight thousand Levites into four groups, and assigned them to continually administer to the "ark."[598] Jehovah, claiming Jerusalem as "the city of his name," declared that he "loved the gates of Zion more than all the dwellings of Jacob."[599]

After enlarging the borders of Israel, David wanted to build a "house" for Jehovah, but was told that he had too much blood on his hands from the battles Jehovah had directed him to fight.[600] Promised that his future son would build it, he was given a "pattern" and began to collect supplies for the building.[601] When David and Bathsheba's love-child, Solomon, was born, Jehovah promised to give the child "rest from all his enemies," so the holy house could be built during peaceful times.[602]

When David was at death's door, he was provoked by Satan or Jehovah--the scriptures are contradictory, one indicating that Satan and Jehovah are the same person--to "number" the inhabitants. But when he did so, Jehovah sent a "plague" upon the people.[603] When seventy thousand people died, David, like Moses, pleaded with him not to be so harsh. After David's death, his son Solomon donned the crown, and when Jehovah asked him what he wanted, Solomon answered: "Wisdom."[604] Thus "Solomon's wisdom [knowledge] excelled the wisdom of all the children of the east country."[605] In the fourth year of his reign,

---

[598] 1 Sam. 18:6; 1 Chron. 15:16; 16:4-6, 42; 23:3-5; 2 Chron. 5:13; 7:6; 23:13; 34:12; Neh. 12:36.

[599] Ps. 78:60, 67-68; 87:1-2; 132; 13-14; Dan. 9:18-19.

[600] 2 Sam. 6:17; 7:2; 1 Chron. 6:31-48; 16:1-6, 37; 17:1; 2 Chron. 1:4; Ps. 76:2; 144:1.

[601] 2 Sam. 7:5-17; 1 Kings 8:17-19; 1 Chron. 17:1-15; 22:1-8, 14; 28:2-10, 12-19; 2 Chron. 29:1-17.

[602] 1 Chron. 22:9.

[603] 2 Sam. 24; 1 Chron. 21:1; 27:23-24.

[604] 1 Kings 1:5-40; 3:5-15; 1 Chron. 29:22-23; 2 Chron. 1:7.

[605] 1 Kings 3:3-14; 4:30-32; 8:22-30; 10:1-7; Ps. 72; Prov., Song of Solomon, Eccl.

four hundred and eighty years after the Hebrews had left Egypt, Solomon hired trained stone masons[606] to build the "house of the Lord" on Mount Moriah, a sacred thirty-five acre tablelike hill that had been used for threshing, a hill that David had bought from the Jebusites.[607] (The crown of Mount Moriah is presently enclosed within the Islamic "Dome of the Rock".) The name "Zion" was then extended to include both hills and sometimes all of Jerusalem.[608] It took Solomon seven years to complete the massive thirty by ninety foot, three-storied structure, with its forty-foot pillars, its fifteen foot porch, running the full length of the building, and its walls and floors overlaid with gold.[609] He created a special "oracle" for the "ark of the covenant," which was placed under two fifteen foot high cherubim that each had a fifteen foot wing span.[610]

When the "ark" was finally brought out of the tent and placed in the new temple, Solomon had a great celebration with a huge sacrifice. When Jehovah appeared to Solomon a second time to reestablish the "covenant" with Israel, a "cloud of thick darkness, filled the house of the Lord, so that the priests could not stand to minister because of the cloud."[611] Solomon then built an elaborate palace, fortified Jerusalem, created a vast navy, and established foreign alliances, but as he grew older, his seven hundred wives and three hundred concubines, many of whom were foreigners, turned his heart to other 'gods.'"[612] Jehovah warned angrily: "I will surely rend the kingdom from thee, and

---

[606] These stone masons, sent by King Hiram, are believed to have been a part of the Masonic Fraternity, hence the famous legends of "Hiram Abiff." See: 1 Kings 5:1-12; 7:13-14, 40. 45; 9:10-12, 26-28; 2 Chron. 2:3-16; 8:1-2.

[607] 2 Sam. 24:18-25; 1 Chron. 21:15-28.

[608] 1 Kings 6:1; 1 Chron. 21:15-28; 22:1; 2 Chron. 3:1-2; Ps. 48; 65:1; 102:21; Isa. 2:3; 8:18.

[609] 1 Kings 6; 7:1; 9:10; 2 Chron. 8:1.

[610] 1 Kings 6:2-31; 8:1-11.

[611] 1 Kings, chapter 8; 9:1-9; 2 Chron. 5:1-14; 6:1.

[612] 1 Kings 3:1; 5:1-12; 9:26-28; 10:11, 22; 11:3-4.

will give it to thy servant. In thy days I will not do it for David thy father's sake, but I will rend it out of the hand of thy son. I will give one tribe [Judah] to thy son for David my servant's sake and for Jerusalem's sake."[613]

A point that is often missed is what Solomon actually did with his gift of "wisdom [knowledge]". He married foreign women; tolerated all religions, and encouraging unity. He surpassed the Hebrew idea of separatism by making foreign alliances; delegated authority to others; and hired foreign craftsmen (stone masons) to build the temple.[614] He was not narrow minded, arrogant or exclusive, and had a great appreciation for craftsmanship. But these qualities greatly displeased Jehovah; broad-mindedness and free thinking are always a threat to a dictator.

JEHOVAH DIVIDES THE KINGDOM

After Solomon's death around 976 BC, the vengeful Jehovah divided the kingdom. One of Solomon's sons, Rehoboam, reigned over the "Southern Kingdom of Judah," while his other son, Jeroboam, ruled over the other ten tribes, the "Northern Kingdom of Israel."

Samaria became the capital of Israel, while Jerusalem remained the capital of Judah.[615] As the two kingdoms warred continually, the temple was robbed of its treasures.[616] It hardly seems fair that the people suffered for Solomon's "idolatry," especially since Jehovah had promised that "the sins of the fathers should not be visited upon the children."[617] The "twelve tribes" never reassembled!

---

[613] 1 Kings. 11:9-14, 23.

[614] 1 Kings, chapters 1-12.

[615] 1 Kings 16:24; Isa. 28:1

[616] 1 Kings 14:23-28; 2 Chron. 12:9, 15.

[617] De. 24:16; 2 Kings 14:6; 2 Chron. 25:4; Ezek. 18:4, 20.

During the next two-hundred-fifty-year period, the majority of the kings of the divided kingdom were "evil," building pagan altars, worshipping other "gods" and making priests of those who were not Levites. In addition to having a lack of compassion for one's fellowmen, Jehovah listed their sins as idolatry and trusting in foreign alliance instead of trusting in him, an act which was forbidden. I wonder how he feels about America. The Hebrews were not allowed to intermarry or associate with "heathen Gentiles, lest they be contaminated by their idols."[618] They were also forbidden to perform any rituals or to worship in their own "high places" or "groves." All worship was to be under the auspices of the priests. King Uzziah was struck with leprosy because he burned incense in the temple instead of letting the priest perform the rite.[619] Knowledge and philosophy were discouraged; the people were not to indulge in culture or free thinking, but only to obey.

A few of the early kings, such as Asa, Jehosophat, Joash, Jehoash, Uzziah and Hezekiah, were faithful to Jehovah and cooperated with the prophets, but, due to the wickedness of the masses and the many evil kings, they were unable to sustain the divided territory.[620] When Jehovah gave up on the "Northern Kingdom of Israel" in 722 BC and "cast them out of his sight," they were captured and taken to Assyria.[621] Luckily they were not annihilated like the nations the Hebrews had conquered!

As the Assyrians re-populated the area with captives from other lands, Jehovah, through Micah, warned the "Southern Kingdom of Judah" that as Samaria had fallen, so would

---

[618] Ex. 22:21-22; Lev. 20:22-23; De. 24:27; 1 Kings 14:23; 17:9-11; 23:4; 2 Kings 17:7-18, 35-41; 2 Chron. 9:19-23; Ps. 78:60-61; Isa. 1:17, 29; 16:12; 30:1-2; 36:7; 58:6-7; 65:3; Ezek. 6:3; Jer. 5:28; 7:31; Hos. 4:6, 13; 7:7, 14; Mic. 2:1; 5:12-14; Zech. 7:10; 8:16-17; Acts 10:28.

[619] 2 Kings 15:1-6; 2 Chron. 26:16-21.

[620] 1 Kings 22:1-4, 41-50; 2 Kings 3:6-25; 11:17-19; 12:1-8; 17:3-41.

[621] 2 Kings 18:9-22; 23:5-8; 28:4; 20:3; 2 Chron. 14:3; 16:1-29; Isa.; Hosea; Amos; Jonah; Micah.

Jerusalem.[622]

JEHOVAH SPOKE THROUGH THE PROPHETS

The term prophet was first applied to Abraham, then to Moses and his brother and sister.[623] Joshua was a prophet as were Balaam and Deborah, during the period of the Judges, but the "Nazarite," Samuel, who served as both judge and prophet, gave a new meaning to the word.[624] Because "there was no open vision, and the word of the Lord was precious in those days," the gifted Samuel, who, as a child had been given to the judge and chief priest Eli, and had grown up administering to the "ark," was sought after as a famous "seer." Jeremiah later hailed Samuel and Moses as the two greatest prophets.[625] Due to their divine attunement, they no doubt received messages from a divine source far beyond Jehovah.

Because Jehovah was against the monarchial system, he did not speak directly through the kings, but through the prophets, who became their advisors. Many of the early prophets wrote books that have since been lost.[626] Most of the prophets were dignified and well accepted by the kings, although Hanai and Micaiah were imprisoned for their dire predictions.[627] But the most colorful of all the prophets, Elijah, "clad in a hairy mantle,"

---

[622] 2 Kings 17:3-6; 18:11; 23:26-27; Mic. 3:12.

[623] Gen. 20:7; Ex. 7:1; 15:20; Num. 11:25-26; chapter 24.

[624] Joshua; Judg. 4:4; 6:8-10; 1 Sam., chapters 3, 10; 19:20-24; Ps. 77:20; Hos. 12:13; Mic. 6:4.

[625] 1 Sam. 1:9; 2:18; 3:1-21; 4:18; 9:9-18; 1 Kings 2:27; Jer. 15:1.

[626] Num. 21:14; Josh. 10:13; 18:9; 1 Sam. 22:5; 2 Sam. 1:18; 7:2-17; 10:10-13; 12:1-25; 15:27; 24:11-19; 1 Kings 1:8-45; 4:5; 11:42; 12:22-24; 16:1-47; 18:3-4, 29; 22:8-28; 1 Chron. 17:1-21:8-19; 29:29; 2 Chron. 9:29; 11:24; 12:5-25; 13:22; 15:1-8; 16:7-10; 17:7-9; 18:7-27; 19:2; 20:14-17, 34; 21:14; 24:20; 29:25; 33:19; Ps. 51.

[627] 1 Kings 18:7-27; 22:8-28; 2 Chron. 16:7-10,

was a thorn in the side of the rich kings with their elaborate palaces. The wicked King Ahab and his wife Jezebel, who, around 900 BC, tried to implant the worship of Ba'al, threatened to kill all the prophets, causing Elijah to seek refuge in a cave, where he was fed by a raven.[628]

He was later fed by an angel who told him to "stand upon the mount before the Lord." As Jehovah passed by with a "strong wind that broke the rocks into pieces and caused an earthquake," his voice, instructed Elijah to anoint a king over Syria and Israel, stating that he still had seven thousand faithful souls in Israel who had not bowed to Ba'al.[629] Performing many "miracles," Elijah brought a child back to life, parted the waters and brought fire from heaven to consume a captain and his army.[630] As a grand finale, after "parting the Jordan River, he ascended into heaven in a "chariot of fire!"[631]

When Elijah was "taken up in a chariot [spacecraft]," the people had a curious reaction. Not understanding what had happened, they began to look for him, "lest the spirit of the Lord hath taken him up and cast him upon some mountain or into some valley."[632] Why would they make this assumption unless they had previously encountered this difficulty? Does this remind you of today's "abduction" claims, in which people are taken into a craft, then returned in some remote place? This was mentioned again in the New Testament when Philip was taken up and set down somewhere else.[633]

---

[628] 1 Kings 16:32-33; 17:2-7; 18:1-6; chapter 19; 2 Kings 1:8.

[629] 1 Kings 19:5-18.

[630] 1 Kings 17:17-23; 2 Kings 1:5-16; 2:7-8.

[631] 2 Kings 2:7-11.

[632] 2 Kings 2:16-17.

[633] Acts 8:39-40.

NAMES AND DATES OF KINGS, PROPHETS, PRIESTS

KINGS OF JUDAH	PROPHETS	PRIESTS	DATE BC	KINGS OF ISRAEL
Saul (40 years)	Samuel		1096 BC	
David (40 years)	Gad	Zadok	1056	
	Nathan	Abiathar		
Solomon (40 years)	Iddo		1016	
Rehoboam (17 years)	Ahijah		976	Jeroboam (22 years)
Abijam (3 years)	Shemiah		959	
Asa (41 years)	Hanai		956	
	Jehu		955	Nadab (2 years)
			953	Baashi (24 years)
			931	Elah (2 years)
			930	Zimri (7 days)
			917	Omri (12 years)
Jehosophat (25 years)	Elijah	Elishama	915	Ahab (22 years)
	Eliezer	Jahaziel		
	Micaiah	Jehoram	898	Ahaziah (2 years)
			896	Jehoram (12 years)
Jehoram (8 years)			890	
Ahaziah (1 year)	Elisha		883	
Athaliah, Queen (6 yr)		Jehoiada	882	Jehu (28 years)
Joash (40 years)			876	Jehoash (16 years)
			855	Jehoahaz (17 years)
Amaziah (29 years)			836	
		Zachariah	823	Jeroboam II (41 years)
Uzziah (52 years)		Azariah	805	
			771	Zachariah (6 months)
			770	Shallum (1 month)
			770	Menahem (10 years)
	Amos		761	Pekahiah (2 years)
	Hosea		759	Pekah (20 years)
Jothan (16 years)	Jonah		755	
Ahaz (16 years)	Isaiah	Urijah	739	Hosea (9 years)
	Micah		730	CAPTIVITY TO
Hezekiah (29 years)	Nahum		723	ASSYRIA
	Zephaniah		721	
Manasseh (55 years)			694	
Amon (2 years)	Jeremiah		639	
Josiah (28 years)	Hulda	Hilkiah	638	
	Second Isaiah			
Jehoahaz (3 months)	Zechariah		608	
Jehoiakim (11 years)	Habakkuk		608	
Jehoiachin (3 months)	Daniel		597	
Zedekiah (11 years)	Ezekiel		597	
CAPTIVITY TO BABYLON			586	

155

The "mantle" of Elijah was passed to his son, Elisha, a diplomatic healer, who continued to perform "miracles" and became head of the school of prophets that Samuel had founded.[634] After Elisha's death, even his bones were holy. When a dead man was lowered into Elisha's grave, he came back to life the moment he came in contact with the prophet's bones.[635] Some Biblical scholars believe Elisha, like Melchizedek and David, was a former incarnation of, or was overshadowed by the spirit of, Jesus, who the Bible says: "was in the world and the world knew him not."[636] Elijah later incarnated as John, the Baptist.

The first writings of the prophets to be preserved were those of Amos and Hosea, who prophesied around 760 to 730 BC. Amos, the shepherd and naturalist, who was not trained by any of the schools for prophets, hailed Jehovah as the God of all nations and warned that the "covenant" with the Hebrews could be "broken."[637] Jehovah threatened to destroy Israel by fire, but Amos talked him out of it and Jehovah finally "repented" for his drastic thoughts.[638] Hosea, warning against social injustice, spoke of Jehovah's love, healing and forgiveness for his "betrothed Israel [his bride]."[639] Later, however, Jehovah contradicted this lovely statement declaring that he had "divorced" Israel.[640]

Another colorful prophet was the royal Isaiah, who "walked naked through the streets" of Jerusalem for three years in an attempt to awaken the people to righteousness, lest they be destroyed by Assyria.[641]

---

[634] 1 Sam. 10:10-13; 19:20; 2 Kings 2:14-25; 3:15; chapters 4-7. Out of these schools for prophets, based on the writings of Melchizedek, grew the Essene movement, through which Jesus was born.

[635] 2 Kings 13:20-21.

[636] John 1:1, 5, 10, 14, 23; 8:56, 58.

[637] Amos 1:1; 3:11-15; 5:27; 7:8, 14-15; 8:9-12.

[638] Amos 7:1-6.

[639] Hos. 2:16-17; 11:3-9; 13:10; 14:4, 9.

[640] Isa. 50:1; Jer. 3:8, 14.

[641] Is. 10:11, 21-22; 20:2-3; 37:32.

SOUTHERN KINGDOM THREATENED

Jehovah speaking through Isaiah and Micah just prior to the fall of the "Northern Kingdom of Israel" in 730 BC, warned of impending judgment, but also prophesied the survival of a "righteous remnant" and the coming of "Immanuel," a "prince of peace" and a "branch of David," who would "rule Israel," carrying the "government" upon his "shoulders."[642] Many believe this to be a messianic prophecy about Jesus, but since it was given to the wicked King Ahaz, it seems to refer to Hezekiah, whose name means "Jehovah strengthens."[643] The Bible calls Hezekiah the son of Ahaz, but Hezekiah, born in 755 BC, was twenty-five years old when he took the throne in 730 BC. At that time Ahaz was thirty-six years old, which would have made him only nine when Hezekiah was born. Hezekiah's mother Abi, a virgin temple woman, was the daughter of the martyred priest, Zachariah, who had counselled King Uzziah.[644] Blavatsky declares:

> "Hezekiah, or 'Immanuel,' was doubtless the son of the royal prophet Isaiah himself. It was most likely Isaiah who had gone into the temple virgin "prophetess" (Isa. 8:1-4), for he had announced to Ahaz the extinction of his line, saying 'surely ye shall not be established' (Isa. 7:9). Ahaz had offered his own child to Moloch as a human sacrifice, then died at age thirty-six, while Hezekiah took the throne [around 730 BC] at age twenty-five. As predicted, Isaiah, who belonged to

---

[642] Isa. 4:2; 7:14-16; 8:1-8; 9:6-7; 10:12, 20-21; chapters 11, 35, 40; Mic. 5:1-8.

[643] 2 Kings 16:3-20; 23:12; 2 Chron. 27:9; 28:1-27; Isa. 7:14-17; 8:1-5; 9:1-7; Mic. 5:2.

[644] 1 Kings 18:2; 2 Kings 14:29; 15:8, 11; 2 Chron. 24:20-21; 25:5; 29:1; Isa. 7:14-16; Matt. 23:35; Luke 11:51.

the royal family, placed upon the throne a 'prince of Bethlehem,' Hezekiah (Mic. 5:2)."[645]

If the prophecies were referring to Hezekiah instead of Jesus, then Micah's description of one "whose goings forth have been from of old, from everlasting" would indicate that Hezekiah was the reincarnation of a very old soul.[646] The early "Christians" attempted to relate all Old Testament prophecies to Jesus, when Jehovah actually sent several "saviors" or "messiahs" such as King Josiah, the high priest Jeshua and King Cyrus to assist Israel.[647] Mohammed claimed that his mission was also prophesied in the Old Testament. But the spirit of Jesus is believed to have been the only one of the various "savior/messiahs" who was "Christed."

The "Southern Kingdom of Judah," under the rule of the faithful King Hezekiah, was fearful of the cruel warriors of Assyria, but Jehovah, through the prophets Isaiah, Jonah, Nahum and Zephaniah, assured them that Nineveh, the capital of Assyria, would be destroyed.[648] When Jonah warned against nationalism and Zephniah predicted judgement against the surrounding nations, explaining how it would affect Judah, King Hezekiah called Jehovah "the God of all the kingdoms of the earth."[649] This, however, was not the case; Jehovah was merely a local regent.

When Jerusalem was attacked by Assyria, Jehovah protected them by sending "a blast upon" the enemy. The Bible relates: "The angel of the Lord went out and smote in the camp of the Assyrians an hundred fourscore and five thousand: and when they [the Hebrews] arose early in the morning, behold, they [the

---

[645] Isis Unveiled, Vol. II, pp 166, 439-441.

[646] Mic. 5:2.

[647] Judg. 3:9; 2 Kings 13:4-5.

[648] 2 Kings 14:25; 19:1-35; Jonah; Nah. 2:8, 13; Zeph. 2:13-15.

[649] 2 Kings 19:15, 19; Jonah; Zeph., chapter 2.

Assyrians] were all dead corpses."[650] More of Jehovah's high-tech, and pretty sneaky to attack them while they slept! When Assyria was finally destroyed by the Medes and Babylonians in 612 BC, Judah was warned of being attacked by the Babylonians, but Jehovah continued to protect them as long as they were under the reign of Hezekiah, which lasted until 701 BC.[651]

Other seeming "miracles" manifested for Hezekiah. In addition to the sun's rays going backwards ten degrees on the sun dial (more technology), he had his life lengthened by fifteen years.[652] After a lifetime of "prospering in all his works," thereby allowing Judah to be "magnified in the sight of all nations," he was buried "in the chiefest of all sepulchers of the sons of David, and all Judah and the inhabitants of Jerusalem did him honor."[653] Thus he was indeed a "savior/messiah" a "prince of peace" and a "wonderful counsellor" who "carried the government upon his shoulders" and "set up an ensign" to save the "Southern Kingdom of Judah" from the hands of Assyria![654] The Bible hails: "After him was none like him among all the kings of Judah, nor any that were before him."[655]

Unfortunately, the next two kings were extremely evil, especially Manasseh, who reigned for fifty-five years, nullifying his father, Hezekiah's reforms by building pagan altars and "causing his sons to pass through the fire" as human sacrifices.[656] The Bible says of him: "He built altars for Ba'al and worshipped all the host of heaven, and served them."[657] This brings up a very interesting point and one that is often overlooked. Many Biblical

---

[650] 2 Kings. 19:35; 2 Chron. 32:21-22; Isa. 37:7, 36.

[651] 2 Kings 20:12-19.

[652] 2 Kings 20:1-11; 2 Chron. 32:24; Isa., chapter 38.

[653] 2 Chron. 32:23-33.

[654] Isa. 5:26; 9:6-7; 11:10-12; 18:3; 30:17; 31:9; Zech. 9:16.

[655] 2 Kings 16:20; 18:1-12; 2 Chron. 28:27; chapters 29-31; Prov. 25:1; Isa. 36-37.

[656] 2 Kings 21:1-161; 2 Chron. 32:33; 33:1-9; Jer. 44:17-19.

[657] 2 Kings 21:3-5, 7; 2 Chron. 33:3-7.

scholars believe the "host of heaven," are mere idols, or the sun, moon and stars, but are they? Read the following and decide for yourselves.

WHO ARE THE "HOST OF HEAVEN?"

If Jehovah was an advanced technological space being, as I have postulated, then who are these other "gods" that Manasseh served? Some Biblical scholars believe the "host of heaven" refer to the sun, moon and stars, but the following makes it clear that they are separate: "Ye have borne the tabernacle of Moloch and Chiun or Remphan [Saturn], figures which you made to worship the star of your 'god;' the king put down the idolatrous priests that burned incense unto Ba'al, to the sun, and to the moon, and to the planets, and to all the host of heaven; he cast down some of the host and of the stars to the ground."[658] As mentioned previously, Jehovah promised to gather the Hebrews from captivity, saying: "If any of thine be driven out unto the outmost parts of heaven, from thence will the Lord thy God gather thee, and from thence will he fetch thee."[659] Evidently some of these "other 'gods'" also had the technology to transport their followers as well as their abductees to the stars. There seem to have been many "wars in heaven."

The writers of the Bible, continually hailing the stars as noble creations, were impressed with their numbers, endowed them with personalities, called them by name and said they have an influence over us. It was a star that rose out of the east to guide the wisemen to find Jesus, who holds seven stars in his hand, and is called the "star that rose out of Jacob." The "Mother God" is "clothed with the sun, with the moon under her feet, and upon her head a crown of twelve stars". The "morning stars sang together;"

---

[658] De. 4:19; 17:3; 2 Kings 17:16; 23:3-5; Jer. 8:2; 19:13; Dan. 8:10; Amos 5:26; Zeph. 1:5; Acts 7:42-43.

[659] De. 30:3-4; Neh. l:9.

and the "dayspring" or "daystar, arises in our hearts."[660] The stars are also said to praise God; "seven stars made obeisance to Joseph" and the righteous "shine as a star". But some of the "wandering" stars that "are not pure," will not give light and will eventually fall.[661] Lucifer, "son of the morning," said: "I will exalt my throne above the stars of God."[662] If the "host of heaven" aren't the sun, moon and stars, who were these "other 'gods'?" Space beings from other planets? Let us examine some of them:

ATLANTIS: This "Mother Empire" of culture and home to the "children of Neptune," consisted of a continent that through a series of three major earthquakes became several islands stretching from beyond the "Twin Pillars of Hercules" (Straits of Gibraltar) to America. It flourished for thousands of years before its sinking by a series of violent earthquakes around 10 or 11,000 BC. Although the name "Atlan," meaning "amid the water," has no etymology in any language known to Europe, Columbus found a village named Atlan near Panama. Poseidon, the Atlantean "god," had a son named Atlas. He was fabled to be a giant who supported the heavens on his shoulders. Today, Altlas is still depicted as a muscle man carrying the earth. The Atlas Mountains are said to be King Atlas changed into a mountain. It is curious that a book of maps, called an Atlas, depicts the shallow spots in the Sargasso Sea where the Island of Poseidon once stood. Core samples, taken from two miles beneath the ocean's surface near the Azores, eight hundred miles west of Portugal, which had been the ancient mountain tops of Atlantis, revealed land-grown plants.

---

[660] Gen. 15:5; 22:17; 26:4; Ex. 32:13; Num. 24:17; De. 1:10; Judg. 5:20; 10:22; 28:62; 1 Chron. 27:23; Neh. 9:23; Job 38:7; Ps. 8:3; 19:1; Job 9:9, 38; 22:12; 32:32; Isa. 40:26; 60:3; Jer. 31:35; Amos 5:8; Obad. 4; Nah. 3:16; Matt. 2:2-10; Luke 1:78; 2 Cor. 4:4-6; 2 Pet. 1:19; Rev. 1:16, 20; 2:1, 28; 3:1; 12:1; 22:16.
[661] Gen. 37:9; Ps. 148:2-3; Job 25:5; Isa. 13:10; Ezek. 32:7-8; Dan. 8:10; 12:3; Joel 2:10; 3:15; Matt. 24:29; Mark 13:25; Luke 21:25; Acts 27:20; Jude 13; Rev. 6:13; 8:12.
[662] Isa. 14:12-13.

Mysterious stone structures have also been detected by echo location in both the Azores and Bimini. The surviving Atlanteans migrated to the Pyrenees Mountains and the higher Basque Provinces bordering France and Spain, to the Atlas Mountains in Morocco, and to the Himalaya Mountains of India. Migrating from a land that was sinking into the ocean, they no doubt preferred a mountainous terrain. However, they gradually spread throughout the valleys in India, Egypt, and Mesopotamia, as well as the coasts of Madeira Island, the Canary Islands, and the isles of Britain. It is curious that the name Medeira was used for a river in Brazil and a beach in Florida, and that the name Canarias is found in both Brazil and Cuba. Could the migrating Atlanteans have utilized the names of their sunken homeland? The Basques, who settled in northern Spain, like the Aymaras of Peru, have an ancient ("Eskura") language that is not related to any other. The Aymara tongue was recently used in a computer program because it was deemed the purest of all languages. Evidence of this ancient language has also been found in Malta, the Canary and Easter Islands, areas that were also peopled with the remnants of Atlantis. Other surviving Atlanteans migrated to America. The term America most likely came from Meru, an Atlantean word meaning "sacred mound," home of the "gods." An ancient term for Atlantis was "Mera or "Meron." The "Temple of Meru" is in Peru, and "Pir" is an Atlantean word for light. The most ancient and isolated people of Peru are the "Aymaras," who claimed to have migrated from Atlantis. The Aymaras were also called "Ohums." ("Ohm" or "Aum" is an ancient name for God.) Other ancient Atlanteans settled in British Honduras, Guatemala, and Costa Rica. Huge standing stones, six foot in diameter, have been found in Yucatan and Costa Rica. They sit on a raised platform, surrounded by beds of smaller polished stones. Both the ancient Peruvians and the Mayas of Yucatan placed a great deal of emphasis on Orion, Sirius and the Pleiades. Atlantides, one of the seven stars of Pleiades, was fabled to be the daughter of Atlas. Archaeologists have found ancient sites in Yucatan dating back to 9 or 10 thousand BC. Surviving Atlanteans of the American southwest migrated to the midwest to become mound builders. The Navaho Indians, claiming to have migrated from Peru, also have such a unique language that it was used during World War II as a secret code. The Atlanteans, under the sacred "Law of the One," believed in a triune God. They called the invisible Heavenly Father, "Hu." The manifested deities were Osiris and Isis, also known as Poseidon and Cleito. Freemasonry is believed to have originated in Atlantis, as well as the concept of hierophants, mystery schools, a sacred mystery language, advanced architecture, craftsmanship, astronomy and astrology. Many scholars believe that Noah was a resident of Atlantis and that the "Garden of Eden" was located there.[663] Others, however, believe it was located near Mt. Ararat.

AKKADIA: Because "Akkad" and "Ak-il" are Atlantean terms, the Akkadians are believed to have migrated from Atlantis. Accad was one of the cities of Shinar which formed the early Kingdom of Nimrod.[664] They were later known as Kaldi, which gradually became Chaldea. The ancient name of the Mediterranean was Akkari. Socially organized with advanced laws and a system of writing, they were architects, metal workers, artists, pyramid builders, and engineers who constructed elaborate dams and canals. They worshipped Osiris and Isis and revered the "sacred-mound" concept of Atlantis. It was most likely the Akkadians who built the great pyramid in Egypt, just prior to the sinking of Atlantis. It is no coincidence that the two openings, on either side of the pyramid are aligned with Orion to represent

---

[663] For further information, see: <u>Atlantis Mother of Empires</u>, Robert B. Stacy-Judd, Adventures Unlimited Press, IL, 1999; <u>Atlantis: The Andes Solution</u>, J. M. Allen, St. Martin's Press, VA, 1999; <u>The History of Atlantis</u>, Lewis Spence, 1926; <u>Atlantis in Spain</u>, E. M. Whishaw, Rider & Co. London, 1928; and <u>The Shadow of Atlantis</u>, Col. Alexander Braghine, Adventures Unlimited Press, IL, 1997; <u>The Secret Doctrine</u>, Vol. I and II and <u>Isis Unveiled</u>, Vol. I, by Blavatsky; and the writings of Edgar Cayce, A.R.E. Press, Virginia Beach, VA.

[664] Gen. 10:10.

Osiris and Sirius to represent Isis. The later Indian, Sumerian, Arabian and Persian cultures stemmed from the knowledge of the ancient Akkadians.

INDIA: India may have been the "Land of Nod, on the east of Eden," to which Cain traveled when he left the "Garden of Eden." Cain's descendants, Jubal, the father of music and musical instruments, and Tubal-Cain, "an instructor of every artificer in brass and iron,"[665] may have been the "father" of crafts in which India became famous. The leaders of India, revered by the Hebrews as "the wise children of the east,"[666] had an organized religion with a triune God Brahma/Vishnu/Shiva. The ancient beings Rama and the highly-technical Indra rode in chariots, or "celestial boats," and wielded thunderbolts (spacecraft with laser weaponry). The "'god' of wind" traveled in a chariot that made thunderous noises and whirled dust. Shiva's weapon consisted of arrows like fiery beams emanating from a sun globe.[667] Around 16,000 BC, the ancient Sethite Priesthood of the osisarion religion, was brought to India by the Dravidians and the great teacher Thoth, who was the first to build cities and establish an import/export business. By 2500 BC, they had a language, a unique pictographic script, art and products of craftsmanship, a standardized technique of pottery, weaving, weights and measures, a towering citadel, a public bath in the center of the city, the plough, prosperity from farming, manufacturing and commerce, the use of cotton and large houses with luxurious baths. Their urban organization was superior to that of Mesopotamia and their cities were refined and luxurious. Their historical Mahabharata, Upanishads, Puranic Texts, and Vedas

---

[665] Gen. 4:16-22.

[666] 1 Kings 4:30; Job 1:3

[667] For further information, see: The Religion of the Veda, The Ancient Religion of India, Bloomfield, AMS Press, NY, 1969, p 155; Srimad Bhagavatam, Seventh Canto, Swami Prabhupada, The Bhaktivedanta Book Trust, NY, 1976, p 10.

are revered as sacred writings. Blavatsky says: "The Hindu Aryan, the most metaphysical and spiritual people on earth, belong to the oldest races; the Semite Hebrew to the latest."[668]

EGYPT: It is believed that Egypt's early settlers came from Atlantis and India as a mature civilization. It is obvious that the Great Pyramid was built by technological beings. The water erosion marks on the Sphinx indicate that it was there 13,000 years ago, at the time of, or prior to, the flood and the sinking of Atlantis around 10 or 11,000 BC. The name Egypt, derived from Ageb, means "Land of the flood." Egypt's sixth-dimensional "god" Ra and the triune "godhead" Osiris/Isis/Horus originated in Atlantis thousands of years ago. (Horus was believed to have held the Office of the Christ.) Ra or Rama, son of Ptah, was an unseen celestial "god" who also manifested himself as the Aten. The "gods," who traversed the heavens in "flying boats," or "a winged globe [spacecraft]," were the first rulers of Egypt. The Egyptian word for a divine being means "one who watches." The humans acted as their servants. The later Pharaohs claimed to be direct descendants of the "gods," but they degenerated into worshipping Amon instead of Aten. The great Egyptian sage and teacher, Amenemope, wrote the "Book of Wisdom," parts of which were later translated into Hebrew and became the Old Testament "Book of Proverbs" and the first Psalms. His teachings also influenced the Pharaoh Akhenaten, the Hellenic philosophies, and the Alexandrian philosopher, Philo. Akhenaten, rebelled against the polluted priesthood and reestablished the teachings of Aten, moved the capitol of Egypt to El Amarna in 1375 BC, built a temple in the shape of a cross and taught monotheism. (Note the similarities in the names "Amarna" and the ancient Peruvian tribe, the "Aymara.") In an ancient tablet, he defined the one and only "god," Ra-Aten, as "a solicitous father, compassionate and tender, the 'god' of gentleness and peace, who was found not in battles

---

[668] The Secret Doctrine, Vol. II, p 470.

and victories but in forms of life and growth, and is not limited to human form but belongs to all nations equally." This certainly doesn't sound like the territorial Jehovah, so perhaps he was a higher God. Akhenaten was also a writer; twelve of his songs were included in Old Testament's Psalms. He is also author of the book: Unto Thee I Grant.

SUMERIA: Sumer means "the land of one who watches." Because the early Sumerians were a unified people with a unified religion, they were able to defend themselves against attack. In the fifth millennium BC, they built great cities, organized a system of city-states, contributed the wheel, a money system with gold and silver as standards of value, a system of credit with interest, the calendar based on the lunar month, clocks, a study of the stars, cuneiform writing on clay tablets, a system of weights and measures, medicine and surgery, radiation treatments, the use of petroleum products, a water level and the square, water control gates and reservoirs, the dome, vault and arch. The Akkadians, under their leader Sargon I, around 2300 BC, established the first great empire in history. With Akkad as its capital, it became known as the Sumerian-Akkadian Empire. Sumeria collapsed in 2180 BC, and from 2100 to 1800 BC the Amorites founded dynasties, including Babylon, under Hammurabi, who established an elaborate code of laws. The "god" of these highly civilized Sumerians was seen as a trinity of Anu, the ultimate divine authority in the heavens; his son, Enlil, the "god of earth; and Enki, also known as Ea, the "water god." There were also fifty deities known as the "great 'gods.'" The "gods" who lived on earth chose the land somewhere northeast of Sumer. This land, later named "the land of the living" by the Babylonians, is believed to have been the biblical "Eden." In the Sumerian language, the "gods" were called "DIN.GIR" (DIN meaning "bright," GIR meaning rocket). The home of the "gods" was "E.DIN. [Eden]" Their Ziggurat temples were called the "Hill of Heaven", reminiscent of the "sacred mound." The head of the temple was an "En," under whom served the priests, with many rites, rituals, ceremonies and holy days. The "gods" of Sumer could have been the "Elohim," a plural term for those who "created" in the "Garden of Eden." Perhaps they were fellow astronauts who used artificial insemination to bio-engineer the genes of the native earth people and the early "root races" with their own. According to the Sumerian carvings and records, the "gods," who traveled in sky vehicles and wore helmets with goggles, ruled as their first monarchs, hence the term "royal" or "blue blood." The priests acted as intermediaries between the people and these technologically advanced "gods." The Babylonians were ruled by Enki's evil son Marduk, who may have been Jehovah.

CHINA: Cultural advancement came to China around 15,000 BC, but they did not build cities or engage in manufacture until around 10,000 BC. By 2500 BC, they had set up efficient city-states. By 2357, they had created an empire, and had developed bronze casting, the silk industry, writing, printing and the potters wheel. They were the most consistent race in believing in the one supreme "god," the heaven itself, called "Shang-TI." Their greatest philosophers were Confucius and Lao Tze.

GREECE: The Greek "gods," similar to those of the Vedas, were said to live in a heavenly Olympus, whose earthly counterpart was the lofty Mount Olympus. They were described as being physically similar to mankind, but immortal, and therefore mentally superior. Their blood was said to be golden. Emotional in nature, they were continually embroiled in disputes with each other. Traveling at immense speeds and flashing powerful weapons, they were interdimensional, mysteriously appearing and disappearing. Due to the early influence of the Melchizedek missionaries, Greece was against all forms of priesthood, thus their teachings were philosophical rather than dogmatic and ritualistic; their emphasis was on craftsmanship and intellect.

BRITAIN: The builders of Stonehenge and the later

Druids, who utilized the amazing structures, are also believed to have been the descendants of the Atlanteans. The Norse/Scandinavian "God of Wisdom," Odin, was curiously connected to both the Buddha and the Garden of Eden" (E-Din or O-din). The Odinic rituals were similar to those of the Brahmins, while their initiation rites resembled those of Freemasonry. The sons of the one-eyed "god," Odin, were Thor and Balder. Balder, "the Beautiful," was believed to be a representation of the Christ. Odin built an etheric temple, Asgard, in which the twelve unseen gods dwelt and administered to the twelve Druid priests on earth.[669]

Blavatsky says of these various "gods:"

"We do not worship the 'gods,' we only honor them as being superior to ourselves. History shows in every race and every tribe, especially in the Semitic nations, the natural impulse to exalt its own tribal deity above all others to the hegemony of the 'gods.' Jehovah has ever been in antiquity only a 'god' among other 'gods.' Astronomically, the 'Most High' is the Sun; the 'Lord' is one of his seven planets. As each Persian Dev is chained to his planet, so each Hindu Deva ('Lord') has its allotted portion, a world, a planet, a nation or a race. Jehovah's portion is his 'chosen people' and none else. What then, have other nations, who call themselves Aryans, to do with this Semitic deity, the tribal 'god' of Israel? Let the 'Angel Gabriel,' the 'Lord' of Iran, watch over his people; and Michael-Jehovah over his

---

[669] For further information, see The Secret Teachings of All Ages, pp xxviii, xxxiii.

Hebrews."[670]

It becomes increasingly clear that different "gods" ruled each nation. Some of them may have been divinely ordained, while others were "fallen angels" or space beings. The Supreme Heavenly Father, who resides in "Paradise," does not descend to rule individual nations or planets. He remains on an esoteric level as the "Father Within."

SOUTHERN KINGDOM CONQUERED

For his sins of idolatry and human sacrifice, Judah's evil king, Manasseh, the son of Hezekiah, was captured and taken to Babylon, but was released when he humbled himself.[671] He rebuilt Jehovah's altars and sacrificed only to him, but although he repented of his evil ways and made amends, Jehovah would not pardon him for the "innocent blood" he had shed; human sacrifice is unpardonable.[672]

Jeremiah, the tender prophet of whom Jehovah said: "Before I formed thee in the belly I knew thee and sanctified thee and ordained thee a prophet to the nations," warned that Judah would be taken captive by Babylonia. But due to the faithfulness of Josiah, who became king in 638 BC, the prophecy was stayed.[673] The pious, Josiah, a great soul to whom some of the messianic prophecies seem to refer, found the Book of the Law of Moses that had been lost for nearly two hundred seventy-five years (around the time of Solomon). After being verified by the prophetess Hulda, it was read to the people.[674] Josiah, in his

---

[670] The Secret Doctrine, Vol. II, p 507-508, 537-538.

[671] 2 Chron. 33:11-13.

[672] Lev. 18:21; 20:2-5; 2 Kings 21:11, 16; 23:26; 24:3-4; 2 Chron. 33:10-20; Jer. 15:4.

[673] 2 Kings, chapter 21; 22:1-2; Jer. 1:5; 20:4-5.

[674] 2 Kings 22:3-20; 23:1-3; 2 Chron. 17:9; 34:14-33.

rampant religious reformation, repaired the temple, broke down the idolatrous altars, and held a Passover. He was killed in 608 BC, by the invading Pharaoh-Nechoh of Egypt.[675] The Bible says of Josiah: "No king before him turned to the Lord with all his heart, and with all his soul, and with all his might, according to all the law of Moses; neither after him arose there any like him."[676] Like Hezekiah, he was a "savior/messiah" to his people! The "ark of the covenant" was mentioned during his reign, but was lost after his death, and not mentioned again until John saw it in "heaven."[677] According to the book of Maccabees in the Catholic Bible, Jeremiah placed it in a cave on Mount Nebo just before the Babylonian exile.[678] It is rumored to have been taken to Ethiopia, where many believe it still remains.

After Josiah's death, the crown was placed upon his son, Jehoahaz. He ruled only three months before the Pharaoh dethroned and exiled him, then appointed his older brother, Jehoiakim, to rule in his stead.[679] When Egypt was conquered by Babylon in 605 BC, Judah came under the rule of King Nebuchadnezzar II, builder of the famed "Hanging Gardens."[680] Three years later, Jehoiakim revolted against the Babylonian king, who in turn invaded Jerusalem and imprisoned him.[681] The prophet Habakkuk complained of the indifference of Jehovah and wondered how the holiness of God could be reconciled with his choice of punishment.[682] In addition to punishing Israel, Jehovah also doled out punishment to the Ammonites, Moabites, Edomites, Phoenicians, and the Philistines of Tyre, Sidon and

---

[675] 2 Kings 22:1-7; 23:4-30; 2 Chron. 34:1-13; 35:1-24.

[676] 2 Kings 23:25; 2 Chron. 35:25.

[677] 2 Chron. 35:3; Jer. 3:16; Rev. 11:19.

[678] 2 Maccabees 2:4-6.

[679] 2 Kings 23:31-37; 2 Chron. 36:1-5; Jer. 22:10-12.

[680] 2 Kings 24:1; 2 Chron. 36:6; Jer. 46:2.

[681] 2 Kings 24:1-6; 2 Chron. 36:5-8; Jer. 22:13-19; 26:20-24; 36:16-26; Dan. 1:1-2.

[682] Hab. 1:1-4, 12-17

Egypt.[683] Finally, someone had began to question Jehovah's tremendous sense of injustice! No wonder the Book of Habakkuk was revered by the Essenes!

In 597 BC, Josiah's grandson, Jehoachin, became king of Judah, but ruled only 3 months before being attacked by Nebuchadnezzar. Seeing the futility of resistance, he surrendered and was carried, with his family and ten thousand inhabitants, into Babylon.[684] The youngest son of Josiah, Zedekiah, became king, but when he revolted, in 586 BC, Nebuchadnezzar captured him, destroyed Jerusalem, confiscated the temple vessels, burned the temple and exiled the leading citizens to Babylonia.[685] After a two year siege on the city, Nebuchadnezzar compelled total surrender and took the remainder of the people into Babylon,[686] thus ending the Hebrew monarchy and beginning their Babylonian captivity.

From the reign of King Josiah to the Babylonian exile (forty-one years), during which Josiah's three sons and his grandson had ruled, Jehovah, through Jeremiah, had continually warned the inhabitants of Judah of their impending destruction, but his messages fell on deaf ears. When Jeremiah, who hailed Jehovah as being the god of all nations, wrote his prophesies and read them to the people, he was put into stocks, held in prison, beaten, and cast into a dungeon. The princes did not dare to kill Jehovah's chosen prophet, but they did all they could to keep him out of the public, finally exiling him to Egypt, where he continued to prophesy.[687] Jehovah emphasized that he was punishing Israel because they had worshipped other "gods," but promised, through Jeremiah, Zechariah and second Isaiah, that a

---

[683] 1 Chron. 18:2, 13; 25:14-19; Ezra 9:1; Ezek. 25:2-16; 29:7-20; 30:4-25; Joel 3:4; Amos 1:8-21; Nahum 3:8-10.

[684] 2 Kings 24:8-16; 2 Chron. 36:8-16.

[685] 2 Kings 24:17-20; 25; 2 Chron. 36:10-21; Jer. 38:1-6; 39:1-14; 52:1-30; Lam. 2:4, 6; Dan. 1:1.

[686] 2 Kings 25:8-30; 2 Chron. 36:11-21.

[687] Jer. 20:2; 32:2; 33:1; 36:19-26; 37:15; 38:6; 43.

"remnant" would return after a "seventy year" exile at which time he would "pardon them" and "raise unto David, a righteous branch."[688]

Rather than Jesus, this prophecy of the "righteous branch," most likely refers to the high priest Jeshua, who an angel clothed with a "change of raiment," set a "fair mitre upon" and "laid before him a stone with seven eyes."[689] Since "eyes" generally symbolize reincarnation, Jeshua, like Melchizedek, David and Elisha, may have been a previous incarnation of, or overshadowed by the spirit of, Jesus. The high priest, Jeshua led the first band of exiles back from their Babylonian captivity. The Persian King Cyrus, another predicted "shepherd," was "anointed" by Jehovah, and had been taken into Jehovah's "secret place" (mothership) and given treasures.[690] Cyrus was not even a Hebrew; again Jehovah went international, but it was only an act of manipulation!

PROPHETIC GUIDANCE DURING THE EXILE

After Daniel, a descendant of David, and his three companions, Shadrach, Meshach and Abed-nego, were carried into Babylon by Nebuchadnezzar, Daniel interpreted the king's dream and was made ruler over the province of Babylon and chief governor over the wisemen.[691] When Jehovah protected Daniel's three companions in a blazing furnace, the king was so impressed he declared: "Your God is a God of 'gods,' a Lord of kings, and a revealer of secrets," yet he still spoke of "gods [plural]."[692] After

---

[688] Isa. 42:1-4; chapters 49-55; Jer. 3:18; 18:15; 19:4; 21;5; 23:3-6, 20; 24:6; 29:10-14; 30:9; 33:7-16; 44:3; 50:4; Lam. 2:1-6; 3:43-44; 4:11; Zech. 3; 6:12; 8:14; (first Isaiah is represented by chapters 1-40; second Isaiah, by 40-55; third Isaiah, 55-66).

[689] Jer. 30:9; Zech., chapter 3.

[690] 2 Chron. 36:22-23; Ezra 1:1; Isa. 44:28; 45:1-5.

[691] Dan., chapters 1- 2.

[692] Dan., chapter 3-4.

the king's death, Daniel interpreted the writing on the wall for King Belshazzar, who made him third ruler.[693]

Daniel also had visions and experiences with angels, including Archangel Gabriel, "who stands in the presence of God," and who later came to arrange the birth of John, the Baptist, and Jesus, then guided Mohammed to establish the Islamic religion.[694] When Darius, the Mede, became king, he made Daniel the first of three presidents over one-hundred-twenty princes of the realm.[695] A jealous group of leaders then cast Daniel into a lion's den where he remained unharmed. The king was so impressed with the power of Jehovah, he called him "the Living God" and demanded that the kingdom "tremble and fear before the 'god' of Daniel."[696]

Daniel continued to have visions of angels.[697] The message that one of the "angels," or astronauts, gave Daniel sheds light on the subject of various "gods" having charge over the different nations: "Fear not, Daniel for from the first day that thou didst set thyself before God, I am come, but the prince of the kingdom of Persia withstood me one and twenty days, but lo, [Archangel] Michael, one of the chief princes, came to help me; and I remained there with the kings of Persia. . . . And now will I return to fight with the prince of Persia: and when I am gone forth, lo, the prince of Grecia shall come. But I will shew thee that which is noted in the scripture of truth: and there is none that holdeth with me in these things, but Michael your prince."[698] Who were these other "princes" of Persia and Greece?

The Bible, speaking of Satan as the "prince of this world; the prince of the power of the air; the spirit that now worketh in

---

[693] Dan., chapter 5.

[694] Dan., chapter 7-9; Luke 1:8-20, 26-38; see the Koran.

[695] Dan. 6:1-3.

[696] Dan. 6:4-28.

[697] Dan., chapters 11-12.

[698] Dan. 10:12-13, 20-21.

the children of disobedience," relates: "Michael the archangel, when contending with the Devil [Satan] disputed about the body of Moses, durst nor bring against him a railing accusation, but said, the Lord rebuke thee. And there was war in heaven: Michael and his angels fought against the dragon . . . and the dragon was cast out into the earth, and his angels were cast out with him."[699] Perhaps "Star Wars" is not only in the movies! As stated earlier, India's "Mahabharata" also relates many of these heavenly wars and describes their high-tech air machines and weaponry.

When Babylonia was conquered by the Persian King Cyrus, the Great, who overthrew the Median supremacy in 539 BC, Daniel continued to commune with angels.[700] Referring to the Hebrew exile as a "curse," he agreed with Jeremiah that it would take "seventy years" to "make reconciliation for their iniquity," but he also promised a "messiah," an anointed one.[701] This prophecy, like that of Jeremiah, also seems to refer to Jeshua, who returned to Jerusalem with the first band of exiles from Babylon.

Another powerful prophet during the time of the exile was the Zadok priest Ezekiel, who was carried into Babylon during the first exile in 597 BC.[702] Jehovah, or "the angel of his presence," came to him in an elaborate spacecraft. Manifesting within "a whirlwind, a cloud and a fire infolding itself," the brilliant "amber" craft revealed "four beings, cherubim, wings and wheels" and made the sound of "great waters."[703] Ezekiel describes the space gear the four beings were wearing as: boots ("feet were straight" and "the sole of their feet was like the sole of a calf's foot"); space suits ("like the color of burnished brass"); and helmets with loud speakers ("firmament upon the heads of

---

[699] John 12:32; 14:30; 16:11; Eph. 2:2; Jude 9; Rev. 12:7-9.

[700] Dan., chapter 10.

[701] Dan. 7:13; 9:11, 24-27; 12:1-3.

[702] 2 Kings 24:10-16; Ezek. 1:1-3.

[703] Ezek. 1:3-28; 3:15.

the living creature was as to the color of the terrible crystal, stretched forth over their heads above . . . and there was a voice from the firmament").[704] Above the four creatures was a shining "throne" that looked like a sapphire, upon which sat another man, perhaps the captain of the shuttle craft, who was wearing a shining one-pieced space suit ("from his loins upward, and from his loins downward"), the "color of amber."[705]

What was Jesus wearing when he appeared to John? The Bible describes "a great voice, as of a trumpet, as the sound of many waters [loud speakers], his head and his hairs were white like wool" [a white helmet?]; "out of his mouth went a sharp two-edged sword" [some type of breathing tube?]; "clothed with a garment down to the foot and girt about the paps with a golden girdle" [a one-pieced jump suit?]; with "feet like unto fine brass" [boots?].[706] Daniel's description of visitors was nearly identical: "A man clothed in linen, loins girded with gold, body like beryl, face as lightning, eyes as lamps of fire, arms and feet like polished brass [spacesuit], and his voice like the voice of a multitude [loud speaker]."[707] The angel that appeared to Balaam had "his sword drawn in his hand, and Ezekiel's vision of the temple revealed "six men," each with "a slaughter weapon in his hand."[708] How appropriate that Jehovah's mothership would be equipped with "slaughter weapons"!

During Ezekiel's encounter, after being fed "a roll" which he was to digest--this may have been a type of drug, for the same thing happened to Jeremiah and John--spirit "lifted Ezekiel up and took him away in a noise of a great rushing."[709] Sounds like the description of modern UFOs! Ezekiel didn't want to go, but

---

[704] Ezek. 1:7, 22, 25.

[705] Ezek. 1:26-27; 8:2.

[706] Rev. 1:10-16; 2:18; 15:6; 19:6.

[707] Dan. 7:9; 10:5-6; 12:6-7.

[708] Num. 22:23; Ezek. 10:1-2.

[709] Jer. 15:16; Ezek. 2:9-10; 3:1-2, 12-15; Rev. 10:8-9.

the hand of the Lord was strong upon him."[710] After receiving instructions, he was made a "watchman."[711] Later, when he saw Jehovah in "great glory, the spirit entered into him" and he was given additional instructions.[712]

About a year later, Jehovah appearing in an amber fire, took Ezekiel by his hair and lifted him "between the earth and the heaven and brought him to Jerusalem," where, he was shown visions of the idolatrous Hebrews, the "image of Jehovah's jealousy."[713] He was "lifted and brought to the east gate of the temple," where he was given further instruction.[714] He reported: "Then did the cherubims lift up their wings, and the wheels beside them; and the glory of the God of Israel was over them above. And the glory of the Lord went up from the midst of the city, and stood upon the mountain which is on the east side of the city. Afterwards the spirit took me up and brought me to them of the captivity."[715]

Jehovah, calling Israel "rebellious, impudent and hard-hearted," said: "they are against me; have forgotten and forsaken me."[716] Listing their sins as: "idolatry, serving wood and stone, weeping for Tammuz, worshipping the sun, burning incense, polluting the sabbath and whoring with other nations," he added that he would be "comforted" only when his anger was accomplished". He said he was "against Israel" and had "no pity;" that he would destroy them with fire, for he rules all nations and does as he sees fit.[717] Another arrogant tirade! He promised to save a "remnant," not for their sakes, but for "his

---

[710] Ezek. 3:14.

[711] Ezek. 3:16-27; 33:7.

[712] Ezek. 3:23-27, chapters 4-7.

[713] Ezek. 8:1-18; 16:38.

[714] Ezek. 11:1-3.

[715] Ezek. 11:22-24.

[716] Ezek. 2:3-4; 3:7; 6:9; 8:12; 9:9; 22:12.

[717] Ezek. 5:8-13; 6:9; 7:4; 8:14, 16; 9:1-5; 16:3, 26-29, 45-50; 20:13-32; 22:1-12, 21; 23:38; 33:25; 36:18-22; Dan. 4:17, 26, 35; 5:21.

holy names' sake;" that it should not be "polluted in the sight of the heathen" so all would know that he is "the Lord" and that his threats "had not been said in vain."[718] He stated later: "Give not thine heritage to reproach, that the heathen should rule over them; wherefore should they say among the people, where is their 'god'? Then will the Lord be jealous for his land, and pity his people."[719] Does this appear to be a genuine pity for the people or was he merely saving face with the heathen? It would appear that Jehovah was as petty as he was violent!

Nineteen years after being teleported to Jerusalem, Ezekiel was transported to Israel and "set upon a very high mountain" where he was met by a man whose appearance was "like the appearance of brass." Given a detailed tour of Jehovah's elaborate "three-storied temple [mothership]," he saw gates, chambers, windows with arches, courts, porches, temple ornaments, and posts and pillars decorated with palm trees and crerubims."[720] Some of the chambers were for singers, others for priests, and some contained hewn stone tables for cutting up sacrifices.[721] Where did they get the meat? Did they beam up animals? Perhaps cattle mutilation is not such a new thing!

When Jehovah entered the temple, with "great glory" and a voice "like a noise of many waters [loud speakers]," Ezekiel was "taken up and brought to the inner court" where Jehovah said: "Show the house to Israel and let them measure the pattern. Show them the fashion, and the goings out, and the comings in, and all the forms thereof, and all the ordinances, and the laws, and write it in their sight."[722] He was then shown the altar and given new instructions about sacrifices, garments and ordinances

---

[718] Isa. 43:25; 48:9-11; Ezek. 6:8-10; 12:20; 20:5-9, 22; 28:25; 30:19; 36:22-28, 32.

[719] Joel 2:17-18.

[720] Ezek. 40:1-49; chapters 41-43.

[721] Ezek. 40:38-42, 44-45.

[722] Ezek. 43:1-11.

for the priests, and the division of the land when they returned to Judah.[723]

Ezekiel also prophesied that David would be a "king, a prince and a shepherd" over them--again referring to the soul of Jesus who had already incarnated several times, or whose spirit had overshadowed several individuals, and was now, as Jeshua, to receive the "new covenant."[724] There are many scriptures indicating that the old "covenant" had been "broken" and that a "new covenant" had been promised.[725] Malachi says the "covenant" would be with "Levi," representing the priests; Jeshua was a Levite and a high priest; Jesus, of the lineage of David, was not.[726]

Jeremiah wrote to the exiles from Egypt, and during that time wrote the book of Lamentations to console them. Job, written prior to the exile, was hailed by Ezekiel as one of three righteous men; the other two being Noah and Daniel.[727] When Job asked Jehovah why the righteous had to suffer, Jehovah appeared to him "in a whirlwind [spacecraft]," stating that his "own right hand" could save him.[728] Isn't that true of all mankind? We make our own heaven or hell right here on earth!

THE HEBREWS RETURN TO JERUSALEM

Finally seeing the error of his ways and realizing the harshness of his punishment, Jehovah proclaimed: "Behold, the days come that I will make a new covenant with the house of Israel and with the house of Judah. I will put my law in their inward parts and write in their hearts; I will forgive their iniquity,

---

[723] Ezek. 43:13-27; chapters 44-48.

[724] Isa. 55:3; Jer. 31:28-33; Ezek. 16:60; 34:23-25; 37:24-25; Dan. 11:22.

[725] 1 Kings 19:10, 14; Ezra 10:3; Neh. 9:38; Isa. 24:5; 33:8; Jer. 11:3, 10; Ezek. 16:57; Hos. 2:18; 8:1; Amos. 1:9; Zech. 11:10.

[726] Mal. 2:4.

[727] Ezek. 14:14, 20.

[728] Job 38:1; 40:14; 42:1-6.

and I will remember their sin no more."[729] Did he attempt to do this through Jeshua?

In 536 BC, seventy years after the Hebrews had been placed under Babylonian rule, they, including the many who had intermarried with the "Gentiles," were "delivered" by the Persian King Cyrus, who had been "anointed" by Jehovah to issue a decree allowing them to return to Jerusalem to rebuild their temple.[730] With the help of the Hebrew high priest, Jeshua, (the "anointed savior/messiah" that Jehovah had promised) and Shashbazzar (who was entrusted to carry the temple vessels), Zerubbabel (a descendant of David, who is listed as one of the ancestors of Jesus) led a band of fifty thousand people to Judah, where he became governor.[731] Encouraged by the prophets Haggai, Zechariah and Obadiah, the Hebrews built an altar, offered sacrifices and began laying the foundation for their temple, which they completed in 516 BC. The courts of the new temple were built after the pattern of Ezekiel's vision. At the dedication ceremony, they sacrificed a hundred bullocks, two hundred rams, four hundred lambs and twelve goats.[732] What a barbecue!

---

[729] Jer. 31:28-33.

[730] 2 Chron. 36:22-23; Ezra 1:1-11; 4:3, 5; 5:13-17; 6:3-5; Isa. 44:26-27; 45:1-13; 46:11.

[731] 1 Chron. 3:19; Ezra 1:5-11; 2:1-67; 3:2; Neh. 7:6-7; Hag. 1:1, 14; 2:21-23; Hag. 2:23; Zech. 3, 4; Matt. 1:12; Luke 3:27.

[732] Ezra 5:5, 7; 6:1-15-22.

	RULERS	PROPHETS	PRIESTS	DATE
Babylonian Kings:	Nebuchadnezzar	Daniel		586
	Belshazzar	Ezekiel		
	Darius, the Mede			
Persian King:	Cyrus, the Great			536
Governors of	Zerubbabel	Haggai, Zechariah,	Jeshua	
Jerusalem:		Obadiah,		
		Joel, Malachi	Ezra	457
	Nehemiah	Third Isaiah		445

In 457 BC, Jehovah guided the priest and scribe Ezra to lead another band of exiles to Jerusalem, where he restored singing into the services, established a library, revived the schools for prophets, and initiated drastic reforms, including the dissolving of interracial marriages.[733] In 445 BC, Nehemiah led a band of exiles to Jerusalem, where he became governor, rebuilt the city walls, had a great sacrifice, took a census, promoted religious revival, which included having Ezra read the Book of the Law of Moses, and had the people sign a covenant.[734] The five sacred books that were read during the Feast of Purim were: Esther, Ruth, Ecclesiastes, Solomon's Song and Lamentations. Jehovah spoke through the prophets Joel, Malachi and third Isaiah, promising a "messiah" who would bless all nations.[735] These are the only prophecies that actually refer to Jesus.

The foregoing scriptures were taken from the King James Version of the Protestant Bible. The Catholic Bible has seven Old Testament books that were omitted from the Hebrew Old Testament and the later Protestant Bible. The reason for this is anyone's guess, for these seven books are of the same caliber as

---

[733] Ezra, chapters 7-10; Neh. .

[734] Ezra 8:1-8; Neh. chapter 1; 2:1-20; chapters 4-9; 10:28-39; 12:26-47; chapter 13.

[735] Isa. 63:16-17; Joel 2:28-29; Mal., chapter 2.

the others in the Old Testament. Tobias is similar to the story of Noah; Judith is similar to Esther; Wisdom and Sirach are similar to Proverbs and Ecclesiastes; Baruch, written by the Prophet Jeremiah's secretary during the exile, is similar to Jeremiah; and Maccabees 1 and 2 relate the history of Israel from 175-135 BC. Especially noteworthy is a summary of Israel's greatest ancestors given in Sirach; the book of Wisdom, calling Wisdom, "She," and defining her as "an aura of the might of God and a pure effusion of the glory of the Almighty;" and Maccabees explaining how the ark of the covenant and altar of incense were hidden by Jeremiah in a cave atop Mt. Nebo just before the Babylonian assault on Jerusalem.[736] All serious students of the Bible will find these seven books informative and helpful.

During the sixth and fifth centuries BC in other parts of the world, the Buddha was teaching in India, Confucius and Lao-Tze in China, Zoroaster in Iran, the Delphic Oracle was active in Greece, and the Hebrew tribes that migrated to America, as described in The Book of Mormon, were setting up great cities. The Hebrews in Israel were still offering sacrifices while the Chinese were becoming enlightened and the Buddhists were experiencing Nirvana! Perhaps they were more interested in spiritual advancement than nationalism, or perhaps the people, free from the interference of polluted priesthoods, had esoterically tapped into the mystical force of the Heavenly "Father Within." It is well to remember that the dark ages only occurred in Christian nations.

---

[736] Catholic Holy Bible, Sirach, chapters 44-50; Wisdom 7:25; 2 Maccabees 2:4-6.

PART VI

JEHOVAH'S LAW FULFILLED
BY JESUS

ISRAEL BETWEEN THE OLD AND NEW TESTAMENT

According to the "Teachers Edition" index of the Oxford Bible:

"Ezra and Nehemiah left a settled form of government, which laid the groundwork for the Talmud. Under Persian rule, the elders were allowed to administer the government with the high priest as their responsible head. The body of elders lasted about one-hundred-fifty years. The conquest of Alexander, the Great, in 331 BC, broke down the barriers separating one kingdom for another, and especially those between the Asiatic and European states. Men learned to understand each other's thoughts, while Greek literature and intelligence spread over the east, and the language became almost universal. After the Battle of Ipsus in 301 BC, Palestine was a kind of neutral territory between the rival empires of Syria and Egypt. With Ezra's Constitution fully developed, a powerful hierarchy had substituted the idea of a church for that of a nation. While they learned independence from the example of Greece, and soon became divided into sects, this freedom of thought was modified, in their case, by the contemplative temper of the east. Ptolemy's invasion led to a further settlement of Jews at Alexandria. The most important result of this was the translation of the Hebrew scripture into Greek, which became known all over the world, and thus prepared the way for the universal spread of Christianity. In 141 BC, Simon, the Just, was appointed leader and high priest over the Jews, and thus began the Maccabeean dynasty of Independence. In 128 BC, his son, Hrycan succeeded him and made an alliance with the Romans. Judea became more powerful than it had been since Solomon's time. Several books were assembled, which were later referred to by the Jews as the Apocrypha. In 63 BC Rome laid siege to Jerusalem, incorporating Palestine into the Roman Empire as part of the province of Syria. The loss of political freedom drove the Jewish spirit to an inward self-exaltation and spiritual pride, with a senile fondness for dwelling on the glories of the past. The Jews turned to minute interpretation of the refinements of the Laws, to exaggerated expectations of fulfillment of prophecy and literal attention to trivial acts of worship. Pharisees, Scribes and Lawyers were more in esteem than priests and Levites, and the teaching was rhetorical and disputatious, rather than dogmatic and authoritative. The Pharisees were strict observers of external rites and ceremonies beyond the requirements of the Law. The Sadducees, denying the authority of all revelation and tradition, subsequent to Moses, were skeptical with regard to the miraculous and supernatural (see Acts 23:6-8). King Herod made use of his position to betray his country to the Romans by fostering immorality, cultivating alien customs, sapping religious faith, encouraging mutual distrust, corrupting the priesthood, and massacring the nobles. He rebuilt the temple on the most glorious scale, intending it to be the proud monument of his dynasty; but it was really the 'whitened sepulchre' that concealed the foul impurity of his family and the loathsome corruption into which he had plunged his people."[737]

In addition to dividing their religion into Pharisees and Sadducees, the Jews had also explored the teachings of Pythagoras, Zoroaster, Freemasonry, the Kabala and the Essenes. So why did they continually "backslide?"[738] Failing to view their mission as spiritual instead of political, they expected a military leader rather than a divine teacher. Striving to regain their outer kingdom, they were not interested in an "inner" one, hence the gentle Jesus did not fulfill their exoteric expectations. Paul says they: "Sought not by faith, but as it were by the works of the law."[739] Jesus, distinguishing between the spirit and the letter of the law, taught no dogma, advocated no priesthood, avoided the outer political scene, and stressed the "inner kingdom," saying we enter by "faith, not works."[740]

JESUS AND THE "FATHER WITHIN"

The auspicious birth of Jesus and the promise of his divinity was heralded by Archangel Gabriel, who appeared to the Virgin Mary, a young lady approximately fourteen years of age.[741] When she asked how this could be, the angel explained: "The Holy Spirit shall come upon thee, and the power of the Highest shall overshadow thee."[742] Artificial insemination? When Jesus was born, he was visited by angels, shepherds and wisemen

---

[737] Brief Historical Summary of the Interval Between the Old and New Testaments, from Josephus and the Book of Maccabees and the Teacher's Edition of the Holy Bible, Oxford University Press, NY, 1860, pp 42-44.

[738] Jer. 3:6-22; 8:5; 31:22; 49:4; Hos. 4:16; 11:7; 14:4.

[739] Isa. 28:16; Jer. 6:21; Ezek. 3:20; 14:3; Rom. 3:20; 9:31-33.

[740] Matt. 22:21; John 18:36; Rom. 2:29; 7:6; 2 Cor. 3:6.

[741] Luke 1:26-33.

[742] Luke 1:35.

from the east, who had been guided by a "star."[743] This "Star of Bethlehem" was no doubt a spacecraft, or an ethereal "Merkaba Vehicle." A mysterious "cloud" or craft also hovered during the baptism of Jesus, appeared with Moses and Elijah at his transfiguration, transported him to heaven during his ascension, and will bring him back at his "second coming," when "we shall be caught up together . . . in the clouds to meet the Lord in the air."[744]

Although fathered by the "Holy Spirit," Jesus was called the son of Joseph, of the royal lineage of King David,[745] but he himself spoke of the "Father Within." Could this loving "Father," as portrayed by Jesus, possibly refer to Jehovah? Joe Lewels, author of The God Hypothesis, explains:

> "As early as 85 AD Christian scholars questioned the connection between Jesus and the old Testament God. Marcion, a formidable scholar of scripture, believed that the kind and good Jesus couldn't possibly be the son of the wrathful, vengeful and materialistic God of the Hebrews. He believed, as did the Mandaeans and other Gnostic sects, that Jehovah was the creator of the physical world, while Jesus was the Son of the Prime Creator. His denial of Jesus' connection to the God of the Hebrews, of course, outraged the Christians of Rome whose views ultimately became the consensus Christian doctrine. Marcion

---

[743] Matt. 2:1-12; Luke 1:78; 2:1-18. In mystical terms, "star" also indicates the Divine Self or "I Am Presence" of an individual. Jesus was the "daystar" who promised to shine in our hearts, 2 Cor. 4:4-6; 2 Pet. 1:19; Rev. 2:28; 22:16.
[744] Dan. 7:13; Matt. 2:2, 9-10; 3:13-17; 16:27; 17:1-15; 24:29-31; 25:31; 26:53, 64; 28:2-3; Mark 1:9-11; 3:21; 9:2-13; 13:26-27; 14:62; 16:19; Luke 2:8, 15; 8:27; 9:28-36; 21:27; 24:51; Acts 1:9; Eph. 1:20; 1 Thes. 4:16-17; 2 Thes. 1:7-8; Rev. 1:7; 14:14.
[745] Matt. 1:1-27; Luke 3:23-38.

and his followers believed that Jehovah was in fact evil incarnate. They reasoned that if Satan tempted Jesus with earthly power and riches, and if the material world is Satan's domain, then the creator of the world, (the Old Testament God) was, in fact, Satan. They noted that Jehovah had tempted Abram, the Hebrew patriarch, with lands and riches and made a pact with him to deliver to him the Jewish people. Such a bargain would only be made by the ruler of the physical world, not the Prime Creator."[746]

During the temptation of Jesus, the tempter Satan (Jehovah?), offered him the world. As the "prince of this world,"[747] it was evidently his to offer. Jesus incarnated upon this planet to overcome the rulership of the "fallen" Luciferic prince. When he established a dispensation of Truth to free the various lifewaves from the lies of the dark forces, it affected the entire universe.[748]

Blavatsky also denies that Jehovah was the father of Jesus:

"It is only through the doctrines of the more ancient philosophies that the teachings of Jesus may be understood; through Pythagoras, Confucius and Plato that we can comprehend the idea which underlies the term 'Father' in the New Testament. Plato did not conceal the fact that he derived his philosophical doctrines from Pythagoras, who like Hermes, got his doctrines from the Brahmans of India. The concepts of the

---

[746] The God Hypothesis, Joe Lewels, Wild Flower Press, NC, 1997, p 260.

[747] John 12:32; Eph. 2:2.

[748] Eph. 1:10; Col. 1:20; Phil. 2:9-10.

Christ and the Logos existed ages before Christianity. Baptism is one of the oldest rites and was practiced by all the nations in their mysteries. The cross was not unique to Christians, and Jesus was not the first crucified savior; there is record of sixteen of them. . . . In view of so much evidence to show that Christian theology is only a pot-pourri of pagan mythologies, how can it be connected with the religion of Moses? . . . When Paul, believing in occult [hidden mystery] powers in the world unseen, says: 'Ye walked according to the Archon [Course] of this world, according to the Archon that has the dominion of the air,' and 'we wrestle not against flesh and blood, but against the dominations, the powers, the lords of darkness, the mischievousness of spirits in the upper regions'[Eph. 2:2; 6:12], it shows that . . . he was fully aware that this Demiurge, whose Jewish name was Jehovah, was not the God preached by Jesus."[749]

As quoted previously: "The Hebrew God [Jehovah] is sometimes called 'The First Archon.' The archons [including Jehovah] were considered evil by the Gnostics. The Demiurge [Jehovah] claimed to be the only God, but was actually under the authority of the Highest God."[750]

The first Christian martyr, Stephen, told the Jews: "Ye received the law by the disposition of angels,"[751] indicating that they had been guided by the "fallen ones" under Jehovah, rather than by the divine messengers of the Supreme God. When Jesus

---

[749] Isis Unveiled, Vol. II, pp 134, 155, 162-163; 206-207, 290. 344, 525-526, 557; See also: The Secret Teachings of all Ages, Hall, pp clxxxi-clxxxiv.

[750] The Complete Jesus, Mayotte, pp 264-265.

[751] Acts 7:53.

performed "miracles," the Jews "glorified the God of Israel [Jehovah]," yet Jesus declared: "The Father himself, which hath sent me, hath borne witness of me, ye have neither heard his voice at any time, nor seen his shape, and ye have not his word abiding in you."[752] When they argued with him, he said, "Ye believe not because ye are not of my sheep. . . . O, generation of vipers. . . Ye are of your father the Devil [Jehovah?]. . . . The hour cometh, and now is, when the true worshippers shall worship the Father in spirit and in truth. God is a spirit."[753] This "Spirit," a divine spark of which dwells within each of us as the "Father Within," can only be known through a spiritual experience; hence Paul added that God is "unknown" and "invisible."[754]

Was the exoteric Jehovah this "unknown" and "invisible spirit?" Could Jesus have been merely presenting a different aspect of Jehovah? Did the Old Testament purposely present Jehovah as a fierce disciplinarian to keep the unruly people in line, or because that was the only concept of God they could understand at the time? Perhaps even the disciples were confused, for Paul said: "So worship I the God of my fathers, believing all things which are written in the law and in the prophets; for there is no difference between the Jew and the Greek; for the same Lord over all is rich unto all that call upon him."[755] Peter said: "The God of our fathers [Jehovah] hath glorified his son, Jesus."[756]

But was Jesus the son of Jehovah, or of a much higher God?[757] Although Jehovah claimed to be the "Most High God,"

---

[752] Matt. 15:31; John 5:37-38; 8:19, 42, 54-55; 5:37-38; 6:46; 7:28-29; 15:21; 16:3; Acts 13:27.

[753] Matt. 3:7; 12:34; 13:38; 23:33; Luke 15:6; John 1:10-11; 4:23-24; 8:38-47; 10:26; 17:2-24; 18:9; 1 Cor. 2:11; Pet. 2:25; 1 John 3:8-10.

[754] Acts 17:23; Rom. 1:20; Col. 1:15-16; 1 Tim. 1:17; Heb. 11:27.

[755] Acts 24:14; Rom. 3:29; 10:12.

[756] Acts 3:13; 4:30.

[757] Mark 1:24; 5:7.

it is apparent that he is but "one of the lower Sephiroth."[758] If Jehovah had been the "Most High," why was he given only one tiny area and one small group of people for "his inheritance," even though it was a crossroads for the then known world? Some Biblical scholars theorize that instead of being Jehovah's son, Jesus, who was "with God from the beginning," may have actually been Jehovah's guide, since he was described as the "rock" who was with Moses in the wilderness.[759] If so, Jehovah evidently didn't listen very well!

Jesus, who was "after the Order of Melchizedek," stated: "I was in the world, but the world knew me not." Who was he? He may have been Melchizedek, and his spirit may have been in, or overshadowing, David, Elisha, the priest Jeshua, and perhaps even Adam and Joshua.[760] The Book of Sirach, in the Catholic Bible, describes Joshua as being: "the great savior of God's chosen ones."[761] This certainly sounds like Jesus. Edgar Cayce says he was Amilius (in Atlantis), Adam, Enoch, Melchizedek, Zend, Ra, Joseph, Joshua, Asaph (chief musician and seer to King David), and Jeshua. Students of other philosophies believe that Jesus was also Vishnu, Krishna, Bacchus, Horus, Zoroaster, Buddha, the Egyptian Sun "god," Ra,[762] Apollonius and Quetzalcoatl. (It is interesting that Jesus, Vishnu and Bacchus are

---

[758] The Secret Doctrine, Vol. I, pp 196-197.

[759] Ex. 17:6; Num. 20:11; Ps. 78:15; John 1:1-5; 8:56-58; 1 Cor. 10:4; Eph. 3:9; Col. 12:17; Heb. 1:2; 1 Pet. 1:20; 1 John 1:1-3; 2:14; Rev. 1:8; 3:14; 21:6; 22:13.

[760] Gen. 14:18; 2 Sam. 7:12-13; 23:1-5; 1 Kings 19:16-19; 2 Kings 2:1-11; 3:11-14; 4:1-38; 5:8-25; 6:1-32; 7:1; 8:1-4; 9:1-21; Ps. 110:4; 132:11; Isa. 1:1; Jer. 23:5; 30:9; Amos 9:11; Zech. 13:1; Luke 1:31-33, 69; 4:27; John 1:1, 10-23; 8:56, 58; Acts 13:23; 15:16; Rom. 1:3-4; 5:14; 1 Cor. 15:22, 45; 2 Tim. 2:8; Heb. 5:6, 10; 6:20; 7:1-21; Rev. 3:7; 22:16.

[761] Sirach 46:1.

[762] The Bible says: "Out of Egypt have I called my Son." Ra means Sun, or Son. Jesus, referred to as the "Sun of righteousness," said, "I am the Amen; Son of man." Hos. 11:1; Mal. 4:2, 5; Matt. 2:15; Luke 12:10; Rev. 3:14.

each symbolized by a fish.) It seems logical that if the spirit of Jesus had been sent by the Supreme God, he would have incarnated, or overshadowed others, many times in order to teach all nations, rather than confining himself to one tiny area. Before beginning his ministry as Jesus, he is believed to have traveled for eighteen years, studying in Egypt, Greece and Asia. Records in a Buddhist monastery show they were visited and taught by "Saint Issa [Jesus]."[763] Legends say that while in India, he encouraged the natives to break their caste system. Unfortunately, they have not yet done so.

THE "KINGDOM WITHIN"

If the Father of Jesus was the True God, whose spiritual energy dwells within us, how did Jesus teach his followers to find and communicate with this Invisible Spirit? First of all, he eradicated the fundamentalist idea that we are miserable sinners whose only hope is to seek atonement from the priests or through animal sacrifices. Instead, he taught that we are "gods;" "children of the light."[764] Secondly, he taught that our divine heritage qualified us to enter into the "Kingdom of God," a "kingdom" that resides within us.

To set the stage for this great teaching, Archangel Gabriel proclaimed that John, the Baptist, second cousin of Jesus, had come "in the spirit of [reincarnation of] Elijah." (The Jews believed in and taught reincarnation. See note #11.) Born to elderly parents and raised as a "Nazarite," he heralded the coming of the Christ and the emergence of the "Kingdom of God." Like Elijah, John was large, rugged, independent, boisterous, defiant

---

[763] For further information, see: The Lost Years of Jesus Revealed, Charles Francis Potter, Fawcett Publications, Inc., CT, 1962; The Jesus Mystery; Janet Bock, Aura Books, CA., 1982; The Aquarian Gospel of Jesus the Christ, Levi, DeVorss & Co., Publishers, CA, 1972.

[764] Ps. 82:6; Matt. 5:14; Luke 6:35; John 10:34; 12:35; Eph. 1:5, 11; 5:8; 1 Thes. 5:5.

and was "clad in a hairy mantle."[765] The Old Testament strengthens the John/Elijah connection by giving a harsh warning to certain people, then writes their names in a "Book of Remembrance," stating that they will "return [reincarnate] and discern."[766] While John was preaching in Israel, he realized that he was once again with these same troublesome people who had "returned' (reincarnated), thus he said rather harshly: "O generation of vipers, who hath warned you to flee from the wrath to come? Bring forth therefore fruits meet for repentance, and begin not to say within yourselves we have Abraham to our father: for I say unto you, that God is able of these stones to raise up [reincarnate] children to Abraham."[767] Thus they were no longer to rely on Abraham, but to place their faith in Christ and his inner "kingdom."

John, preaching repentance, taught that mankind could prepare for the emerging "kingdom" by being baptized to eradicate their past sins. After centuries of being told that nothing but animal sacrifices could atone for their sins, this news attracted an enormous following that spread into Asia Minor. People were happy to learn that there was finally something that they, as individuals, could do. This was the first step in freeing the masses from the control of the priesthood; the first step in the "libertine" movement.

When Jesus was baptized by John, he was blessed by the descent of the Holy Spirit, the feminine/intuitive side of the Godhead in the form of a dove.[768] Many scholars consider that Jesus was at this moment "Christed," with the presence of Lord Maitreya, who then held the "Office of the Christ." (Jesus

---

[765] 1 Kings 17:1; 2 Kings 1:8; 2:11; Isa. 40:3; Mal. 3:1; 4:5-6; Matt. 3:1-17; 11:1-15; 14:1-5; 16:13-17; 17:10-13; Mark 1:2-9; 6:14-16; 8:27-28; 9:11-13; Luke 1:11-19, 76; 3:4-15; 7:24-28; 8:18-28; 9:7-8, 18-20; John 1:15-42; 3:28; 7:24-28; Acts 12:24-25.

[766] Malachi, chapter 3; see also: Isa. 40:3-8.

[767] Matt. 3:7-9; Luke 3:7-8.

[768] Matt. 3:13-17; Mark 1:9.

presently holds this Office.) In whatever manner he was blessed by his Divine Spirit, he gave it credit for all that he accomplished, saying: "The Father that dwelleth in me, he doeth the works. . . . I can of mine own self do nothing."[769] He promised that in like manner, we too could be guided by the inner Christ Spirit.

Jesus heralded John as being greater than the prophets. But, great as John was, his message of an emerging "kingdom" and his criticism of King Herod's divorce were as abrasive as his manner of dressing. He was killed by the king, who selfishly feared the emergence of an outer kingdom.[770] Perhaps John suffered the violence of imprisonment and being beheaded due to his misuse of divine power when he, as Elijah, invoked fire from heaven to kill two bands of soldiers who had come to bring him before the king.[771] The Law of Karma -- "whatsoever a man soweth, that shall he also reap"[772] -- always manages to catch up with us! In one lifetime or another, he had to face the king!

John had promised a "kingdom" that was to come, but when Jesus began his ministry, he proclaimed that it had arrived! He revealed an "inner kingdom" that "is not of this world;" one that cometh not with "observation," but is "within" us.[773] What is the "kingdom?" The term symbolizes the higher states of consciousness that are "above" the "carnal mind," a mind that looks only on the "outward appearances" and brings "warring to the soul." It is this lower, "carnal mind" that we are striving to

---

[769] Matt. 12:18, 28; Mark 2:8; Luke 4:1, 14, 18; 10:21; John 5:30; 14:10. See also: Luke 1:47; 2:27;

[770] Matt. 4:12; 11:1-3, 7-13; 14:3-12; Mark 1:4, 14; 6:16-25; 9:7-9; Luke, chapter 3; 7:19-23, 23-28.

[771] 2 Kings 1:9-15.

[772] Gal. 6:7. See also: 1 Kings 17:18; Job 4:8; Prov. 22:8; Isa. 33:1; Ezek. 35:15; Obad. 15; Matt. 7:1-2; Mark 4:24-25; 12:40; Luke 6:37-38; John 8:34; 2 Cor. 2:10; Rev. 13:10;

[773] Matt. 4:17; 6:10; Luke 11:40; 17:20-21; John 8:23-29; 14:10-20; 16:27-32; 17:11, 21-22; 18:36-37; 20:17; Acts 1:6.

"overcome."[774] The eastern religions refer to the worldly state as "maya" or "illusion." Jesus said: "The kingdom of heaven is like unto leaven, which a woman took, and hid in three measures of meal, till the whole was leavened."[775] The "three measures" are three states of consciousness: body, soul and spirit. In his parables he compares our higher thoughts to "seeds" sown in the field of consciousness; our lower thoughts to "tares."[776] Because our thoughts and words are important; Jesus said: "Every idle word that men shall speak, they shall give account thereof . . . Not that which goeth into the mouth defileth a man; but that which cometh out of the mouth."[777]

How is the "kingdom," or higher state of consciousness, entered? As you can see by the above, it certainly helps to have positive speech and positive thought, but it is not something that we can do entirely on our own. Jesus said: "I am the door [the mediator]. . . no man cometh unto the Father, but by me," thus, the esoteric, occult "kingdom within" cannot be entered without first uniting with, or being initiated into the frequency of the "mind of Christ."[778] Just as the Holy Spirit entered Jesus during his baptism, the Christ Spirit enters us. This "transforming mind of the Christ," is the "door" that leads us down the "yellow brick road" to the "Wizard of Oz," our Divine Spirit.[779] Realizing our oneness with God awakens us to our oneness with all mankind. This is the beginning of divine love and compassion, a spiritual love that knows no judgement, sees no boundaries, and harbors

---

[774] Matt. 10:36; 24:15; Mark 13:14; John 16:33; Rom. 7:23; 8:7; 12:21; 1 Cor. 3:3; 13:12; 1 John 2:13-14; 5:4-5; Rev. 2:7, 9-13, 17; 2:26; 3:5, 12, 21; 21:7.

[775] Matt. 13:33; Luke 13:20-21.

[776] Matt. 13:24-30.

[777] Matt. 12:36; 15:11.

[778] Matt. 13:11, 35; 24:45; Mark 4:11; Luke 8:10; 12:42; John 4:32-34; 10:9; 14:6; Rom. 8:7, 27; 12:2; Heb. 5:6; 1 Cor. 2:7-8, 16; 3:2; 4:1; 13:2; 14:2; Eph. 3:3; Col. 1:26; Heb. 5:6, 12-14; 1 Pet. 1:12.

[779] John 5:58; Rom. 12:2; 1 Cor. 2:16; Phlp. 2:5; 1 Pet. 3:8; 4:1.

no fears.

Lest you be confused by the terms Holy Spirit, Christ Spirit, Christ Mind, and our own Divine Spirit, which is a spark of the "Father God," suffice it to say that in the spiritual realms beyond duality, all things are one. It is only in the material realms that we perceive separation. Spirit means one substance; one life. In our pre-existent state we were aware of our oneness, but when we were born into form, our memory was veiled. Our greatest task, during our many incarnations on the wheel of rebirth, is to awaken to our Real Self; to see ourselves as more than the body we inhabit. Hence Jesus said: "He that findeth his life shall lose it, and he that loseth his life for my sake shall find it."[780] We identify with our "carnal mind"-ego self (with a little "s") until we awaken to our Divine Self (with a capital "S"). This is why enlightenment is called Self-realization, with a capital "S."

But although the realm of spirit is one, the energies are focused by a hierarchy of various beings. Hence, we find the "Office of the Christ," the "Office of the Holy Spirit," etc. When Jesus said he puts his spirit and light within us, it is like giving us a jump-start, allowing us to "have life more abundantly."[781] This awakens us to our own Divine Spirit, the spark of the "Father Within." It is not Jesus, the man, that enters us, but the Christ Spirit (energy) that he radiates, hence it is referred to in the Bible as being "quickened;"[782] by the mystics as being "initiated."

Jesus said he "stands at the door" of our heart and "knocks," that he might come in and "sup" with us; that we might set down together to "eat bread in the kingdom."[783] Breaking bread and drinking wine is a symbol of "communion," which esoterically means communication. We communicate with Divine Mind through intuition and meditation; by "taking no thought, by

---

[780] Matt. 10:39; 16:25; Luke 17:33; John 12:25.

[781] John 10:10,

[782] Matt. 10:20; Mark 13:11; Luke 11:13; John 6:63.

[783] Matt. 26:29; Mark 14:25; Luke 14:15; 22:29-30; Rev. 3:20.

being still;" "led beside the still waters" to hear the "small still voice" within.[784] After we peel away the layers of ego and illusion that cloud our Divine Spirit, our Real Self, then we, like a drop of water, unite with the sacred ocean of Cosmic Consciousness. This intimate experience of merging with the one life of the Absolute, is what Jesus meant when he said: "I am in my Father, and ye in me, and I in you."[785]

It is not so much something that we have to add unto ourselves, but that which we need to subtract or peel away in order to find our Divine Spirit that has always been there, but was hidden deep within our heart. The teachings of Jesus concerning the "kingdom" were not new; they had been taught throughout the world. The initiated Jews of the Tanaim Order and others knew these esoteric "mysteries," but were evidently not sharing them, for Jesus said: "Woe unto you, lawyers! ye have shut up the kingdom of heaven . . . taken away the key of knowledge: ye entered not in yourselves, and them that were entering in ye hindered."[786] Since few people were able to comprehend the "keys" to the "mysteries," they were carefully guarded, lest they be profaned.[787] But these teachings are freely given when the student is deemed ready.

Jesus assists us by radiating the Christ Spirit to help us find the inner "kingdom." The spirit of Jesus had come to earth many times to teach this great truth. As Blavatsky stated, there have been sixteen incarnations of the Christ. Actively searching for his "sheep" as our "friend" and "wayshower," he also promised to send the Holy Spirit, the feminine aspect whose

---

[784] Gen. 24:63; Josh. 1:8; 1 Kings 19:12; Ps. 1:2; 5:1; 19:14; 23:2; 46:10; 49:3; 63:6; 77:12; 119:15, 23, 48, 78, 97, 148; 143:5; Isa. 30:7; Matt. 6:25-34; Luke 12:17-26; John 11:20; 1 Tim. 4:15.

[785] John 14:20.

[786] Matt. 23:13; Luke 11:52; John 7:49.

[787] Ps. 25:14; 78:2; 139:15; Isa. 65: 8; Matt. 6:4, 6, 18; 13:11, 35; Mark 4:11; Luke 8:10; Rom. 9:27; 11:1-5, 25; 16:25; 1 Cor. 2:7; 15:51; Eph. 3:3-4, 9; 5:32; 6:19; Col. 1:26-27; 2:2; 4:3; 1 Tim. 3:9, 16; Rev. 1:20.

"Spirit of Truth" dwells within to "comfort" us.[788] (The Holy Spirit has always been here--it is even mentioned throughout the Old Testament--but Jesus arranged the dynamic outpouring that had been predicted in Joel 2:28-29.) According to Paul, the Holy Spirit brought with it nine spiritual gifts: "The word of wisdom, word of knowledge [note the difference between the two], faith, healing, working of miracles, prophecy, discerning of spirits, diverse kinds of tongues, and interpretation of tongues."[789] The dynamic outpouring of the Holy Spirit was accomplished on the "Day of Pentecost," a last-ditch effort to free mankind from the fetters of the Jewish religion that stressed self-examination and self-denial rather than selflessness. Teaching others to unite with their Inner God Force, Jesus fulfilled the need for exterior ceremonies and sacrifices. He indicated that in an intimate family relationship, as represented by the "fatherhood of God and the brotherhood of man," one did not need ceremonies. These outer practices have a tendency to stifle one's deep, inner, spiritual attunement.

The Buddhist teachings have a parable: "If you see the Buddha on the road, kill him," meaning if you begin to see the Divine Source as an external being, you have missed the truth of the inner connection with the divine spark of God residing within your heart. When Jesus said: "I am in the Father, and the Father in me," he was referring to an inner spiritual "kingdom within," rather than to a physical manifestation. This is entirely different from Moses being visited by the external Jehovah, who arrived in a noisy, smoking spacecraft and sat down with him to eat and drink fatty meat and wine.[790] The "Father Within" does not travel in a spacecraft or drink wine. Instead, he emanates an energy, or shares his Spirit, to allow an inner mystical attunement. William

---

[788] Matt. 28:20; John 8:32; 10:1-9; 14:16, 26-27; 15:13-15, 26; 16:7; Rev. 3:20.
[789] 1 Cor. 12:1-11.
[790] Ex., chapter 24; John 14:10-11.

Kingsland, in his delightful mystical book, <u>Christos</u>, stated: "When man has realized his oneness with the imperishable reality, there is no longer room for the personal gods which he formerly worshipped."[791]

Stressing the reality of the inner spiritual world, Jesus further explained: "Except a man be born of water (the Living Water) and of the spirit, he cannot enter into the kingdom . . . flesh and blood cannot inherit the kingdom."[792] The "carnal mind" or ego is not uplifted or reprogrammed, it is "overcome." This "death of the ego," also referred to as the "dark night of the soul," allows the birth of spirit. Direct experience with Spirit allows us to "put on the mind of Christ" that enlightens and transforms.[793] Because Jesus radiated the Christ Spirit and forgave the sins of those who followed his teachings, he went beyond John's "baptism of water;" he truly "baptized with fire."[794] The divine spark of God burns dimly in most of mankind, but Jesus brings it to birth and fans it to shine as a "daystar."[795] This is what Paul meant when he said: "Awake thou that sleepest, and arise from the dead, and Christ shall give thee light."[796]

To enter the "kingdom," Jesus said we must be "poor in spirit;" we must "come as a little child."[797] He also warned: "The way is narrow, the gate is straight; anyone who enters not by the door," is like a thief.[798] The correct way is through prayer, fasting

---

[791] Christos, William Kingsland, John M. Watkins, London, England, 1929, p 19.

[792] Matt. 25:34; 26:41; Mark 14:38; John 1:12-13; 3:3-8; 4:10-11; 7:38; 14:16-17, 26; 15:26; 16:7-8, 13; 20:22.

[793] John 3:5-6, 8; 16:33; Rom. 12:2, 21; 1 Cor. 2:12, 16; 15:38-49; 1 John 5:4-5; Rev. 2:7.

[794] Matt. 3:11; 12:18; Luke 3:16; John 3:5-8; 4:23; 8:12; 9:5; 2 Cor. 4:4-6; 1 Pet. 1:19.

[795] John 15:9-10, 13; 2 Cor. 4:4-6; 2 Pet. 1:19.

[796] Eph. 5:14.

[797] Matt. 5:3-20; 18:10; Mark 10:14; 19:14; Luke 18:16.

[798] Matt. 7:14; Luke 13:24; John 10:1.

and meditation; the wrong way is through the use of drugs, body mutilations, wild rhythms, ceremonial dancing, or other artificial means. One may experience a temporary, solar-plexus, astral, "high" through these avenues, but it won't be a true, sustainable spiritual experience of entering into the heart to commune with the "Father Within." If you blast your way through the "door," you may be awed by the psychedelic colors of the blast, but you will still need to learn to properly open the doorway of your heart chakra.

While experiencing long periods of meditation in this inner "kingdom," one becomes detached from the outer world; lives "in" the world, but is not "of it." Jesus said he was not "in the world" and called us "out of the world," admonishing us to "savor things of God, not of man; to seek first the kingdom"[799] by surrendering to God's Will. Thus the "kingdom" is not entered only by the works we do, but the goodness that we are. It is our devotion to God and the fruits of our loving service that makes us a truly spiritual being, a member of the family of God who can wear a crown, symbolizing enlightenment, and can dwell in the "inner kingdom" where we are one with the Christ Spirit.[800]

The Jews, not interested in an "inner kingdom," were expecting another "savior/messiah" like Joshua, Hezekiah, Josiah and Jeshua, to establish an outer kingdom against the Romans. But since Jesus is "the true tabernacle," while Moses had merely served the "shadow of heavenly things," it was finally time for the "shadows" to pass; it was time to go "within the veil" which was "rent" while Jesus was on the cross, hence the "veil" was "done away in Christ."[801]

---

[799] Matt. 6:33; 7:7; 16:23; Mark 8:33, 36; Luke 9:25; 11:19; 12:31; John 8:23; 15:19; 16:28, 33; 17:11-18; 18:36.

[800] 1 Cor. 12:21-27.

[801] Isa. 25:7; Matt. 27:51; 28:3; Mark 15:38; Luke 17:24; 23:45; 2 Cor. 3:14-16; Heb. 6:19; 8:1-5; 9:3; 10:20; 1 John 2:8; Rev. 1:16; 4:5-6.

JESUS TAUGHT HIS OWN "SHEEP"

The teaching of law and justice had produced a law-abiding people with high moral standards, but heavily steeped in tradition, there was little love or mercy in their hearts. Jesus came to teach love and forgiveness rather than vengeance. Although he denied that some of the Jews were "his sheep," he honored them by telling a "Gentile" woman in Samaria: "Ye worship ye know not what: we know what we worship; for salvation is of the Jews." He said he had come only to "his own lost sheep," but the Bible says he had also been sent "as a light to lighten the Gentiles," who although not as moral as the Jews, were more gentle and loving.[802] He told the Jews, "Jerusalem shall be trodden down of the Gentiles until the times of the Gentiles be fulfilled."[803] When he said: "Other sheep I have, which are not of this fold: them also I must bring,"[804] he may have been referring to the "lost tribes" that had spread throughout Europe and Asia as well as the Americas. The Book of Mormon relates that after the crucifixion of Jesus, he visited the tribe of Joseph in America. There are also many legends of a white, bearded "savior" visiting throughout Polynesia. The Bible speaks of "those whose names were recorded from the beginning," and "those whose names were not written in the Book of Life. Some have no "inheritance," while some have been "adopted" as a "son of God,"[805] so obviously, there are various lifewaves or "sheep" upon this planet.

Unlike the vengeful Jehovah, who looked upon mankind

---

[802] Matt. 10:5-6; 15:21-28; 18:11-13; Mark 7:25-30; Luke 2:32; 15:4-6; 19:10; John 4:1-42; 6:39; 10:2-16, 27-29; 15:19; 16:15; 17:6-12; Acts 3:26; 13:47.

[803] Luke 21:24.

[804] John 10:16; 11:52.

[805] Matt. 7:23; 25:12; Luke 13:25, 27; Acts 26:18; Rom. 8:15-17, 21, 23; 9:8, 26; 11:17-24; Gal. 4:5-7; Eph. 1:5, 11, 14, 18; Col. 1:12; Heb. 9:15; 1 Pet. 1:4.

as "nothing," the loving Father God sent Jesus to be the "good shepherd," who searches for his "lost sheep." He said: "My sheep hear my voice and I know them, and they follow me. . . And there shall be one fold, and one shepherd."[806] Like the "prodigal son," we are welcomed back with loving arms.[807] How different from the roaring, vengeful god of fear, who had to be continually appeased with priests, ceremonies and sacrifices! Indeed it was good news ("gospel") to hear of a loving, merciful "Father" who not only welcomes his children with open arms, but also sends his beloved messenger to search for them.

JESUS FULFILLED THE LAW OF MOSES

The Jews feared that Jesus would "change their customs," but his method of teaching was not to contradict the beliefs of others. Instead, he told them of the "inner kingdom," knowing it would eventually clarify their external beliefs. He said: "Think ye not that I am come to destroy the law, or the prophets: I am not come to destroy but to fulfill. . . . The law and the prophets were until John: since that time the kingdom of God is preached."[808] Well versed in the Old Testament, he reduced the ten commandments to two: "love God and love your neighbor as thyself."[809] (He knew that we cannot love others until we first love and accept ourselves.) He honored the Law of Moses, yet warned his disciples to beware of the doctrine of the Pharisees and Sadducees that "pass over the love of God" and "abandon the commandments" to keep their own "traditions."[810] He prepared

---

[806] John 10:3, 16, 27.

[807] Luke 15:11-32.

[808] Matt. 4:17; 5:17 23:13; Mark 1:15; Luke 9:56; 16:16-17; 24:27-28, 44; John 4:34; 5:36; 17:4; Acts 6:14; Rom. 10:4.

[809] Matt. 22:36-40; Mark 10:19; 19:19; Mark 12:30-33; Luke 10:27; 18:20; John 13:34-35; 14:21; 15:12, 17; 21:15-17.

[810] Matt. 15:2-6; 16:6-12; 23:1-3; Mark 7:9; Luke 11:42; 12:1; 20:46-47.

for the Passover by throwing the money changers from the temple, which he called "my Father's house;" by feeding his followers with loaves and fishes; and by scheduling his own crucifixion, during that time.[811] He honored the role of the priests by sending those who he had healed to them to "offer the gift that Moses commanded."[812] He observed the practice of sacrifice by telling his disciples to prepare for it, yet he indicated to them that his crucifixion, the fifth initiation, would fulfill the need for sacrifice, saying: "Moses gave you not that bread; but my Father giveth you the true bread from heaven. . . . I am the Living Bread of Life: he that cometh to me shall never hunger; and he that believeth on me shall never thirst. . . . To him that overcometh will I give to eat of the hidden manna."[813] Paul referred to this as sacrificing the "carnal mind" to put on the "mind of Christ."[814] At the "Last Supper," Jesus said of the wine: "This is my blood of the new testament, which is shed for many for the remission of sins."[815] Hall adds:

> "Jesus disclosed to his disciples that the lower world is under the control of a great spiritual being which has fashioned it according to the will of the Eternal Father. The Eternal Father sent unto creation the eldest and most exalted of His powers--the Divine Mind. This Divine Mind offered itself as a living sacrifice and was broken up and eaten by the world. Having given its spirit and its body at a secret and sacred supper to the

[811] Matt. 6:2, 17-19; 14:15-21; 21:12-13; Mark 6:38-44; 8:5-19; 11:15-17; 14:12-16; Luke 9:13-16; 19:45-46; 22:7-15; John 2:13-16, 23; 6:4-14; 11:55; 12:1-2; 13:1-2; 18:28, 39; 19:14.

[812] Matt. 8:4; mark 1:44; Luke 5:14; 10:25-29; 17:14.

[813] John 6:32-35, 51; Luke 22:8; Rev. 2:17.

[814] Rom. 8:7, 27; 12:2; 1 Cor. 2:16; 5:7; 10:16; Heb. 9:1, 26; 10:3-12; 12:24; 13:10-12.

[815] Matt. 26:26-28; Mark 14: 22-24; Luke 22:17-20.

twelve manners of rational creatures, this Divine Mind became a part of every living thing. Man was thereby enabled to use this power as a bridge, across which he might pass and attain immortality. . . . The sacrificing of beasts, and in some cases human beings, upon the altars of the pagans was the result of their ignorance concerning the fundamental principle underlying sacrifice."[816]

Since Jesus had "fulfilled" the old "covenant" and offered a "new testament," which included the Gentiles, he updated the Law of Moses, saying: "Ye have heard that it hath been said, an eye for an eye, and a tooth for a tooth: but I say unto you, that ye resist not evil; ye have heard that it hath been said: Thou shalt love thy neighbor and hate thine enemy, but I say unto you; love your enemies, bless them that curse you."[817] He taught unconditional love and passiveness, while Jehovah was a "man of war."[818] Jehovah had ordered that witches be killed, but Jesus healed those who were possessed of demons; the Law of Moses had prescribed the death penalty for adultery, but Jesus prevented the stoning of an adulteress, saying: "The son of man is not come to destroy men's lives, but to save them."[819] The Old Testament is based on punishment and fear of the dark forces, while Jesus stressed love and forgiveness, teaching his disciples to "cast out

---

[816] The Secret Teaching of all Ages, pp xci, cxxxv, clxxix.

[817] Ex. 21:23-25; De. 7:10; Isa. 59:18; Matt. 5:38-39, 43-44; Luke 6:27-28; Heb. 8:6; 9:15.

[818] Ex. 15:3; Matt. 5:39, 43; 19:19; 22:17-21, 39; Mark 12:14-17, 31, 33; Luke 6:29; 10:27; 20:22-25.

[819] Ex. 21:17; 22:18; Lev. 20:10; Matt. 4:14; 7:1-2; 8:16, 28, 33; 9:32; 12:22; Mark 1:32; 5:15-18; Luke 6:17; 8:36; 9:56; 12:14; John 7:24; 8:6-11, 15; 12:47.

devils."[820] Fearing nothing, he mastered all!

In addition to honoring the rights of women and allowing them to anoint his feet and travel with him, he spent time with the publicans, prostitutes and sinners, refused to abide by the traditional rules of fasting or washing of his hands, and told the people to pray in private, to take no oaths, and to do their good deeds secretly.[821] While healing on the sabbath, a day in which Jehovah had forbidden any form of work, Jesus said: "The son of man is Lord even of the sabbath."[822] He had also been given "the keys to all kingdoms of heaven and earth," a divine power which he shared with those he "ordained."[823] But most of all he gave to mankind the teachings of "eternal life,"[824] while Jehovah had guarded the "tree of life" with "flaming swords," lest man regain his twelve-strand DNA, the trunk of the "tree," and discover the secret of immortality.[825] Jehovah wanted to rule mankind; Jesus wanted to set them free!

These teachings were offensive to the Jews, but it was his claim of divine heritage, his "new covenant" that surpassed the Law of Moses, and his blatant forgiveness of sins, that caused them to consider him dangerous and blasphemous. They knew that Jehovah could place his spirit, or other spirits, within an individual, but they could not accept that the human Jesus could do so. And of course they had no understanding of the

---

[820] Matt. 7:22; Mark 3:15; 16:17; Luke 9:1; 11:20; Acts 5:16; 8:7; 16:18; 19:12; Jas. 2:19.

[821] Matt. 5:33-34; 6:1-4, 16-18; 9:10-12; 15:2; Mark 2:15-17; 7:5-7; Luke 5:30-32; 7:36-50.

[822] Ex. 16:23-29; Matt. 12:1-12; Mark 2:23-28; 3:2-4; Luke 6:1-9; 13:10-16; 14:1-6; John 5:9-18; 7:22-24; 9:14-16.

[823] Matt. 9:6; 10:1; 16:19; 28:28; Mark 2:10; 3:13-14; 9:1; 12:24; Luke 4:6-36; 5:24; 9:1; 10:17; John 10:18; 15:16; Rev. 1:18.

[824] Eternal Life is the continuity of consciousness; in spirit there is no beginning or end.

[825] Gen. 3:24; Mark 10:17, 30; John 3:15; 4:36; 5:39, 68; 10:28; 12:25; 17:2-3; Acts 13:48; Rom. 2:7; 5:21; 6:23; 1 Tim. 1:17; 6:12, 29; 2 Tim. 2:10; Titus 1:2; 3:7; 1 Pet. 5:10; 1 john 1:2; 2:25; 5:11, 13, 20.

overshadowing "Office of the Christ" working through Jesus. Oriented to politics rather than spirituality, they also feared that Jesus, the "son of," or reincarnation of, David,[826] who was actively gathering members for his "kingdom," would usurp their political power. They wanted a powerful king, not a meek teacher who spoke of a God superior to Jehovah. One who established a "new covenant" that went beyond their beloved Law of Moses! To them, this was blasphemous!

MATERIALISM VS "ONENESS"

The greatest difference between the teachings of Jesus and those of Jehovah, in addition to the "Holy Spirit of Truth" vs the Luciferic "Father of Lies," is the issue of exoteric materialism, the realm of Ahriman. Jehovah, the tribal "god" of the physical world, granted land to his "chosen people," alienating them from the masses, while Jesus, whose "kingdom" is not of this world, shared his spirit in an effort to unite all mankind. Not impressed with land owners, religious leaders, the rich, or the self-righteous who stood on the street corners to pray, Jesus, making no class distinction, went to the poor and downtrodden, feeding and healing them.[827]

Assuring his followers that they were "one" with him and with the "Father Within," that they were "gods" and "children of light," Jesus did not set himself apart or claim to be God, or the one and only "Son of God." Calling himself the "son of man," he asked: "Why callest thou me good? None is good save one, that is, God."[828] He told his followers not to pray to him but to the "Father;" that the works he did, they could do also; that just as he was "one" with the Father, and had been with God "from the

---

[826] Matt. 1:1; 9:27; 12:8; 15:23; 20:31; 21:9, 15; 22:42; Mark 10:47-48; 12:35; Luke 20:41.

[827] Matt. 6:5-6.

[828] Matt. 12:31-32; Mark 3:28; Luke 12:10; 18:19.

beginning," so they had been also.[829]

He stressed this universal interconnectedness by saying: "Inasmuch as ye have done it unto the least of one of these, my brethren, ye have done it unto me."[830] Because our every thought and action affects everything and everyone in the universe, like ripples in the water, our karmic actions return to us to be redeemed. The further we are along the path, the quicker the karma returns.

Striving to "save" mankind by liberating us from our physical and material entrapments--the lures of Ahriman--Jesus urged his followers to sell their material possessions and "follow" him, thereby "storing their treasures in heaven."[831] Aware that possessions cause attachments which bind us to the world, he also urged us to transcend the material world to regain our immortality, the "tree of life;" our "twelve-strand DNA," that was removed in the Garden of Eden.[832] Knowing this awakening to oneness allows us to transcend into the timeless, spaceless, dimension to experience the true nature of Divine Mind, he emphasized that we are not merely humans trying to be gods, but pre-existent, immortal "gods" temporarily encased within a physical body. This truth had been expressed in the Vedic philosophies for centuries, but we of the western world, thanks to the vast efforts of Madame Blavatsky, Vivikananda, and others who came from the east during the nineteenth century, are just discovering it.

Because Jesus stressed detachment from the world, it is interesting to note that the motto for the Internet is: "The Internet brings the world closer to you." Perhaps this is a good reason not to become overly involved, plus the fact that the early computer

---

[829] John 10:20; 14:12; 15:27; 16:25-26; 17:11, 21; 2 Thes. 2:13; Eph. 1:4.

[830] Matt. 25:40; Mark 9:41; John 14:20; 17:21; Rom. 8:16; Eph. 5:8; 1 Thes. 5:5.

[831] Matt. 4:19; 6:19-20; 16:24; 19:21, 27; Mark 10:21, 28; 16:17; Luke 12:33; 18:22; John 10:5; 12:26; 13:36-37.

[832] Gen. 3:11-24; Rev. 2:7; 22:2, 14.

programs are set up with eighteen digits: six digits, dash, six digits, dash, six digits. Is this technology the dreaded "666" of Revelation? When the entire planet vibrates at the frequency of 666, cataclysms occur. The "Golden Age of Peace" will commence when the planetary frequency is lifted to 888. One makes their ascension when they reach the frequency of 999.

Why is the government pushing the Internet? Control? Are they aware that an abundance of left-brain addiction to intellect prevents the development of right-brain feeling and intuition? If we have an available source of exoteric information, why bother to look within? It was stated on a newscast that anyone not familiar with computers and the Internet, is considered "illiterate." Jesus said: "My kingdom is not of this world; render unto Caesar that which is Caesar's; unto God that which is God's." Perhaps being "illiterate" to worldly intellectual pursuits allows one to discover their inner intuitive abilities. Remember that it was the "carnal mind" that was "beguiled,"[833] because it "desired to be wise (knowledgeable)".

Wisdom and knowledge are not the same. Wisdom comes from the crown chakra's attunement to Divine Mind, while "the wisdom (knowledge) of this world is foolishness with God."[834] Paul, warning against serpentine knowledge and intellect, said: "Beware lest any man spoil you through philosophies and vain deceit, after the tradition of men, after the rudiments of the world, and not after Christ."[835] The Internet offers world-wide communication, a step toward oneness, which is good, but it also requires a great deal of discernment.[836]

Lewels makes an interesting observation about "civilized" man, who is disconnected from spirit, as opposed to the simple native, who is aware of the sacredness of Mother Earth:

---

[833] Gen. 3:3-7.

[834] 1 Cor. 3:19.

[835] Col. 2:8.

[836] 1 Cor. 2:13-14.

"How is it that indigenous people of the world . . . were able to remain connected to God and to nature, while another branch of humanity became separated and lost sight of its true nature? . . . Their deeply spiritual communion with the cosmos provided them with the knowledge that the gathering of material possessions was also unnatural and contrary to spiritual law. . . . Psychic abilities demonstrated by the natives . . . seemed so interconnected by some invisible force that they, in fact, acted in unison. [They] lead their lives in tune with nature, taking only what they need, leaving behind no pollutants that poison the soil or the waters, and loving and caring for all of God's creation. Without religious institutions, they instinctively live by the spiritual laws of the universe and practice a spirituality that makes them one with their Creator. . . [As 'civilized' man] began to perceive himself as master of his environment, he lost his spiritual connection to plants and animals, as well as to his fellow man and to the Creator."[837]

Another analogy of the native connection to Spirit and their awareness of the sacredness of Mother Nature, is beautifully expressed by Charles A. Eastman, in his delightful book: The Soul of the Indian:

"There were no temples or shrines among us save those of nature. Being a natural man, the Indian was intensely poetical. He would deem it sacrilege to build a house for Him who may be met face to face in the mysterious, shadowy aisles

---

[837] The God Hypothesis, pp 288-289, 291-295.

of the primeval forest, or on the sunlit bosom of
virgin prairies, upon dizzy spires and pinnacles of
naked rock, and yonder in the jeweled vault of the
night sky! He who enrobes Himself in filmy veils
of cloud, there on the rim of the visible world
where our Great-Grandfather Sun kindles his
evening camp-fire, He who rides upon the
rigorous wind of the north, or breathes forth His
spirit upon aromatic southern airs . . . He needs no
lesser cathedral!"[838]

Although Genesis instructs us to "replenish the earth and
subdue it and have dominion," we can do so with love and respect
instead of recklessly slaughtering, polluting, and exploiting.
Mother Earth is not just an inanimate ball of rock, but a living,
breathing entity. Many other religions have a great respect for
nature. We need to remember that in the priestly document,
which comprises chapter one of Genesis, God created the animals
first then created the androgynous beings. After declaring them
as "good," he gave them no eating restrictions and told them to
take "dominion." But in the Jehovistic document, which
comprises chapter two of Genesis, the creation was not declared
"good," hence they were given eating restrictions and were not
given dominion. Because we are not one of the first androgynous
beings, we cannot claim this "dominion,"[839] therefore, we have no
right to destroy the planet. It is not ours; we are merely visiting
"pilgrims."[840]

---

[838] The Soul of the Indian, Charles A. Eastman, Houghton Mifflin, Ms.
1911, p 5.
[839]

[840] Heb. 11:13; 1 Pet. 2:11.

THE CHRISTED JESUS

Paul, realizing the difference between the man, Jesus, and his "Christed" Spirit said: "For there is one God, and one mediator between God and men, the man Christ Jesus."[841] To say "Jesus Christ" as if it were a first and last name is incorrect. Jesus, the man, was "Christed" during his baptism, hence Paul called him "Christ Jesus" or the "Lord's Christ."[842] (The same is true of Buddha. The man, Gautama, held the office of Buddha, meaning "awakened one," just as Jesus was overshadowed by the Christ, meaning "anointed one.") Hall says of becoming "Christed:"

> "Mortal man achieves deification only through at-one-ment with his Divine Self. . . . This Christos, or divine man in man, is man's real hope of salvation--the Living Mediator between abstract Deity and mortal humankind. . . . Jesus has been confused with the Christos, or god-man, whose wonders he preached. Since the Christos is the god-man imprisoned in every creature, it was the first duty of the initiate to liberate, or 'resurrect,' this Eternal One within himself. He who attained reunion with his Christos was consequently termed a Christian, or Christened man."[843]

Blavatsky enlarges upon the subject:

> "From the very day when the first mystic found that means of communication between this world and the worlds of the invisible host, between the

---

[841] 1 Tim. 2:5; Heb. 9:15.

[842] Matt. 3:16; 16:20; Mark 1:10; 8:29; Luke 3:22; 5:32; John 1:32-33; Acts 18:5, 28; Rom. 8:1-2, 39; 15:5; 16:3; 1 Cor. 1:2, 30; Gal. 4:14; Eph. 1:1; 2:6-7; Phlp. 2:5; 1 Tim. 2:5; 2 Tim. 1:9; Heb. 13:1.

[843] The Secret Teachings of All Ages, p clxxviii.

sphere of matter and that of pure spirit . . . he recognized his God and felt the great being within himself. Once man knew the 'Atman,'[Spirit], the 'I Am' showed his full power to him who could recognize the 'still small voice.'. . . It was the same mystical contemplation as that of the Yogin: the communion of the Brahman with his own luminous Self. . . . the Supreme God."[844]

This "Inward Man, Hidden Man in the Heart" is what Jesus called the "Father Within."[845]

THE INTERNATIONAL JESUS

Having traveled throughout Egypt, Greece, Mesopotamia, India and Tibet, Jesus was well versed in the teachings of the Kabalists, Nazarites, Essenes, Freemasons and Buddhists. Blavatsky explains:

"Although called a 'wine bibber' and using oil for healing, Jesus was an Essene and a Nazarite, for we not only find him sending a message to Herod, to say that he was one of those who cast out demons, and who performed cures, but actually calling himself a prophet and declaring himself equal to the other prophets (Luke 13:32). He never ate a meal without saying "grace" and he divided his teachings into exoteric and esoteric, dividing his followers into 'neophytes,' 'brethren,' and the 'perfect.' He had long hair, wore a seamless garment, and believed in reincarnation, but is also found disagreeing with his early

---

[844] Isis Unveiled, Vol. II, pp 317-318, 342, 565-566.
[845] John 5:19, 30; 8:28; 2 Cor. 4:16; 1 Pet. 3:4.

teachers on several questions of formal observance. . . . He preached the philosophy of Buddha. . . . The true spirit of Christianity can alone be fully found in Buddhism. . . . His motive was evidently like that of Gautama Buddha to benefit humanity at large by producing a religious reform which should give it a religion of pure ethics; the true knowledge of God."[846]

Jesus was a Nazarite, an order dedicated to guarding the sacred wisdom teachings, but he was not a Nazarene; the town of Nazareth did not even exist during his ministry.[847] Although Jesus agreed with many of the Essene teachings, he was more open; less disciplined; not so organized with group hierarchy, priests, temples, rituals and purification; and although often surrounded by angels, he did not teach "angelology."[848] Making it clear that he had not come to earth to maintain the status quo, but to make changes, he stated adamantly: "Think not that I am come to send peace on earth: I came not to send peace, but a sword. For I am come to set a man at variance against his father, and the daughter

---

[846] Isis Unveiled, Vol. II, 123, 132-134, 143-144, 147, 240, 324, 338-342, 537-539, 556.

[847] Nazareth - According to Steven Sora: "In AD 65 Simon led his followers, who called themselves Nazoreans, away from Jerusalem. They may have founded the town of Nazareth. In the year AD 66, we know they were forced into hiding. In another town called Nazara, and in Cochaba, the family of Jesus, known as the "Heirs," lived and survived persecution. The Nazarene Church became completely separate from the Pauline Christian Church. . . . Nazoreans and Ebionites, known as "Poor Christians" were by then just small sects hiding in southern Lebanon and near the Euphrates River." The Lost Treasure of the Knights Templar, Steven Sora, Destiny Books, an imprint of Inner Traditions International, Rochester, VT, copyright 1999, pp 137-138.

[848] Matt. 1:20-24; 2:13, 19; 4:11; 13:41, 49; 24:28-31; 25:36; 26:53; 28:2, 5; Mark 1:13; 8:38; Luke 1:11-38; 2:8-15, 21; 22:43; John 1:51; 20:12. For further comparisons, see: Jesus and the Dead Sea Scrolls, by James H. Charlesworth.

against her mother, and the daughter-in-law against her mother-in-law."[849]

Jesus, the Christ, and Gautama, the Buddha, taught many of the same concepts: "Love, compassion and mercy; lay not up for yourselves treasures upon earth; be non-attached; know ye not ye are the temple of God; be ye perfect; do unto others as ye would have them do unto you; turn the other cheek; blessed are the pure in heart; God sends rain on the just and on the unjust alike; and if thy hand offend thee, cut it off." It is curious that both the Christian rosary beads and the Buddhist mala beads each have one hundred-eight beads in a string. Jesus, like Krishna, Buddha, and Horus (the son of Osiris and Isis) was born of a line of royalty. All were born of a virgin mother; all were believed to have been an incarnation of Vishnu, the Holy Spirit; all taught the common people; all were said to have crushed the head of the serpent; all rebelled against priests; all were persecuted; and all ascended into heaven in a craft. Blavatsky says: "We can assert, with entire plausibility, that there is not one of all these sects--Kabalism, Judaism and our present Christianity included--but sprung from the two main branches of that one mother trunk, the once universal religion which antedated the Vedic ages; prehistoric Buddhism which merged later into Brahmanism."[850] This "mother trunk" of "prehistoric Buddhism," no doubt, came from Atlantis.

But although teaching some of the same concepts as Brahmanism and Buddhism, Jesus went a step beyond by informing his followers of the intimate connection we have with the Father God, who projects a fragment of himself to dwell within each of us, thereby establishing a parent/child relationship. After making this mystical connection, we will never again think of God in abstract, philosophical terms, but as our constant companion; our ever-guiding Light; our Divine Spirit. Whatever

---

[849] Matt. 10:34-35; Luke 12:49-53.

[850] Isis Unveiled, Vol. II, p 123.

we are doing, no matter how menial, we will do it with God. Many times I find myself thinking inwardly, "God, let's do the dishes," etc. With this inner awareness, I am never alone. This relationship is beautifully expressed in The Practice of the Presence of God[851] and The Urantia Book.

"Practicing the Presence," had been preserved in the mystery schools, but had not been taught openly since the days of the Osirian, Sethite and Melchizedek teachers. It was alluded to in Buddhism, but many look to their leader, Buddha, rather than to the indwelling Father God, a mistake that Jesus endeavored to avoid by emphasizing the "Father Within." (Some philosophies tend to impersonalize God as merely a Force for good or a universal mind substance, rather than an intimate, loving "Father.")

There is a possibility that when Jesus studied internationally, then taught many of the esoteric teachings, that he could have overstepped his bounds with Jehovah. Perhaps he was expected to continue with the limited "obedience" teachings of the Jews rather than exposing them to the liberating concepts of Buddhism. When Moses and Elijah came to him during his "transfiguration" to speak "of his decease," Jesus did not want to go through with the death plan.[852] While in the Garden of Gethsemane, "his soul was exceedingly sorrowful, even unto death." It was the first time he had ever asked anyone to stay with him, and even after an angel came to comfort him, he was still "in an agony . . . his sweat was as it were great drops of blood falling down on the ground."[853] He pleaded: "Father, all things are possible unto thee; take away this cup from me." The next day, while on the cross he cried, "Why hast thou forsaken me?"[854] Did

---

[851] The Practice of the Presence of God, Brother Lawrence, Fleming H. Revell Company, NY, 1895.

[852] Luke 9:31.

[853] Matt. 26:36-38; Mark 14:32-34.

[854] Matt. 26:39-46; 27:46; Mark 14:35-42; 15:34; Luke 22:42; John 12:27-28.

Jehovah silence him because he taught too much? William Bramley comments:

> "Jesus wanted to bring to Palestine a genuine spiritual science of the type the mavericks [those who are unowned or unbranded] were still attempting in India. Jesus therefore became a rebel inside of the very brotherhood organization backing him. Jesus' greatest mistake was believing that he could use the channels of the corrupted brotherhood network to spread a maverick religion, even if he had many close friends and loved ones in the Essene Order. Jesus never had time to establish his maverick religious system because some of his Essene backers and according to the Bible, even some . . . 'angels,' quickly got him into trouble by proclaiming him the messiah."[855]

TEACHINGS TAKEN TO THE "GENTILES"

After his crucifixion, the apostles took the teachings first to the Jews, then to the "Gentiles" as Jesus had instructed them to do.[856] Paul said of the Jews, who he called "the children of disobedience:" "Through their fall, salvation is come unto the Gentiles for to provoke them to jealousy. . . . Blindness in part is happened to Israel, until the fullness of the Gentiles be come in."[857] When the Jews insisted that the "Gentiles" be circumcised and follow the Law of Moses, Paul said it was not necessary and instead gave them four new rules: "Abstain from meats offered to

---

[855] The Gods of Eden, William Bramley, Avon Books, NY, 1993, p 132-133.

[856] Matt. 10:5; 12:18;21:43; Luke 2:32; 21:24; Acts 7:45; 9:15; 26:23; 28:28; Rom. 10:20.

[857] Rom. 11:11, 25; Eph. 2:2; 5:6; Col. 3:6, 14.

idols, from blood, from things strangled, and from fornication."[858]

Paul explained, as Jesus had done, that they were no longer under the Law, but had gone beyond it; that Jesus had "justified" them from "all things which could not be justified;" that the followers of Moses didn't understand the Law; and that even the prophets didn't understand the "mysteries."[859] Stressing that "without love there is nothing," Paul said: "The Law was added because of transgressions, 'till the seed [Jesus] should come. . . . If ye be led of the spirit, ye are not under the Law, but under grace; the letter killeth, but the spirit giveth life . . . all the law is fulfilled in one word, even in this: Thou shalt love thy neighbor as thyself."[860]

But not everyone, especially the apostles Peter and James, were happy about Paul and his new rules, even though he was merely following the teachings of Jesus. Some of the early followers of Jesus, who were leery of Paul, because he had not been one of the original apostles, were even circulating a document called: Kerygmata Petrou, which stated that Paul had changed the teachings of Jesus. Why were so many at odds with Paul, a Jew as well as a Roman citizen, who made three great missionary journeys into Asia Minor, Europe and Arabia?[861] Peter was arrogant because Jesus had called him the "rock," hence he had taken the most active part in the affairs of the infant church. It was he who had elected a successor for Judas and who was the main speaker on the "Day of Pentecost." James was arrogant because he was the brother of Jesus and therefore the next heir in the royal bloodline of King David.[862] (Jesus had several brothers and sisters who were younger than James, but James had become

---

[858] Acts 15:20, 29; 21:21, 25; Rev. 2:20.

[859] Matt. 12:7; 13:17; Acts 13:39; Gal. 2:16.

[860] Rom. 2:9-10; 4:15; 5:20; 6:14-15; 7:6-8; 8:2; 13:8-9; 1 Cor. 13:1-13; 2 Cor. 3:6; Gal. 3:19, 25; 5:14, 18; 1 Tim. 1:9; Heb. 2:2; 7:11.

[861] Acts 14:12; Rom. 11:13.

[862] Matt 13:55; Mark 3:17; 5:37; 6:3; 15:40; 16:1; Luke 24:10; Acts 21:17; Gal. 1:19; Jude 1.

head of the family.)[863]

It was difficult for either Peter or James to believe that Paul, who had formerly persecuted the "Christians," had been personally chosen by him.[864] If reincarnation were not a reality, there would have been absolutely no logic in Jesus having chosen Paul. The bond between them cannot be fully understood until one reviews the Old Testament account of the interactions between King Saul (the former incarnation of Paul) and King David (who had lived in the spirit of Jesus).[865] King David, through Jesus, was giving King Saul (Paul) another chance. The ancient King Saul had actually been a "goodly man" until Jehovah, enraged because he did not kill King Agag and all of his livestock, had put an "evil spirit" into him.[866]

In turn, one cannot fully understand Peter without first understanding his previous incarnation as Jonah, who had lived around 800 BC. Jesus called Peter "Simon, son of [reincarnation of] Jonas."[867] ("Son of," in mystical terms, means the incarnation of, hence Jesus was the "son of David."[868]) The obstinate yet humorous personality of Jonah and Peter, who were both involved in a storm at sea, was almost identical.[869] The possibility of Peter having been Jonah is strengthened by the fact that Jesus had told the Scribes and Pharisees that the men of Nineveh, to whom Jonah had prophesied, would "rise" [reincarnate] with their

---

[863] Matt. 12:46; 13:55; Mark 3:31; 6:3; 15:40; Luke 8:19; John 2:12; 7:3-5; Acts 1:14; Gal. 1:19; 1 Cor. 9:5.

[864] Acts 9:15.

[865] I Samuel, chapters 16-31; Acts 7:58; 8:1-4; 9:1-20; 13:22; 18:9-10; 22:4-21; 23:11; 26:13-18; 1 Cor. 2:3; 15:8-9; 2 Cor. 11:30; 12:7-9; Gal. 4:13-14; Eph. 3:8; Phlp. 3:6; 1 Tim. 1:12-15.

[866] 1 Sam. 15:1-35; 16:14; 28:18.

[867] Matt. 12:39-42; 16:17; John 1:42; 21:15-17.

[868] Matt. 15:22; 20:30-31; 21:9, 15; 22:42; Mark 10:47-48; 12:35; Luke 18:38-39; 20:41; Rev. 22:16.

[869] Jonah 1:15-17; 2:1; Matt. 14:27-32; 16:22; Mark 8:32; Luke 5:8; 22:31-33; John 13:8-11.

generation to condemn it.[870]

Peter, having been a disciple of John, the Baptist, was much more rigid and disciplined than Jesus. It was because of his strength of character that Jesus had called him the "rock," had given him the "keys to the kingdom of heaven," and had made him the "spokesman" for his group of followers.[871] But Peter made ridiculous requests, protested against Jesus when he washed the feet of the disciples, impulsively cut off the ear of the man who wanted to arrest Jesus, and denied Jesus three times.[872] He was evidently forgiven, however, for after the crucifixion, Peter, the leader on the "Day of Pentecost," had a vision, and was miraculously delivered prom prison.[873] James, who had not even believed in the messiahship of Jesus during his lifetime, took over as head of the church after Peter had been thrown into prison by King Herod Agrippa I around 42 AD. At the "First Council of Jerusalem," conducted by James, he addressed the conflict between his group, the "legalists," those who still adhered to the Law of Moses, and the "libertines," those who agreed with Jesus and Paul that they were no longer under the Law.[874] Paul said "where the Spirit of the Lord is, there is liberty," but James was so orthodox that some of his representatives even frightened Peter and Barnabas into observing the Jewish food laws.[875] Peter was

---

[870] Jonah 1:17; Matt. 12:37-43.

[871] Matt. 16:13-19; John 1:42.

[872] Matt. 17:4; 26:33-35, 51, 69-75; Mark 14:47; Luke 22:50; John 13:6-8; 18:10.

[873] Acts 2:14-38; 10:11; 12:1-17.

[874] For more information see: Rosslyn Guardian of the Secrets of the Holy Grail, Tim Wallace-Murphy and Marilyn Hopkins, Element, MA, 2000, pp 64-68; Jesus the Heretic, Douglas Lockhart, Element, Shaftesbury, 1997, p 230; History of Christianity, Paul Johnson, Penguin, London, England, 1978, p 41; James the Brother of Jesus, Robert Eisenman, Faber & Faber, London, England, 1997. See also: Acts 15:1-31; 21:1-30; I Cor. 9:5-6; 2 Cor. 3:17; Galatians, chapters 1-2, Hebrew, chapters 11-12, and James, chapter 2.

[875] 2 Cor. 3:17; Gal. 2:11-21.

overly cautious about angering the Jews, who were a constant threat over the early "Christians," while Paul, being a Roman citizen, stood up to them.

The Christian and the Jewish religions were distinctively different. Jesus came to fulfill the Law of Moses, to reveal the "Kingdom of God," and to preach a gospel of love and forgiveness. Peter and James, who considered the teachings of Jesus to be mainly for the Jews, wanted to use these new teachings to purify the existing Jewish faith. But Paul, who considered the teachings to be for both the Jews and the "Gentiles," wanted to supersede the Law of Moses by blending the teachings of Jesus with the deeper esoteric teachings, which were comparable to those of the Book of John and the Book of Revelation. Paul, who combatted Jewish errors and prejudices, and cautioned against Judaizing teachers, emphasized faith instead of law, and upheld Christian liberty. Peter and James and their followers apparently did not understand Paul's mystical terms such as: "caught up into the third heaven; incorruptible bodies; Unknown, Invisible Father; master builders; babes;" and "reborn."[876] Paul, whose teachings were later incorporated into Gnosticism, made such mystical statements as:

> "Leaving the principles of the doctrine of Christ, let us go on unto perfection; not laying again the foundation of repentance from dead works, and of faith toward God, of the doctrine of baptisms, and of laying on of hands, and of resurrection of the dead and of eternal judgement. . . for it is impossible for those who were once enlightened, and have tasted of the heavenly gift, and were made partakers of the Holy Ghost, and have tasted the good word of God, and the powers of the world to come. . . . When I was a child I spake as

---

[876] 1 Cor. 15:42-52; 2 Cor. 11:30; 12:2-5, 9; Heb. 6:1-5.

a child, I understood as a child, I thought as a child: but when I became a man, I put away childish things. For now we see through a glass, darkly; but then face to face: now I know in part; but then shall I know even as also I am known."[877]

In addition to disliking Paul, the apostles were also aware of his inability to form relationships with women, his infirmities, and his obvious fanaticism, which were carry overs from his difficult lifetime as King Saul. Madame Blavatsky sheds light on this Pauline/Petrine controversy:

"The Apostle of the Gentiles [Paul] was brave, outspoken, sincere, and very learned; the Apostle of Circumcision [Peter], cowardly, cautious, insincere, and very ignorant. That Paul had been, partially, at least, if not completely, initiated into the theurgic mysteries admits of little doubt. . . . In his Epistles to the Corinthians [speaking of 'Archons' or angels] . . . Paul [is] abounding with expressions suggested by the initiations of Sabazius and Eleusis. . . When Paul entitles himself a 'master-builder,' he is using a word pre-eminently kabalistic, theurgic, and masonic. . . . He thus declares himself an adept, having the right to initiate others. . . . What Paul preached, was preached by every other mystic philosopher. . . . Paul admitted to belonging to the sect of the Nazarenes [Nazarites] . . . Warning his converts against the worshipping of angels . . . [he] was fully aware that this Demiurge, whose Jewish name was Jehovah, was not the God preached by Jesus. . . . The Reformation . . . and Marcion. . .

---

[877] 2 Cor. 4:4-6; Heb. 6:1.

abandoned Peter and alleges to have chosen Paul
for its only leader. . . . The Jewish Tanaim . . . [is]
composed of the followers of Peter and John; the
Christian kabalists of the Platonic Gnosis . . .
ranged with the Pauline Christianity. . . . However
disfigured were his Epistles by dogmatic hands
before being admitted into the Canon, Paul's
conception of [Jesus] . . . can still be traced in his
address to the various Gentile nations. Only, he
who would understand him better yet must study
the Philonean Logos reflecting now and then the
Hindu Sabda (logos) of the Mimansa school. . . .
Take Paul, read the little or original that is left of
him in the writings attributed to this brave,
honest, sincere man, and see whether any one can
find a word therein to show that Paul meant by
the word Christ anything more than the abstract
ideal of the personal divinity indwelling in man.
For Paul, Christ is not a person, but an embodied
idea. . . . Paul was the real founder of
Christianity."[878]

Without Paul, the Christian religion would have merely
been an extension of Judaism. Presently known as Hilarion,
Master of Truth, Paul is still actively channeling to reveal the
deeper esoteric meanings concerning the teachings of Jesus. He
is still striving to enlighten the veiled "Christians," who have
received from their church leaders a watered-down version of the
true teachings. Lifetime after lifetime, the spirit of King Saul/Paul
continues to expound the esoteric teachings of Jesus.
　　Peter and some of the apostles also disputed the teachings
of Mary Magdalene, who is believed by many to have been the

---

[878] Isis Unveiled, Vol. II, pp 84, 89-91, 137, 161-162, 179-180, 198, 206,
241, 277, 574.

reincarnation of King David's beloved wife Bathsheba, and to have been the wife of Jesus, who he "often kissed upon the lips."[879] The fact that Jesus was called "Rabbi" also indicates that he was a married man.[880] (Jesus and Mary Magdalene were believed to have been married at Cana, hence Mary, the mother of Jesus, was responsible for furnishing the wine. It was her feeling of duty that had prompted her to push Jesus into performing his first miracle of turning the water into wine.)[881] Why else did Jesus, after his resurrection, appear first to Mary Magdalene and allow her to be the carrier of the good news?[882]

She was believed to have been carrying the child of Jesus at the time of his crucifixion and to have travelled to France where she was honored as a representation of the Mother Goddess, symbolized by a dove. The church at Rennes-le-Chateau was found to have been built over the ruins of a Visigothic church that was dedicated to her. The later Cathedral at Chartes was also built in her honor, rather than to the Virgin Mary, as many have believed.

If this is true, why would something as important as the marriage and offspring of Jesus be denied by the latter church? After Jesus made his triumphant entry into Jerusalem as the "son of David," the threat of kingship became very real, hence the mocking sign above his head on the cross read: "King of the Jews."[883] To the people of that time the terms "savior" or "messiah" were synonymous with kingship. The royal bloodline of Jesus, who may have had children by Mary Magdalene, is

---

[879] See <u>Nag Hammadi Texts</u>, Gospel of Mary (Magdalene).

[880] John 1:38, 49; 3:2; 6:25; 20:16.

[881] John 2:1-11.

[882] Mark 16:9; John 20:1, 16.

[883] Ps. 118:25; Matt. 21:9; 27:37; Mark 11:9-10; 15:26; Luke 23:38; John 12:13; 19:19.

considered by many to be the true meaning of the "Holy Grail."[884] The holy cup held the bloodline, as well as the blood of the Christ.

This political point of view is explained by Steven Sora, in The Lost Treasure of the Knights Templar:

> "The church, as directed by Constantine sought to stamp out any earthly line of descendants who would threaten its authority. . . . Not intent on crowning an earthly king and wishing to avoid what Rome might misconstrue as a threat, the family and descendants of Jesus were a topic to be avoided and soon denied. . . . When the marriage of Jesus was left out of the Gospels, it was not because the Church was against marriage . . . [it] was not being debated as a religious issue--it was a political question. . . . The Church sought to remove James from the historical records and raise the status of Mary to a virgin [having no other children than Jesus]. . . . Rome had reason to take seriously the threat of a king emerging from the bloodline of David. . . . The message of Jesus had been love; the message of the Roman Church was power."[885]

Thus the apostles and the early "Christians," with their talk of a "kingdom," were considered a threat by the Romans, who had no concept of a spiritual "kingdom within." To them Jesus was the reincarnation or the spirit of King David and his followers ("members of his kingdom") were revolutionaries!

If you find it hard to accept that Jesus was married and had a child, you may be totally overwhelmed by another ancient legend that is presently being researched. It fosters the belief that Jesus did not die on the cross, but survived, lived in France for

---

[884] For further information, see: Holy Blood, Holy Grail, Baigent, Michael and Leigh, Richard, NY, Dell Publishing, 1983.

[885] The Lost Treasure of the Knights Templar, pp 132-137, 176.

many years, had several children, and still has a line of living descendants. This theory is based on the fact that the "sponge of vinegar" that was given to him while he was on the cross may have contained a solution of mandrake root which made him appear to be dead. Due to this appearance, his legs were not broken.[886] It was unusual for anyone to die on a cross in only six hours. And if one of the Roman guards was in on the plan to switch the vinegar sponge to mandrake, he would have pierced the side of Jesus very gently. When Jesus appeared to his apostles after the crucifixion, he allowed them to touch the wounds in his hands, feet and rib, stating that he was not a "spirit," but was still "flesh and bones."[887] Legends say that after a long life, based in France while traveling throughout the world, he returned to India to die. A tomb has recently been found there upon which is engraved the wounds in his feet.[888] This is an interesting controversy, but more evidence is still needed to deem it a fact.

It has been predicted that ancient scrolls and records will be found in the "last days" prior to the emergence of the Golden Age. That time is now, but even when ancient writings are found, the problem is in getting them out to the public. Luckily the Nag Hammadi Codices, the Emerald Tablets and The Secret Gospel of Mark, were quickly revealed, but such was not the case with the Dead Sea Scrolls, which were scrutinized for nearly fifty years before being presented to the public. Were they changed or were some of them withheld?

Whenever a text is unearthed, the "Christians" become alarmed. Why? If Jesus is their leader, why aren't they delighted to find some of his original teachings? What are they afraid of?

---

[886] Matt. 27:34, 48; Mark 15:36; John 19:29-33.

[887] Luke 24:39.

[888] For further information on the controversial subject of the offspring of Jesus and his crucifixion survival, see: Holy Blood, Holy Grail, by Michael Baigent; Bloodline of the Holy Grail, by Laurence Gardner; The Lost Treasure of the Knights Templar, by Steven Sora; Jesus Died in Kashmir, by Faber-Kaiser, Andraeus, Abacus/ Sphere, London, England, 1978.

It has been rumored that sacred writings are buried within the shoulder of and beneath the foot of the sphinx, but there is a blackout on information concerning them. Does the possibility of discovering that the pyramids of Giza were build by Atlanteans pose a threat to their long-held theories of Egyptology? Great shades of The Celestine Prophecy! Why does the world continually block the emergence of truth?

THE FOLLOWERS OF JESUS VS THE EARLY CHRISTIAN CHURCHES

Jesus was obviously of a higher lifewave and taught a greater truth than his predecessors, but unfortunately only a few of his original teachings were preserved. One of the greatest of all human tragedies is the way in which the so-called "Christian" churches altered his message, especially since he wasn't even in favor of churches, but preferred teaching outdoors.[889] Speaking against the way in which the Sadducees, Pharisees, and lawyers had abused the teachings of Moses, he predicted the collapse of the temple, telling them that the body is the "temple of the Holy Spirit" and "the light of the body is the eye,"[890] another direct reference to the "kingdom within." When he said: "Upon this rock [Peter] I will build my church," he was referring to the heavenly "houses not made with hands,"[891] (elevated states of consciousness) rather than to a physical building. When Jesus returns, he will no doubt reject the massive churches with their exoteric teachings. However, there is much truth, faith and goodness in these institutions.

According to Blavatsky, the original followers of Jesus knew the truth:

---

[889] Matt. 5:l; 10:1; Mark 4:1; Luke 6:12; 9:1.

[890] Mark 13:2; Luke 4:1; 11:34; 19:44; 1 Cor. 3:16; 6:19; 2 Cor. 6:16; Col. 2:9; Heb. 8:2.

[891] Matt. 16:18; John 14:12; Acts 7:48; 17:24; 2 Cor. 5:1-3; Eph. 2:20; Heb. 9:11; 2 Pet. 1:13-14; Rev. 21:14.

"History finds the first Christian sects to have been either Nazarenes, like John, the Baptist; or Ebionites, among whom were many of the relatives of Jesus; or Essenes. . . . They united together in opposition to the synagogue and the tyrannical technicalities of the Pharisees, until the primitive group separated in two distinct branches . . . one represented by the followers of Peter and John; the other with the Pauline Christianity. The Gospel according to Matthew in the New Testament is not the original Gospel. . . . Around the end of the fourth century, Saint Jerome, who found the authentic and original evangel, written in Hebrew, by Matthew, in the library collected at Caesarea, confesses that he had to ask permission of the Nazarenes to translate it. . . . Jerome knew that this original Gospel of Matthew was the expounder of the only true doctrine of Christ . . . [but he] became more zealous than ever in his persecutions of the 'Heretics,' because to accept it was equivalent to reading the death sentence of the established church."[892]

The same is no doubt true of the modern-day "Fatima Prophecy!" Could it destroy the Catholic church?

The date of the original Gospel of Matthew, which was written to Jewish converts to show them that Jesus was the predicted messiah of the Old Testament, is uncertain. The letters of Paul, who had traveled and studied from the time of his encounter with Jesus in 33 AD until 50 AD, were written from the year 52 until his death in 65. The Epistle to the Thessalonians, giving a treatise on becoming one with the Christ Spirit, written

---

[892] Isis Unveiled, Vol. II, pp 1-9, 127, 134-135, 144, 154-156, 168-171, 180-183, 197-198, 210, 307.

in 52 AD, is the earliest and most valuable book of the New Testament. The Epistle to the Corinthians is the most elegant, while Philemon is a masterpiece of composition. James, a sermon by the brother of Jesus, is an early writing directed to the Jews. Many scholars feel this writing is in conflict with the letters of Paul. After the death of Peter in 65, John Mark, most likely using his words and views, wrote the Gospel of Mark. Written to the Romans, it depicted the actions of Jesus, rather than a discourse about him. Around 80, Luke, the only "Gentile" writer of the New Testament, wrote his Gospel, using the Gospels of Matthew and Mark, other written sources and oral testimonies for his information.

The Acts of the Apostles, a record of the apostles from the ascension of Jesus to around 70 or 80 AD, was most likely written by Luke, who had traveled extensively with Paul and had kept a diary. Luke had also seen Peter and John Mark in Rome and Philip and Cornelius in Caesarea. Although many new churches had been established throughout the Mediterranean world, the multitudes of "Christians" were still unacquainted with the nature of the mission which had been Jewish and was now becoming predominantly "Gentile." The purpose of the book of Acts, to answer their questions, was both religious and historical. Both Luke and Acts of the Apostles leaned toward the Gentiles rather than the Jewish converts.

The Gospel of John, as well as John I, II and III and the Revelation, all containing greater metaphysical depth, were written by John around 96. (John, the most beloved of the disciples, was a prophet as well as an Apostle. He had been asked by Jesus to take care of his mother and was the only one of the twelve who was not crucified. He was the reincarnation of Jonathan, the son of King Saul, and beloved friend of King David. He and Jesus had retained their love. Centuries after the crucifixion of Jesus, John incarnated as Nostradamus.)[893] The

---

[893] John 12:23; 21:20-23.

First Book of Peter was written by a Christian elder. The Second Book of Peter, the latest book of the New Testament, was written nearly one hundred years after the crucifixion. Written some 62 years after Peter's death, it refers to Paul as a "beloved brother," and labels his letters "scripture." This would certainly indicate that Peter himself did not write it! Peter, like James, was adamantly against Paul.

Many of these early writings were altered by the various church councils. Unfortunately, most of the references to the feminine aspect were deleted in an effort to prevent our "mystical marriage" of soul and spirit and thereby keep us ever-dependent upon their controlling priesthood. The churches taught that one's sins (failures) would condemn them to "hell"--that they have but one chance--while Jesus, confirming reincarnation, said: "You must be born again."[894] Perhaps the original version, stressing the importance of reincarnation, read: "You must be born again and again and again!" Paul said: "If in this life only we have hope in Christ, we are of all men most miserable."[895] The Nag Hammadi Codices, found in Egypt in 1945, are believed to be authentic and less altered than those of the Bible. The Gospel of Love a Gnostic variation upon the Gospel of John, survived for many centuries and was used by the Cathars. In 1958, a secret Gospel of Mark was discovered at the Monastery of mar Saba.[896] This Gospel explained an initiation rite given by Jesus in which, after a six-day purification, the initiate dressed in white linen to be baptized. This was alluded to by the young man who stood near Jesus at the time of his arrest.[897] Such purification and initiatory rites, given by Jesus, were also explained in the Essene Gospel of Peace. Other wonderful scriptures are found in The Lost Books of The

---

[894] Matt. Matt. 11:11-15; 16:13-17; 17:10-13; Mark 8:27-28; 9:11-13; Luke 7:26-28; 9:18-20; John 1:1, 10-23; 8:56, 58; Rev. 3:14.

[895] 1 Cor. 15:19.

[896] See The Secret Gospel, by Morton Smith, The Drawn Horse Press, CA, 1960.

[897] Mark. 14:51-52.

Bible and The Forgotten Books of Eden. By the end of the first century, at least thirty sects of Christianity had sprung up in Asia Minor, Syria, Alexandria, and Rome. Each sect had a different version of the "gospels."

The churches ignored the mystical union with the Christ Spirit and discounted the nine spiritual gifts of the Holy Spirit. Anyone manifesting these mystical gifts was considered a witch or a heretic.

The Urantia Book has some interesting things to say about the "inner kingdom" vs the church:

> "The kingdom of heaven is neither a social nor economic order; it is an exclusively spiritual brotherhood of God-knowing individuals. . . . True religion is to know God as your Father and man as your brother. . . . The religious man who finds God in nature has already and first found this same personal God in his own soul. . . . It is high time that man had a religious experience so personal and sublime that it could be realized and expressed only by 'feelings that lie too deep for words.'. . . The church, as a social outgrowth of the kingdom, would have been wholly natural and even desirable. The evil of the church was not its existence, but rather that it almost completely supplanted the Jesus concept of the kingdom. . . . The old religion taught self-sacrifice; the new religion teaches only self-forgetfulness, enhanced Self-realization in conjoined social service and universe comprehension. . . . The old religion was motivated by fear-consciousness; the new gospel of the kingdom is dominated by truth-conviction. . . . Paul's successors partly transferred the issues of eternal life from the individual to the church. Christ thus became the head of the church rather than the elder brother of each individual. . . . The

231

early Christians (and all too many of the later ones) generally lost sight of the Father-and-Son idea embodied in Jesus' teaching of the kingdom. . . . Jesus taught men to place a high value upon themselves in time and eternity. . . . He revealed and exemplified a religion of love, security in the Father's love, with joy and satisfaction consequent upon sharing this love in the service of the human brotherhood. . . True religion is delivered from the custody of priests and all sacred classes and finds its real manifestation in the individual souls of men. . . . Jesus did not die to ransom man from the clutch of the apostate rulers and fallen princes of the spheres. . . Neither was the master's death on the cross a sacrifice which consisted in an effort to pay God a debt which the race of mankind had come to owe him. . . . Jesus lived and died for a whole universe, not just for the races of this one world. Though it is hardly proper to speak of Jesus as a sacrificer, a ransomer, or a redeemer, it is wholly correct to refer to him as a savior. He forever made the way of salvation (survival) clear and certain."[898]

Those who receive the "Spirit of Truth" and enter the "kingdom within," have no need of the manipulating priesthoods. The so-called "Christian" churches added the concept of "original sin" in order to become the only avenue through which we could be "saved from sin." Their emphasis on sin and their ignoring of the scriptures that describe us as "gods" and "children of the light," have held us in an insecure state of dependency upon them. The time is long overdue for this yoke to be broken!

---

[898] The Urantia Book, pp 1088, 1091, 1106, 1829, 1864-1865, 1951, 2016-2017, 2063, 2071, 2092-2095.

Spirituality is an inner and a very personal experience. It is not the business of the church or the priests to oversee our progress. We are guided by Jesus, our "friend" and "wayshower," who not only loves us, but has also endowed us with the Christ Spirit to shine as the "daystar" in our heart. The illumination of this inner light is the beginning of true service; a time when our every thought and action is for the upliftment of others. I once saw a billboard that read: "Spread the teachings of Jesus; use words only if necessary." An enlightened being, who has subdued his "carnal mind," overcome his ego, and allowed his inner divinity to shine through, radiates divine light to uplift all mankind. Jesus, stressing the importance of the inner kingdom, did not teach external churchology. Blavatsky says of the early Christian churches, who outlawed truth:

> "The Christians did not kill the pagans because they thought they were evil, but because they wanted to reign supreme as the only ones who could perform 'miracles' or receive revelation. Instead of burning the pagan books, they kept them in the Vatican library so their priests could learn to perform these 'miracles.' The church did not know the secrets of the mysteries. They tortured the initiates to learn these secrets, but the initiates, bound by their oath of secrecy, would not tell them. The church feared the secret societies because they had higher truths. They killed them so they would have no competition. They did not want the pagans to reveal the antiquity of the teachings or the truth about the Trinity or Jehovah, or that there had been several embodiments of the Christ [Spirit]. But although the Christians copied the ancient mysteries of the so-called 'pagans,' there are also many differences between them. The Christians teach about the Devil [Satan] and hell; there is no devil and hell

in paganism. The Christians teach 'miracles,' saying only the priests can perform them; paganism teaches no 'miracles,' but the natural and scientific use of the laws that anyone can learn. The church discourages study, making it illegal to read books on magic and keeping the writings in Latin that only the priests can read; paganism encourages study and independent thinking. The church disagrees with science; paganism explores and promotes it. The church burns and destroys ancient teachings, professing that all enlightenment begins with them; paganism spreads and fosters ancient wisdom. The church won't tolerate mythology or philosophy; paganism blends with it. The Christians teach creation; pagans teach emanation. The Christians taught that the Son was God, and that the Trinity is one; pagans taught that the Son was an emanation from a higher 'First Cause'; that Jehovah was a lesser being."[899]

Hall agrees:

"The early Christians used every means possible to conceal the pagan origin of their symbols, doctrines, and rituals. They either destroyed the sacred books of other peoples among whom they settled, or made them inaccessible to students of comparative philosophy, apparently believing that in this way they could stamp out all record of the pre-Christian origin of their doctrines. In some cases the writings of various ancient authors were tampered with, passages of a compromising

---

[899] <u>Isis Unveiled</u>, Vol. II, pp 10-53.

nature being removed, or foreign material interpolated."[900]

During the reign of the Emperor Trajan in 96 AD, Rome was troubled by revolts throughout Asia and Asia Minor. When the Jews, in 115, under their leaders Akiha and Bar Cocheba, joined the rebels, Judea was nearly destroyed and the Jews were forbidden to visit Jerusalem except on the anniversary of the destruction of their temple. After this dispersal, the Jews, without a nation or a common language, were a people by religion only. But Jesus promised that after the "time of the Gentiles" is "fulfilled," they will be allowed to return and rebuild their temple.[901] Is that time now?

Christianity did not become an official religion until the time of the Roman Emperor, Constantine, the Great, who in 312 AD, saw a vision of a pillar of light in the form of a cross upon which was written the message: "In this, conquer." Those who were with him also saw the vision. More holograms and space technology? In a dream the following night, Constantine saw Jesus, who instructed him to make a flag containing the symbol of the vision. He claims that in the dream, Jesus assured him that the flag would grant him victory over his enemies. Does this sound like Jesus who did not involve himself with worldly matters? With his "Edict of Milan," Christianity, after three centuries of persecution, became Rome's official religion.

Constantine, after establishing a church in the name of Jesus, later, through the Council of Nicaea in 325, removed many of the references to reincarnation. He then declared Jesus to be the sun/son of God; adapted the pagan celebration of the rebirth of the sun on December 25th to be his official birthday; adopted the pagan fertility festival, Easter, as his resurrection; and changed the sabbath day of worship to Sunday, the day of the

---

[900] The Secret Teachings of all Ages, p clxxxi.
[901] Luke 21:24; Rom. 11:11, 25; Eph. 2:2; 5:6; Col. 3:6, 14.

sun. He stilled the complaints of the original groups by making "heresy" and "paganism" a crime. Thus Christianity was changed, but like the Jewish religion before them, several esoteric branches of the mystery teachings have survived.

The Emperor Theodosius I fostered the emergence of the dark ages by issuing laws of punishment, destroying pagan temples, and burning the Alexandrian library. Around 550, at the Council at Constantinople, his wife, Justinian, enacted the death penalty and began burning at the stake the "heretics"--that is anyone who disagreed with their dogma. She also removed Origen's teachings of the true message of Jesus. Even the Pope himself was not allowed to attend this Council. Theodosius also transformed the church into a war machine that performed what they termed "just wars." This is ironic since the early Christians did not even allow soldiers to join their groups, and of course Jesus advocated a path of non-resistance. Theodosius also issued a decree to remove some of the remaining references to reincarnation and pre-existence from the Bible. Fortunately, they missed many, for some six hundred references still survive.

During his reign, the "bubonic plague" spread throughout the Roman Empire and into Europe. It was not unusual for Jehovah to engage in such germ warfare; he had done so many times before.[902] But this "plague" was different, for even at night, the sky seemed to be on fire. Historical accounts report "lights around the sun" and a huge "dragon [spacecraft]" traversing the heavens. Due to the frequent appearance of unusual aerial phenomena, it was referred to as "God's disease." The plagues could have been the result of man's negative thoughtforms, but the Old Testament continually attributed the plagues to Jehovah. According to the prophecies, such phenomena was to be the herald of a "new messiah." Was it a mere coincidence that the "plague" that was killing off many of the Christians, was still

---

[902] Lev. 26:21; Num. 11:33-34; 16:46-49; 25:8-9; 31:16; Josh. 22:17; 1 Sam. 5:6-12; 6:4; 2 Sam. 24:12-25; 2 Chron. 21:14-15; Zech. 14:12-13.

raging when the prophet Mohammed was born? Was he a "new messiah?"

Perhaps Jehovah had given up on both the Jews and the Christians and had attempted to gain control through Mohammed. Or perhaps this was another of his Machiavellian ploys to create conflict between two opposing nations, as was the case with Abraham's son Isaac from his wife Sarah, and Ishmael, Abraham's son by his handmaid, Hagar, (the two tribes who became the Jews and the Arabs). Legend claim that Hagar brought two sacred black stones from Abraham to Arabia.

Many different nations were expecting a "savior/messiah." Abraham's wife Keturah gave birth to the line that produced Zoroaster, around 600 BC, and later Baha'u'lla, around 1850 AD, who is believed by many to be the reincarnation of, or overshadowed by the spirit of, Jesus. Martin Luther, founder of Protestantism, is considered by some to be a "messiah," but in his protest against the Catholic Church, he didn't regain any of Christianity's purity. His rebellion against the priesthoods was admirable, but the Protestants threw out the baby with the bath water by disregarding the Mother God aspect, the saints, and exorcism.

The "return" of many great "savior/messiahs" has been predicted: the Hindus expect a Kalki Avatar; the Buddhists expect a greater Buddha, who many believe to be Nichiren Daishonin, who began teaching in 1253 AD; the Mazdeans expect a Sosiosh; the Hopi expect a Pahana; and the Islamics expect a Mahdi. The Hindus believe the tenth and last incarnation of Vishnu will manifest during the "Golden Age of Peace." Jesus may have been one of the incarnations of Lord Vishnu of the triune Godhead of Brahma, Vishnu and Shiva. His "second coming" would certainly usher in a millennium of peace. But peace will most likely come only after a purification, for "new wine" is not placed in "old bottles."

Just as Jesus fulfilled the limiting Law of Moses during his sojourn on earth, he, during his "second coming," will no doubt fulfill the jumbled mess that has mistakenly been called

"Christianity." He will no doubt reestablish a mystical school of truth. Fundamental churchology and religion, meaning "to bind," will be abandoned in favor of true spirituality; union with Spirit. How can beliefs that are based on literal interpretations possibly endure mankind's budding understanding? The Old Testament predicted that "at the time of the end," which is now: "knowledge shall be increased."[903] Paul said:

> "'Till we all come in the unity of the faith . . . . That we henceforth be no more children, tossed to and fro, and carried about with every wind of doctrine, by the sleight of men, and cunning craftiness, whereby they lie in wait to deceive; but speaking the truth in love, may grow into him in all things, which is the head, even Christ."[904]

When all faiths look to that which they have in common rather than upon that which they differ--their underlying sameness--they will finally realize that "Christ" is a universal cosmic principle, distinct from any person in which this principle may have manifested. Then they will know that whether we call it Christ, Krishna, or Horus, the principle is the basis for true mysticism. One of the fundamental churches greatest barriers to achieving this "unity of the faith" is their lost belief in reincarnation. The Jews believed in it and the early Christians believed until it was abandoned by the church Council in 553 AD. When this teaching is restored, the barriers will fall like the Berlin Wall!

Perhaps elaborate churches, rituals, vestments, masses, music and incense inspire the feelings needed to turn within, but can you imagine Jesus wearing papal robes or swinging an incense burner? When we mistake the props for the real thing, we

---

[903] Dan. 12:4.
[904] Eph. 4:13-15.

miss the deeper esoteric teachings. Spirituality is a quality of life rather than a belief; being rather than doing. Religion of the future will not be new, it will merely be an understanding of that which has been called "the mysteries". When elaborate churches are replaced by simple meditation rooms and initiation chambers, we will finally come into alignment with the teachings of Jesus, who advocated simplicity, despised priesthoods, and had no temple, altar, rites or rituals. He emphasized that the temple is man; that the divine nature of man is the Christos.

Mystical writer, Edouard Schure, in his book, <u>From Sphinx to Christ</u>, summarizes:

"What Christ brought to the world was a new life, a sovereign impulsion, an immense faith in earth made new, and heaven reopened, by means of the Divine Presence that radiated from His Person. . . . When Jesus said to his followers: 'The Kingdom of heaven is within you,' he was promising the conquest of heaven through the inner life. . . . This radiation prolonged for a time by the phenomenon of spiritual resurrection, created the first Christian communities and was sufficient for them. . . . During the first two centuries a number of Christian communities maintained the ancient hierarchial tradition of graduated initiation. This was called the Gnosis. But after Saint Augustine's pronouncement that faith in the Established Church should take the place of everything else, the principle of initiation was suppressed and blind faith superseded true knowledge. Submission to the Church and to her ordinances replaced union with the living Christ. . . . No more need of Jesus Christ, since we have the Pope! Let darkness reign in the mind, so long as the body of the Church survives! . . . Reestablishing graduated initiation would despoil the Church and her uncontrolled power. . . . The Cosmos of Wisdom must be changed into a Cosmos of Love. All that the self can produce within itself must become Love, and the greatest and most comprehensive example of Love is the Christ, the sublime Solar Spirit. . . . The new temple will aim at representing the influx of divine powers to the earth and to the heart of man, and at expressing their reciprocal interpenetration through an ascending and descending movement. The plan of the building will no longer be based on the square, but on the circle, or several intersecting circles. The inner freize will be ornaments with the symbols of the planets and the signs of the zodiac. . . . This religion will be explained and supported by a new science, which might be called the Science of Spirit. Its aim will be to seek for the principles and causes that lie behind all phenomena, and to rise from the visible to the invisible, from the material to the spiritual. . . . The principle apostle and preacher of these new forms of knowledge will be Art, the initiator and redeemer. Human language will once more become creative, and poetry a sacred thing. Drama will again become the representative of the sacred Mysteries. No rules and no dogmas will be imposed, save nobleness and dignity. In the words of Christ, it is by their fruits that works and men shall be judged. Enlightened humanity will choose what beautifies the body, widens the mind, and illumines the spirit, while refusing all that might injure, contaminate or dissociate them. . . . Woman, intuitive and endowed with spiritual sight, will have her place in the temples under the control of the initiates. . . . But let us not think that it will be formed or maintained without a struggle. . . . On the one side will be ranged egoism, hatred, and the spirit of negation, armed with black magic; on the other, love, wisdom and faith, armed with white magic (the royal art of initiates in all ages). . . . The only weapons of the chosen ones will be divine knowledge, and divine love, and their only ambition to save as many souls as possible from perversion, destruction and death. . . . By this time the Christ will be completely identified with the earth and with humanity."[905]

[905] From Sphinx to Christ, Edouard Schure, English translation of L'Evolution Divine, by Eva Martin, printed in Great Britain, reprinted by David McKay Company, Philadelphia, PA, 1920, pp 272-283.

PART VII

JEHOVAH GUIDES MOHAMMED

WHO IS MOHAMMED?

Mohammed, the prophet of Islam, born during the time of the great plague in 570 AD, was of the lineage of Abraham's son, Ishmael. After the death of his parents, he was raised by his grandfather. Upon his grandfather's death, he was taken in by an uncle. Around twelve years of age, he traveled with his uncle on a caravan to Syria, where he learned several religious and philosophic traditions. On his trip, he was impressed with a group of mystical Nestorian Christian monks, who warned him against idolatry. (It is interesting that he found truth in Syria, since it was in "Haran", near Edessa, on the bank of the Balikh River, where his ancestor, Abraham, had traveled when he left his birthplace, Ur.)

Mohammed revisited the Monastery in Syria and studied with them when he was in his twenties. At age twenty-six, he married a wealthy widow and had six daughters. Of the six, Fatima, was the only one to survive him. Later he took other wives and had a son who died. It was legal for the Prophet to have many wives, but it was not legal for his followers,[906] hence he was heavily criticized for his harem.

After years of intense study and devotion and spending the month of Ramadan doing ascetic rites in a cave in Mount Hira, he was visited by Archangel Gabriel. Overcome with peace and understanding, he lost consciousness. When he awoke, the angel stood before him, declaring him to be the prophet of the Living God (Allah, or Jehovah). After seven years of preparation, he began to receive the Surahs (chapters of the <u>Koran</u>). Each time they were dictated to him, he broke out in a cold sweat and fell into a trance-like state. His followers then wrote or memorized the messages. In the satiristic book: <u>The Satanic Verses</u>, the author Salman Rushdie indicates that during Mohammed's

---

[906] <u>Koran</u>; Surah 33:50.

"dreams," he received both divine and satanic verses and was unable to distinguish the difference.[907] This book, however, is controversial.

After four years of teaching a small group of followers, Mohammed was commanded to teach publicly. By 622 AD as he continued to grow in popularity, the city leaders feeling threatened by his revelations, planned an assassination. Warned by Archangel Gabriel to flee his home town of Mecca, he and his family moved to Medina. When he revisited Mecca, eight years later, he circled the Kabba seven times, ordered the 360 idols within its precincts to be hewn down, then re-dedicated the structure to Allah.

MOHAMMED VISITS THE SEVEN HEAVENS

In the twelfth year of his mission, Mohammed was roused in his sleep by Archangel Gabriel, who brought a strange creature that was different from any upon earth. It had a human face, the body of a horse, the wings of an eagle and eyes like stars. It was called "Al Borak," meaning lightning. Mounting the creature (no doubt some type of shuttle craft), Mohammed was carried over Mount Sinai and Bethlehem, then landed at the holy temple of Jerusalem. There, Mohammed was met by a man, who offered a cup of wine and a cup of milk. Gabriel approved when he chose the milk. Entering the temple, he saw Abraham, Moses, Jesus and many other prophets, who he joined in prayer. The sky opened and a golden ladder of light descended from heaven until the lower end of it rested upon the holy "Rock of Moriah." Assisted by Gabriel, Mohammed ascended the ladder to see the celestial regions divided into seven zones. In other words, he was taken into a multi-storied mothership, which was most likely the same one the Bible refers to as "Zion," however, the <u>Koran</u> uses the

---

[907] <u>The Satanic Verses</u>, Salman Rushdie, Viking Penguin Inc., NY, 1989.

term "Illiyum."

After entering the gate of the first heaven, he saw silver, with the stars suspended upon chains of gold. Each star had an angel guarding it. Upon seeing Adam, Mohammed paid homage to him. Many animals were present. Approaching the second heaven, he was met by Noah. In the third heaven, he was met by a huge angel of death, named Asrael. In the fourth heaven dwelt the angel of tears, who wept over the sins of men. In the fifth heaven, which was golden in color, he was met by Aaron and the avenging angel of fire. The sixth heaven was composed of an immense transparent stone and was presided over by the guardian of heaven and earth. Beside him was Moses. The final ascent brought them to the seventh heaven, an area of divine light and transcendent glory, where he was met by Abraham and Jesus. There, he saw a sacred building resembling the Kabba at Mecca. Mohammed asked Jesus to intercede for him, and from the seventh heaven, Mohammed passed through a region of light, then one of utter darkness. From the darkness, he emerged into the presence of Allah, whose face was covered with twenty thousand "veils." Allah placed one hand upon Mohammed's breast, the other upon his shoulder, then communicated a message to him. This message is not recorded in the <u>Koran</u>, but is said to have been preserved as part of the secret tradition of Islam. Hall says of Mohammed's journey:

> "The description of the ornamentations of the seven spheres or levels suggests the decoration of a Lodge or sanctuary of initiatory rites. . . . The night journey itself is highly reminiscent of the Apocalyptical vision of Saint John, the account of the ascent through the seven spheres described by Hermes in the Divine Pymander, and the descent of Ishtar through the seven gates in the

Babylonian legend of Tammuz."[908]

Of Mohammed's night journey, the <u>Koran</u> says:

"Glory to Allah, who took his servant for a journey by night from the sacred Mosque to the Farthest Mosque, whose precincts We did bless, in order that We might show him some of our signs: for he is one who hears and sees all things."[909]

The "seven heavens," also mentioned in the <u>Koran</u>,[910] offer a detailed description of "Illiyum." That is reminiscent of Jehovah's "Zion," where the saints are said to reside. The <u>Koran</u> describes:

"The record of the righteous is preserved in Illiyum. The righteous will be amid gardens and fountains of clear-flowing water. Their greeting will be: 'You enter here in peace and security.' And We shall remove from their hearts any lurking sense of injury: they will be brothers joyfully facing each other on thrones of dignity. There, no sense of fatigue shall touch them, nor shall they ever be asked to leave. . . . Truly the righteous will be in bliss: on thrones of dignity they will command a sight of all things. You will recognize in their faces the beaming brightness of

---

[908] <u>The Adepts in the Eastern Esoteric Tradition</u>, Part IV, <u>The Mystics of Islam</u>, Manly P. Hall, The Philosophical Research Society, Inc. CA, 1975, pp 35-36.

[909] <u>Koran</u>; Surah 17:1.

[910] <u>Koran</u>; Surah 2:29; 17:44; 23:17; 65:12; 67:3; 71:15.

Bliss."[911]

THE DEATH OF MOHAMMED

Mohammed traveled to Mecca just before his death in 632 AD. Because he had been poisoned by one of his enemies, he suffered greatly for many years. Mohammed, like the prophets before him, was a faithful servant to his "god." Hall says:

"The pressures of bickering and controversy of the early Christian church impelled him to seek the original and pure religion of the prophets and patriarchs. . . . Because Deity is one and alone and there can be no other God besides Him, Mohammed could not accept the divinity of Jesus or the doctrine of the Holy Trinity. . . . Mohammed went so far as to say that his own coming was prophesied in the Old Testament, and also that after him, another teacher would appear who was to be 'the desired of all nations."[912]

Some of the Biblical "savior" prophecies no doubt referred to Mohammed, while the "desired of all nations" most likely refers to Baha'u'lla, a prophet who manifested in Iran in 1863, and who many believe to be the spirit of Jesus fulfilling the prophecies of the "second coming." Blavatsky adds:

"The Mahometans outnumbered the Christians. Why? Because their prophet never sought to identify himself with Allah. Otherwise, it is safe to say, he would not have lived to see his religion

---

[911] Koran; Surah 15:45-48; 83:18-28.
[912] The Adepts in the Eastern Esoteric Tradition, Part IV, The Mystics of Islam, pp 18-19.

249

flourish. 'Till the present day Mahometanism has made and is now making more proselytes that Christianity. . . . Buddha never made of himself a 'god,' nor was he deified by his followers. The Buddhists are now known to far outnumber Christians. . . Mohamet never was, neither is he now, considered a 'god;' yet under the stimulus of his name millions of Moslems have served their God with an ardor that can never be paralleled by Christian sectarianism. That they have sadly degenerated since the days of their prophet, does not alter the case in hand, but only proves the more the prevalence of matter over spirit all over the world. Besides, they have never degenerated more from primitive faith than Christians themselves. Why, then, should not Jesus of Nazareth, a thousand-fold higher, nobler, and morally grander, be as well revered by Christians and followed in practice, instead of being blindly adored in fruitless faith as a 'god?'"[913]

Good question, but it was not Jesus himself that claimed to be God. He said he was but a "mediator." It was the early Christians who proclaimed his deity, then persecuted his followers who taught the truth.

THE KORAN: THE ISLAMIC BIBLE

The word Koran, or Qur'an, means recitation; Islam means submission to God's Will; Muslim refers to one who submits. Hall says of the Koran:

"The book deals with a variety of subjects,

---

[913]   Isis Unveiled, pp 239-240, 575.

including theology, ethics and jurisprudence. . . .
Idolatry and the deification of human beings are
strictly forbidden. Such religious observances as
fasting and pilgrimage are established and
defined. The Moslem legal code is founded upon
the authority of the <u>Koran</u>, and this brings the
religion into direct contact with the private citizen
and the concerns of his daily living. . . .
Mohammed is not responsible for the
contradictions and inconsistencies in the <u>Koran</u>,
for the volume was not compiled and did not
assume its present form until over twenty years
after his death. In its present state the <u>Koran</u> is, for
the major part, a jumble of hearsay through which
occasionally shines forth an example of true
inspiration."[914]

The "god," Allah, who is obviously Jehovah, since they
are both referred to as "the God of Moses," claims to be the only
God, although other "gods, deities and warners" are mentioned.[915]
Allah uses the plural term: "We;" his angels are also mentioned;
and the terms "worlds" and "heavens" are always used in the
plural. Not only is he punishing and vengeful like Jehovah, but he
also uses some of the same arrogant phrases, such as: "He helps
who he will;" and "Allah grants his authority to whom he
pleases."[916] In addition to instructing his followers not to marry,
befriend or even listen to an unbeliever, he encourages them to
fight for their cause, saying:

---

[914] The Adepts in the Eastern Esoteric Tradition, Part Four, The
Mystics of Islam, p 25; The Secret Teachings of all Ages, p cxcii.

[915] Koran; Surah 5:64; 23:91; 41:48; 43:20, 23; 34:22; 36:23;
38:4-5.

[916] Koran; Surah 2:247; 5:64; 18:211; 24:2; 30:5; 39:52.

"Fight in the cause of Allah those who fight you.
. . . And slay them wherever you catch them, and
turn them out from where they have turned you
out; for tumult and oppression are worse than
slaughter. . . . Therefore, when you meet the
unbelievers (in fight) smite at their necks; at
length, when you have thoroughly subdued them,
bind a bond firmly (on them). . . . Not equal are
those believers who sit (at home) and receive no
hurt, and those who strive and fight in the cause
of Allah with their goods and their persons. Allah
has granted a grade higher to those who strive and
fight. . . . a special reward."[917]

The Koran honors Abraham and the Biblical patriarchs
and gives full credence to the "Law of Moses," saying it was
Allah who spoke directly to Moses, but like Jesus, it teaches that
this "Law" was fulfilled.[918] The Koran says it was Allah who
"confused the people, afflicted the nations, drowned the
Egyptians" and "rained down fire and brimstone."[919] Whenever
listing the patriarchs, Ishmael, the son of Abraham by Sarah's
handmaid, Hagar, is always mentioned. Jehovah had said of
Ishmael: "I have blessed him and will make him fruitful, and will
multiply him exceedingly; twelve princes shall he beget, and I
will make him a great nation. . . . He will be a wild man; his hand
will be against every man, and every man's hand against him; and
he shall dwell in the presence of all his brethren."[920] The Bible
says Ishmael's descendants inhabited Assyria, which is presently
Saudi Arabia. Mohammed lived in Arabia. Did the Islamic people

---

[917] Koran; Surah 2:63, 190-191, 244, 255; 4:95, 144; 5:57; 9:123;
25:52; 47:4; .

[918] Koran; Surah 4:164; 5:44.

[919] Koran; Surah 5:13-14; 6:42; 11:82; 43:55.

[920] Gen. 16:12; 17:20; 21:18; 25:9, 12-18.

252

inherit Ishmael's "wild" personality?

The Koran hails Jesus as a great prophet but does not accept him as "God." It states:

> "The similitude of Jesus before Allah is as that of Adam. He created him from dust. . . . He was no more than a servant: We granted our favor to him, and We made him an example to the Children of Israel. . . . We strengthened him with the Holy Spirit . . . We sent him the gospel. They do blaspheme who say: 'God is Christ the son of Mary.' But Christ said: 'O children of Israel! worship God, my Lord and your Lord.'. . . They do blaspheme who say: God is one of three in a Trinity: for there is no God except one 'god' (Allah). . . . Christ the son of Mary was no more than a messenger."[921]

What does Allah say concerning the practice of sacrifice? The Koran reports:

> "Allah took our promise not to believe in a messenger unless he showed us a sacrifice consumed [beamed up] by fire (from heaven). . . . Whoever holds in honor the symbols of Allah, (in the sacrifice of animals), such (honor) should come truly from piety of heart. . . . To every people We appointed rites (of sacrifice), sustenance He gave them from animals (fit for food). But your God is One God (Allah): submit then your wills to Him (in Islam): and you give the good news to those who humble themselves. . . . The sacrificial camels We have made for you

---

[921] Koran; Surah 2:253; 3:55; 5:46, 72-75; 43:57-59.

as among the symbols from Allah. . . . It is not
their meat nor their blood, that reaches Allah: it is
your piety that reaches Him."[922]

EXPANSION OF THE ISLAMIC RELIGION

Unlike the Hebrews who annihilated those who were not
of their faith, Mohammed assembled an army to forcibly convert
the "infidels." Leaving a trail of blood through Europe and the
Middle East, the militant Islamics forced their way into India. But
in spite of its brutal expansion, Hall defends:

> "To ignore the heritage of culture received from
> Islam would be an unpardonable oversight, for
> when the crescent triumphed over the cross in
> Southern Europe it was the harbinger of a
> civilization which had no equal in its day. . . . The
> results of Mohammedism have been greatly
> underestimated. In the century after Mohammed's
> death it wrested Asia Minor, Africa and Spain
> from Christianity, more than half of the civilized
> world, and established a civilization, the highest
> in the world during the dark ages. It brought the
> Arabian race to their highest development."[923]

Blavatsky agrees:

> "When the Moslems overran Syria and Asia
> Minor for the first time, they were welcomed by
> the Christians of those regions as deliverers from
> the intolerable oppression of the ruling authorities
> of the church. . . . There has never been a religion

---

[922] Koran; Surah 22:32-37.
[923] The Secret Teachings of all Ages, p cxcii.

in the annals of the world with such a bloody record as Christianity. . . . Even the rapid spread of Mahometanism before the conquering sword of the Islam prophet, is a direct consequence of the bloody riots and fights among Christians. It was the war between the Nestorians and Cyrilians that engendered Islamism."[924]

But although Islam surpassed Christianity in culture and avoided the pitfalls of idolatrous paintings and statuary of the divine hierarchy, neither of them adhered to the teachings of Jesus; neither emphasized   direct contact with the "Father Within". Like other religions, Islam divided into an esoteric and an exoteric level. Mohammed himself inspired the Sufi Order, meaning Sophia or Wisdom. The Dervishes and Druses are other mystical branches of Islam.

Five hundred years after the death of Mohammed, in 1099, the Catholics (the so-called "Christian" church) began the Crusades to force the Moslems out of Jerusalem. Like the Jews, each side claimed to be under the guidance of God (Jehovah/Allah); each had been told that theirs was the "only true religion." More Machiavellian ploys; a (divine?) leader pitting one side against the other! The gruesome war, perhaps the bloodiest in history, lasted until the fall of Jerusalem and the final victory of the Moslems in 1291. Two hundred years of Genocide; dark ages indeed! Bramley states:

"When we look at the spiritual practices of the Christian knights and Moslem Ishmaelians, we discover that participation in warfare was often

---

[924]   Isis Unveiled, Vol. II, pp 28, 53-54, 81-82, 238-40, 252-253, 575. Mohammed studied with the Nestorian Monks and adopted many of their teachings. Cyril, Bishop of Alexandria, although canonized, was a murderer and a thief. It was he who had Hypatia put to death for teaching the truth about the origins of Christianity.

exalted as a spiritual quest. Warriors on both sides were inspired by corrupted brotherhood mysticisms which taught that spiritual rewards could be earned by engaging in military endeavors against fellow human beings. This was the mythology of the 'spiritually noble' war in which gallant soldiers were promised eternal salvation and a place in heaven for fighting a noble cause. . . . Societies which exalt criminal actions as a noble quest will suffer a rapid deterioration in the mental and spiritual condition of their inhabitants."[925]

Let us not repeat such a "holy" war in modern times! Jesus said: "Resist not evil; be in, but not of the world."[926] But who has followed his advice? Perhaps the Buddhists and the Taoist, who have never fought about religion, or perhaps rare individuals like Mahatma Gandhi, Nelson Mandella, and Martin Luther King. It is well to remember that while Europe was plagued by the dark ages, India, the Orient and the Americas were experiencing their cultural peak. The religions and philosophies that weren't inspired by Jehovah/Allah didn't proclaim their way to be the only way, and they certainly didn't kill those who believed differently. Spirituality was seen as an inner connection to our Divine Source.

The European dark ages extended to include the horrors of the Catholic Inquisition, which lasted for six hundred years, from the late thirteenth to the nineteenth century. During this time Europe was again besieged with "Black Death" plagues. It is believed that these plagues were once again caused by germ warfare from the "gods" that was spread by the influx of a tremendous number of "comets" which may not have actually been comets at all. The people described them as a "column of

---

[925] The Gods of Eden, Bramley, p 166.

[926] Matt. 5:39.

fire, ball of fire, cigar or beam shaped" or "a sharply pointed wooden beam." Not only were these "comets" accompanied by strange, noxious mists and a fearful stench, but also by strange devilish looking men in black. The following illustration was observed in Arabia in 1479 and published in 1557. The artist's concept, based on eyewitness testimony, looks like a rocket ship with numerous port holes.[927] Was this the "gods" way of thinning out the population?

Although the <u>Koran</u> is moralistic, forbids drinking and gambling, and coerces its followers to pray five times a day, it, like the Old Testament, is exoteric and religious rather than esoteric and spiritual, emphasizing justice rather than peace and love. Jesus taught so simply, but will mankind ever truly understand?

---

[927] This illustration was reproduced from <u>A Chronicle of Prodigies and Portents</u> by Conrad Lycosthenes, published in 1557. For further information, see: <u>Gods of Eden</u>, p 181-195, 250-251.

PART VIII

JEHOVAH GUIDES THE MORMONS

CLOSE ENCOUNTER AT AGE FOURTEEN

Just as Jehovah seemed to have given up on the Jews and the Christians in favor of the Islam, he seems to have given up all on them in favor of Mormonism, officially called "The Church of Jesus Christ of Latter-day Saints." Perhaps he finally realized that the real power was in the teachings of Jesus, and that to have diluted them in Christianity and omitted them from Islam was a grave mistake. The high point of The Book of Mormon is the teachings of Jesus, which he gave to the Hebrew tribes in America, when he visited them three days after his crucifixion. But unfortunately, many of his most valuable teachings were omitted.

How did the Hebrews get to America and how did The Book of Mormon come into existence? Mormonism started in 1820, when Joseph Smith, a fourteen year old boy, living in Manchester, New York, had an unusual visitation while he was praying alone in the woods. It is interesting that he was the same age as the virgin Mary, when the angel first appeared. He describes his close encounter:

> "I kneeled down and began to offer up the desires of my heart to God [Jehovah]. I had scarcely done so when immediately I was seized upon by some power which entirely overcame me, and had such astounding influence over me to bind my tongue so that I could not speak. Thick darkness gathered around me and it seemed to me for a time as if I were doomed to sudden destruction. But exerting all my powers to call upon God to deliver me out of the power of this enemy which had seized upon me, and at the very moment when I was ready to sink into despair and abandon myself to destruction, not to an imaginary ruin, but to the power of some actual being from the unseen

261

world who had such a marvelous power as I have never before felt in any being. Just at this moment of great alarm, I saw a pillar of light exactly over my head, above the brightness of the sun; which descended gradually until it fell upon me. It no sooner appeared that I found myself delivered from the enemy which held me bound. When the light rested upon me I saw two personages (whose brightness and glory defy all description) standing above me in the air. One of them spake unto me, calling me by name, and said, (pointing to the other,) 'This is my beloved Son, hear him.' . . . No sooner therefore did I get possession of myself, so as to be able to speak. . . . I was answered. . . . When I came to myself again I found myself lying on my back, looking up into heaven."[928]

Referring to the experience as a "vision" and a "divine manifestation," young Joseph said, "I had actually seen a light, and in the midst of that light I saw two personages, and they did in reality speak unto me, or one of them did."[929] Doesn't this brilliant "pillar of light" that hovered over his head then "fell upon" him, and the two shining personages who stood above him "in the air," sound like someone in a spacecraft projecting in a teleportation beam? Many of today's abductees describe similar experiences, especially their "being seized upon by some power" and the smothering "darkness" (forcefield) that "gathers" around them.

Three years later, in 1823, Joseph had another "close encounter." He explains:

---

[928] Times and Seasons, a newspaper in Nauvoo, IL, 1842; History of the Church of Jesus Christ of Latter-day Saints, a five volume series printed from 1839-1846 in Nauvoo, IL, chapters 1 to 6.

[929] Times and Seasons; History of the Church of Jesus Christ of Latter-day Saints.

"While I was thus in the act of calling upon God, I discovered a light appearing in the room which continued to increase until the room was lighter than at noonday, when immediately a personage appeared at my bedside standing in the air, for his feet did not touch the floor. He had on a loose robe of most exquisite whiteness. It was beyond anything earthly I had ever seen. . . . He called me by name, and said unto me that he was a messenger sent from the presence of God to me, and that his name was Moroni. That God had a work for me to do. . . . He said there was a book deposited written upon gold plates, giving an account of the former inhabitants of this continent, and the source from whence they sprang. . . . Also that there were two stones in silver bows, and these stones fastened to a breastplate constituted what is called the urim and thummim deposited with the plates; and the possession and use of these stones were what constituted Seers in ancient or former times; and that God had prepared them for the purpose of translating the book. . . . While he was conversing with me about the plates the vision was opened to my mind that I could see the place where the plates were deposited. . . . After this communication I saw the light in the room begin to gather immediately around the person of him who had been speaking to me, and it continued to do so until the room was again left dark except just around him, when instantly I saw as it were a conduit [transporter beam] open right up into heaven, and he ascended up till he entirely disappeared and the room was left as it had been before this heavenly light had made its appearance. . . . I lay musing on the singularity of the scene and marvelling greatly at what had been told me by this extraordinary messenger when in the midst of my meditation I suddenly discovered that my room was again beginning to get lighted, and in an instant, as it were, the same heavenly messenger was again by my bedside. He commenced and again related the very same things which he had done at his first visit without the least variation. . . . Again he ascended as he had done before. . . . Again I beheld the same messenger at my bedside, and heard him rehearse or reappear over again to me the same things as before. . . . After this third visit he again ascended up into heaven as before and I was again left to ponder on the strangeness of what I had just experienced, when almost immediately after the heavenly messenger had ascended from me the third time, the cock crew, and I found that day was approaching so that our interviews must have occupied the whole of that night. I shortly after arose from my bed, and . . . found my strength so exhausted as rendered me entirely unable. . . . My strength entirely failed me and I fell helpless on the ground and for a time was quite unconscious of anything. The first I can recollect was a voice speaking unto me calling me by name. I looked up and beheld the same messenger standing over my head surrounded by light as before. He then again related unto me all that he had related to me the previous night, and commanded me to go to my father and tell him of the vision and commandments which I had received."[930]

---

[930] Times and Seasons; History of the Church of Jesus Christ of Latter-day Saints.

Reminiscent of space-age technology? A brilliant being hovering in mid air, to repeat his tape-recorded holographic message over and over, then ascending into a "conduit," a teleportation beam that opened into heaven (spacecraft). Sounds like he was describing a scene on Star Trek!

Young Joseph found the plates in the hill of Cumorah and unearthed them, but was told to re-bury them, for the time was not yet right. After having visited the site every year for four years, he was finally instructed to re-excavate them in 1827. He translated them through the use of the enclosed "urim and thummim," then after showing them to three witnesses, who were ordained into the Aaronic Priesthood by a "messenger from heaven," he returned them to the angel in 1838. This entire procedure is documented and signed in the front of The Book of Mormon.

CLOSE ENCOUNTERS OF JOSEPH

WHO COMPILED THE PLATES?

How did these plates come into existence? In 597 BC, during the first year of the reign of Zedekiah, the last king of Judah, there came a "pillar of fire and dwelt upon a rock before" a Hebrew named Lehi, "and he saw and heard much."[931] Later, while he was still "overcome with the spirit, he was carried away in a vision [abducted by the spacecraft]," and "saw the heavens [mothership] open, and he thought he saw God sitting upon his throne, surrounded with numberless concourses of angels in the attitude of singing and praising their God. . . . He saw one descending out of the midst of heaven, and he beheld that his luster was above that of the sun at noon-day. And he also saw twelve others following him, and their brightness did exceed that of the stars in the firmament."[932] He was then given a book that predicted the fall of Jerusalem. After reading it and praising Jehovah, he began to prophesy to the people.[933]

The local people became angry due to his dire messages and tried to kill him. Jehovah told him in a dream to take his family and depart into the wilderness.[934] When they reached the Red Sea, they "built an altar of stones and made an offering unto the Lord.[935] Then after some of his sons were sent back to Jerusalem to retrieve the five books of Moses, the prophesies of Jeremiah and Isaiah, and several brass plates, upon which were engraved the record of the Jews and a genealogy of their forefathers, proving they were of the tribe of Joseph. They were sent back a second time to bring Ishmael and his family so Lehi's sons would have daughters to marry.[936] Too bad Jehovah didn't

---

[931] The Book of Mormon, 1 Nephi 1:4-6.

[932] 1 Nephi 1:7-10.

[933] 1 Nephi 1:11-19.

[934] 1 Nephi 1:20; 2:1-2.

[935] 1 Nephi 2:3-7.

[936] 1 Nephi, chapter 3-7.

think of Ishmael's family beforehand, for being sent back to Jerusalem from the Red Sea is quite a trip to make twice! Great shades of poor, elderly Moses having to climb up and down Mount Sinai so many times! But then Jehovah never claimed to be organized!

After the sons of Lehi married the daughters of Ishmael, they continued their journey. Nephi, in the first chapter of The Book of Mormon, explains: "And it came to pass that as my father [Lehi] arose in the morning, and went forth to the tent door, to his great astonishment he beheld upon the ground a round ball of curious workmanship; and it was of fine brass. And within the ball were two spindles; and the one pointed the way whither we should go into the wilderness."[937] More space technology!

After wandering in the wilderness for eight years, Jehovah instructed them in building a special ship that "was not made after the manner of men."[938] Does this remind you of Noah? When they arrived in the "promised land" of the Americas in 589 BC, they tilled the ground and planted. Just after that they found "beasts," including "the cow, the ox, the ass, the horse, the goat and the wild goat, swine, elephant, cureloms and cumoms." They also found gold, silver and copper."[939] Nephi, made golden plates upon which to record their travels. Centuries later Thor Heyerdahl made this same journey in a similar ship, and sure enough the currents carried him from Africa to South America, just where the ancient Hebrews had landed.

The group battled continuously and after Nephi was made king, Jehovah cursed those who rebelled against him by darkening their skin. Thus there were two races, the warring tribes of light-skinned Nephites, who kept the Law of Moses, and

---

[937] 1 Nephi 16:10, 16, 26, 30.
[938] 1 Nephi, chapter 17; 18:2.
[939] 1 Nephi 18:24-25; Ether 9:18-19.

the dark-skinned Lamanites, who became evil.[940] This creation of skin tones, like the "mark" placed upon Cain in the Old Testament, is another of Jehovah's Machiavellian ploys of pitting one group or race against another.

Around 279 BC, the Nephites discovered another group of Hebrews that Jehovah had brought across the ocean during the time Judah's King Zedekiah was carried to Babylon. The two groups united and together they deciphered an engraved stone that told of a tribe of Jeradites that had come to America at the time of the Tower of Babel thousands of years before.[941]

During the reign of King Benjamin, the people continued to sacrifice to Jehovah.[942] Many times during their wars and adventures, the Nephites and Lamanites were visited by "angels descending in clouds [spacecraft]," and "heard the voice of God [Jehovah] as great thunder [loud speakers]."[943] But even more impressive, they were visited by Jesus himself! Just after his crucifixion, the Americas experienced three hours of intense earthquakes. The Book of Mormon describes: "The whole face of the land was changed, because of the tempest and the whirlwinds and the thunderings and the lightnings, and the exceeding great quaking of the whole earth. . . . Only the righteous were spared."[944]

JESUS VISITS ANCIENT AMERICA

This frightening event was followed by three days of darkness, during which Jesus spoke to the people.[945] After the

---

[940] 2 Nephi, chapter 5; Jarom 5.

[941] Omni 13-22.

[942] Omni 23.

[943] 2 Nephi 10:3; Jacob 7:5; Mosiah 3:2; 4:1; 27:11; Alma 8:14; 10:7; 13:22, 24; 19:34; 24:14; 36:8; 38:7; Helaman 5:11, 29, 48; 12:9; 13:7; 16:14; 3 Nephi 7:15, 18; 11:3; 17:24; 19:14.

[944] 3 Nephi, chapters 8-9; 10:11-14.

[945] 3 Nephi, chapters 9-10.

darkness passed, Jesus appeared in the heavens, then descended into their midst to teach them.[946] One big difference between the Koran and The Book of Mormon is that the Koran hails Jesus as a great prophet but says he is not a divine being, while The Book of Mormon says he is synonymous with God; that they and the Holy Spirit are one.[947] Did Jehovah decide to try a new approach? Why wouldn't a space being, who was assigned only one tiny area of the earth for his inheritance, want to claim oneness with Jesus; to hitch his wagon to a star? He no doubt knew that Jesus was the real power, the "Christed" representative of the Supreme Unseen God.

When Jesus visited ancient America, according to the Book of Mormon, he appointed twelve apostles to baptize the people, then with great love and compassion for the people, repeated the "Sermon on the Mount" and other messages that are recorded in chapters five through seven of Matthew in the New Testament. He stated that although the Law of Moses was fulfilled, his covenant with the people was not yet fulfilled.[948] Calling them his "sheep," he said he had other tribes outside of Jerusalem, whose whereabouts he was not allowed to reveal.[949] He then lovingly healed the people and gave them a sacrament of bread and wine. When he ordained the disciples with the power to bestow the Holy Spirit, "many angels descended, encircled as if by fire and did minister unto them," then suddenly "a great cloud [spacecraft with a forcefield] overshadowed them and Jesus ascended into the cloud.[950]

The next day, as word spread, a great multitude came. When the disciples baptized and bestowed the Holy Spirit upon them, "they were encircled about as if it were by fire, and it came

---

[946] 3 Nephi, chapters 11-26.

[947] 3 Nephi, chapter 11; 15:5; 20:35; 28:10.

[948] 3 Nephi 15:8-9.

[949] 3 Nephi 15:12-24; 16:1-5; 17:4.

[950] 3 Nephi, chapters 17-18.

down from heaven and angels did come out of heaven and did minister unto them."[951] Jesus returned a second time and compassionately prayed for the people, fed and taught them and performed several "miracles."[952] When he was ready to leave, three people were beamed up into the mothership with him. Later, they were set back down as immortal, "sanctified" teachers.[953]

But exciting as it was, the teachings of the Old Testament, the Koran and The Book of Mormon, which foster the idea of priesthoods to act as a mediator between man and God, all fall short of the original teachings of Jesus. Jesus healed and performed "miracles" in ancient America, but although the "kingdom" was mentioned, it was not defined as being "within" as it had been in the New Testament. It was described as a place you could "inherit" after you were baptized.[954] And although stating that he and the Father are "one," it was not stated that the people were "one" with them, or that he was the "door" by which they could reach the "Father Within." The words of Jesus were beautiful and loving, but emphasized more of the outer rituals than the esoteric mysteries. Jesus may have taught more that was reserved only for the disciples and their students, or Jehovah could have manipulated the people who were recording the history, or even Joseph Smith, who later did the translating, to omit them. It would certainly go along with his manipulating personality to have somehow prevented the transcription of the deeper esoteric teachings of Jesus that would have by-passed the limiting priesthoods and led them to direct contact with the supreme "Father".

After being visited by Jesus, the Nephites and Lamanites experienced two hundred years of peace, but gradually began to war amongst themselves. Eventually the Lamanites killed the

---

[951] 3 Nephi, chapter 19.

[952] 3 Nephi 19:15-36; chapters 20-28.

[953] 3 Nephi 28:13-40.

[954] 3 Nephi 11:33.

Nephites. One of the last holy men, Moroni, in 421 AD, buried the records of their history in the hill of Cumorah in New York, where the fourteen-year-old Joseph was guided to find them fourteen hundred years later.

The Book of Mormon is filled with descriptions of great cities, cement roads and houses; descriptions of ancient America that the young Joseph, could not have known about. In the 1830's, cement roads had not yet been discovered or reported to exist in South America. The Book of Mormon, therefore, seems to be a valid account--at least as valid as the Bible and the Koran. Joseph did not stand to gain anything by perpetuating a fraud. On the contrary, he was harassed continually and finally killed. Those who continued the religion were run out of town and suffered untold hardships in the Utah desert, where they lived isolated from the rest of the country for many years.

Joseph Smith, like Moses, King David, Mohammed and many others before him, was hard working, faithful and obedient to Jehovah. Any of these great men would have gladly laid down their life for their cause. The fact that the Jewish, Christian and Islamic religions turned out to be so militant is not the fault of these wonderful leaders. And it is certainly not the fault of Jesus!

Of the four Jehovistic religions, Mormonism has the purest morals, history and diet. Although they have missionaries, they have not sent out an army to harass all who will not join them, they don't sacrifice animals, and they certainly have not practiced any acts of genocide or sponsored Crusades or Inquisitions! But if their members begin to receive their own messages from divine beings, instead of adhering to the messages of their appointed prophet, they may be excommunicated! By-passing their priesthoods to go directly to God, is forbidden! Entering the "kingdom within" is evidently not their goal!

It is interesting that during the lifetime of Joseph Smith, around the 1830's, the prophet Baha'u'lla (Allah) was active in Iran. Thus Jehovah was still fanning the flames between the Jews and Arabs. During the same time slot, another group was founded in America. Ironically they called themselves: Jehovah's

Witnesses. Hopefully the spiritual philosophy of the impending "Golden Age of Peace" will surpass these Jehovistic religions to emphasize oneness and the "kingdom within," the true mystical enlightenment of Christ Consciousness!

PART IX

SUMMARY

SUMMARY

While writing this book, I was concerned about its effect on the readers; concerned that it might cause others to lose their anchor and be tossed about in a sea of confusion. I questioned whether or not the public is ready for the truth about the religion/ET connection. Filled with love and compassion for others, it is not my intention to sway anyone from their faith. If you are in a group that's helping you, stay there! It's not a matter of right or wrong groups, religions, or philosophies; they are only different vibrations. Each group is like a grade in school. If you have a greater understanding, say you are vibrating at a tenth-grade level, you are not going to feel comfortable with a kindergarten group. But this does not mean the lower level is wrong. Their beliefs are at their own level of acceptance. To tell them differently--to "cast your pearls"--would merely upset rather than help them. Every individual needs to find a group that gives him/her a sense of belonging. You are free to seek God in your own way; grant others the freedom to do likewise.

It's not my intention to intellectualize God or to create atheism. Learning that some of the ancient "gods" are ETs does not mean there is no God. Our esoteric Divine Source was merely misrepresented, allowing religion and dogma to become a substitute for true spirituality. There is a God! This Divine Energy, our Source, is your Heavenly Father, with whom you can contact and unite. Trust your feelings, for it is your heart that basks in the presence of divinity. Subdue the masculine aspect of intellect long enough to allow your feminine intuition to feel this inner connection.

While seeking guidance, I was given three meaningful dreams. I share them with you to offer another way of looking at divinity.

DREAM #1:

I had just bought a new mobile home that had many windows. (Home represents consciousness; windows represent insight). It was delivered to a lot with a beautiful view, but when I went inside, I found the view blocked by a huge fence that the neighbors had built. I was in a dilemma. Knowing I couldn't remove their fence, I thought of taking out one wall, so there would be a front view, but I knew this would weaken the bearing wall. While contemplating, I was told inwardly: "There are two ways to remedy the situation: 1) Teach your neighbors they don't need a material fence; that they can have an etheric 'Wall of Light;' or 2) put your house on a higher foundation (come up higher in your consciousness) and look over the top of the fence." At this point I realized the dream referred to revealing the truth about Jehovah. I don't want to destroy (tear down) the religious beliefs (fences) of others, yet I know the importance of informing them of the higher truth, 'lest they continue to be duped by the manipulating forces. I sincerely hope and pray that I have "come up high enough in consciousness" to present this book effectively without destroying anyone's sense of love and faith in their Divine Source. To me, God, my inner presence, who is my constant companion, is very real.

DREAM #2:

I had built a large, sprawling house on either side of and including what seemed to be an old abandoned railroad track. After the house was furnished and decorated, a huge, streamlined train came roaring down the tracks, ramming through one side of my house and whizzing out through the other. Seeing that the magnificent, shining train was labeled "Omnipotent," I was thrilled by the sight of it, but was devastated that it had destroyed a portion of my house (state of consciousness). Believing it was the train's fault, I contacted the (divine) workers of the "Omnipotent Company" and asked them to repair my home; to rebuild it over the tracks. But they refused, explaining that the unpredictable train might utilize the tracks again. They suggested bulldozing an area beyond the right side of the tracks to extend the existing house, then closing up the portions that had been damaged, thus forming two houses, one on each side of the track. I agreed, but when the bulldozer pushed its way through my house, it destroyed the furniture and decorations. When I complained, they said, you can't expand your house (consciousness) without removing your previous furnishings (attitudes and concepts). They built the new extension and labeled it "Eastern Religions." They named the remaining house on the left side of the tracks, "Western Religions," then stated firmly: "Although the great and powerful train, 'Omnipotent,' visits everywhere to spread its essence, it cannot be captured or held within an individual house or area. It's essence can only be felt. The tracks must remain clear!" Hearing this, I suddenly realized the dynamity of having had this powerful Force pass through my house (consciousness). I had been filled with a divine force comparable to electricity, something we can plug in to and gradually absorb, yet a force that no individual, religion or philosophy can capture. A house with walls (a state of consciousness with fixed concepts) doesn't allow this attunement. We need to keep an open, ever-expanding, mind; to see truth on both sides of the track. No wonder Jesus generally taught outdoors, free from the confines of limited thinking. Our church is Mother Earth; its roof, Father Sky.

DREAM #3:

A group of us were in a classroom when we heard a whirling sound. We ran to the window and saw a magnificent, shimmering white spacecraft hovering above us. It was nearly as bright as the sun! We watched as it descended, straight down. As it neared the ground, four legs emerged, a ladder ejected and four brilliantly-shining beings stepped out. Tall and thin, they were wearing loose-fitting white silken garments that glistened in the light. They seemed to be men, but were so angelic looking it was hard to distinguish their gender. Almost too brilliant to look at, their vibration was so high it made us feel dizzy. As they stood on the ground, they announced, "We have come to initiate four people." They called out four names; mine was one of them. I watched as they initiated the first three people. As they lovingly passed their hands over them, I saw an array of sparkling lights. When each of them walked past me, they were nearly as dazzling as the space beings. When it was my turn, the emanation of love from the visitors, as they passed their hands over my body, was overpowering. They didn't talk to me directly, but discussed my needs. When they came to one portion of my head, they said, "She needs a little more energy here." It felt electrifying as they waved their hands over the spot. When they had finished, they added: "She still has some attitudes that are blocking the flow, but she has worked her way through them to the degree that they can be removed." At that point I felt a great rush of energy like a strong electrical current; I thought I was going to levitate. When they finished, they said directly to me: "You are now empowered." It felt like I was floating as I walked away. The essence of the dream remained with me for the next couple of weeks, during which I felt an intense heat (shakti) surging through me and was totally engulfed in a radiance of love and bliss. I had no doubt that these "ETs" were the positive angels, the "Christ Forces in Space."

Raise your consciousness to see a greater truth. Don't try to capture God within your own religious walls (concepts); the only wall you need is "Light." Realize that God is Omnipotent--in all things simultaneously. When you inwardly contact your Divine Source, your old attitudes and concepts will expand, for it is the "Christ Forces in Space," the inner space within your heart, the "kingdom within," that empowers you.

A SPIRITUAL MESSAGE FROM GLENN JOHNSON:

Another interesting explanation of "God" was given to me

by an elderly gentleman, Glenn Johnson, who has for the past twenty-five years been receiving messages from a being named "Moses" (not the Biblical Moses, but a being who resides in the higher realms).[955] After asking Glenn a complex question, he gave me the following written message:

> "Dorothy has a question she would like to ask. Would you, Moses, answer a question for her? *This is Moses speaking. I will answer the question Dorothy would like to ask.*
>
> Is Jehovah, the being who appeared to Moses at Mt. Sinai, a God, or the 'Highest God,' or is he merely an ET who traveled in a spacecraft? Is Jehovah the 'Father Within,' who Jesus referred to as God, or is the 'Father' a higher being?
>
> *I thought you could ask some complex questions but Dorothy has you beat. We, spirit beings of the higher levels of consciousness, do not use names except when we communicate to incarnated human beings. Names originating in the physical level living on the earth relate to concepts of the earth. I use the name Moses so you, who live in the physical state, will know who you are communicating with. In my spiritual state I do not have a name. Our Creator who has been referred to as Jehovah, God, or many other names, does not use a name to identify himself. Our God is our Creator who created all human*

---

[955] Glenn Johnson's messages have been compiled, edited and published in a series entitled <u>Messages From Beyond</u> and <u>Sir George, the Ghost of Nyack,</u> by Bill Merrill of Deer Publishing Co., Beaverton, OR, 1993 and 1995. Merrill is currently publishing more of Glenn's messages in <u>The Creating Intelligence Theory</u> and <u>Go To The Light</u>, The Moses Group, Beaverton, OR, 1999.

beings and the spiritual structure within which all spiritual human beings exist. There are many Creators. It would be difficult to say one is above or below another. Our Creator was not the beginning of intelligence. He was the beginning of all human life, spiritual and physical.

Our Creator was created by an intelligence that was before him. He, in turn, was created by an intelligence that was before him. The being who appeared to the Biblical Moses was not our God but a high level human spiritual being. It could have been assumed that it was God who was speaking because the words were God's words, but they were only words conveyed by a messenger. Many times in the past messengers of God have been considered God. They might be considered as Gods or Lesser Gods but that is not true. God seldom speaks to physical human beings. He speaks to high level spiritual beings who in turn speak for him.

Our God does not need a spacecraft to travel from place to place. He travels through the energy frequencies and may be in several places at the same time. I, Moses, can travel through the frequencies but I cannot travel as far as our God can travel. I generally do not communicate directly to our God. I communicate through a higher human spiritual being who is one of a few who communicate directly to our God. I speak his words for him as I speak for many other intelligences who would like to have their words heard by physical human beings. We have made an exception for you, Glenn, by arranging for you to communicate directly to intelligences that normally would not communicate to physical human beings.

How am I to know that you, Moses, speak for our God? All I have is your word.

I am he. Moses is a spokesman for me. I am your Creator. Believe what Moses tells you for he is my messenger. Listen to him carefully.

How do I know you to be my Creator? How can I tell you from Moses?

You have my word.

Can you, Moses, tell me more about the communication I just received?

You have the word of our Creator. He has said that I am his messenger. There are so many messages that exist in the physical world, many of which have been modified, that it will become a difficult job to find the truth. The truth will repeat itself over and over again. Many false words have been attached to words of truth for reasons of the various authors. Do not believe any one source or believe that any one person has all the truth. You have overstayed your time. You must return to your energy frequency now!

(The words from our Creator were written in large letters and seemed to come through with a tremendous burst of energy. Later I had trouble relaxing. It was about twelve hours before I felt normal again. In reading the words from our Creator later I could feel a surge of energy pass through my body. Glenn Johnson)"

Needless to say, I was intrigued and uplifted by his message, and will never forget the blaze of light that shot through me when I first read the words *"I am he."*

Barbara Marciniak's message, as quoted in the introduction, is well worth repeating: "The original planners . . .

intend to alter the frequency of earth to that of love. . . . to reinsert light on this planet and restore earth."[956] My dreams and Glenn Johnson's message assured us that they are already doing so on an individual basis.

In our age of cloning, quantum physics and holographic images, there is a great need to reexamine the ancient writings. We need to rise above blind adoration and seek the truth. Because extraterrestrials have molded our cultures and are the basis of most of our religions, it is imperative that we finally turn from the material, exoteric world to find the spiritual, esoteric "Father Within."

I am grateful to have been one of the messengers of this intriguing field of mysticism. May you enter the "kingdom within" and be filled with the "omnipotent" love and light of our Divine Source, the Heavenly Father, whose divine spark resides within you. "Be still and know," listen for the words, *"I am he,"* for "the truth shall make you free (John 8:32)."

---

[956] Bringers of the Dawn, Barbara Marciniak, pp 4, 6, 14-18.

BIBLIOGRAPHY

Akhenaten, *Unto Thee I Grant*, CA, AMMORC, 1925.

Allegro, John M. *The Dead Sea Scrolls*, Penguin, Harmondsworth, England, 1964.

Allen, J. M., *Atlantis: The Andes Solution*, Saint Martin's Press, VA, 1999.

Amarushka and Joshua, *The Solar Cross 11:11 Stargate*, Ministry of the Children, AZ, 1998.

Baigent, Michael, Leigh, Richard and Lincoln, Henry, *Holy Blood Holy Grail*, NY, Dell Publishing, 1983.

Baigent, Michael and Leigh, Richard, *The Dead Sea Scrolls Deception*, Corgi, London, England, 1992.

Baker, J. A., *The Development of Christian Doctrine Before the Council of Nicaea*, London, England, 1964.

Bergier, Jacques, *Extraterrestrial Visitations from Prehistoric Times to the Present*, Henry Regnery Company, IL, 1973.

Berlitz, Charles, *Atlantis, the Eighth Continent*, G. P. Putnam's Sons, NY, 1984.

Blavatsky, H. P., *The Secret Doctrine*, Vol. I and II, Theosophical Publishing CO., NY, 1888.

Blavatsky, H. P., *Isis Unveiled*, Vol. I and II, Theosophical University Press, CA, 1976.

Bloomfield, *The Religion of the Veda, The Ancient Religion of India*, AMS Press, NY, 1969.

Blumrich, Josef F., *The Spaceships of Ezekiel*, Bantam, NY, 1974.

Bock, Janet, *The Jesus Mystery*, Aura Books, CA, 1982.

The Book of Mormon, The Church of Jesus Christ of Latter-day Saints, NY, 1830.

Borysenko, Joan, *Seven Paths to God*, Hay House, Inc. CA, 1997.

Bramley, William, *The Gods of Eden*, Avon Books, NY, 1993.

Brandon, S. G. F., *The Formation of Christian Dogma*, NY, 1957.

Brett, Gilbert James, *The Bible in Alphabet*, Consolidated Book Publishers, IL, 1947.

Brown, Courtney, *Cosmic Voyage*, Dutton Books, NY, 1996.

Bucke, Richard Maurice, *Cosmic Consciousness*, E. P. Dutton & Co., NY, 1901.

Burrows, Millar, *More Light on the Dead Sea Scrolls*, The Viking Press, NY, 1958.

Charles, R. H., *The Book of Enoch*, Oxford Clarendon Press, 1912.

Charlesworth, James H., *Jesus and the Dead Sea Scrolls*, Doubleday, NY, 1992.

Charroux, Robert, *Forgotten Worlds*, Popular Library, NY, 1973.

Church, W. H. *Edgar Cayce's Story of the Soul*, A.R.E. Press, Virginia Beach, VA, 1971.

Danielou, Jean, *The Dead Sea Scrolls and Primitive Christianity*, New American Library, MY, 1962.

Donnelly, Ignatuis, *Atlantis: The Antediluvian World*, Harper & Bros., 1949.

Doreal (translator), *The Emerald Tablets of Thoth The Atlantean*, available through Source Books, P.O. Box 29231, Nashville, TN 37229.

Downing, Barry H., *The Bible and Flying Saucers*, Marlowe & Co., NY, 1998.

Drake, Raymond W., *Gods and Spacemen in the Ancient East*, Signet Book, The New American Library, Inc., NY, 1973.

Dupont-Sommer, Andre, *The Essene Writings from Qumran*, Oxford, 1961.

Dutt, Romesh, *Ramayana and the Mahabharata*, London, Dent, 1961.

Eastman, Charles Alexander, *The Soul of the Indian*, Houghton Mifflin, MA, 1911.

Eisenman, Robert, *James the Brother of Jesus*, Faber & Faber, London England, 1997.

Essene, Virginia and Nidle, Sheldon, *Becoming a Galactic Human*, S. E. E. Publishing Co., CA, 1994.

Faber-Kaiser, Andraeus, *Jesus Died in Kashmir*, Abacus/Sphere, London, England, 1978.

Filliette, Edith, *Saint Mary Magdalene, Her Life and Times*, Society of St. Mary Magdalene, Newton Lower Falls, MA, 1983.

Fowler, James W., *Stages of Faith: The Psychology of Human Development and the Quest for Meaning*, Viking Press, NY, 1981.

Frissell, Bob, *Nothing in This Book is True, But it's Exactly How Things Are*, Frog, Ltd., Berkeley, CA, 1994.

Gardner, Laurence, *Bloodline of the Holy Grail*, Element Books Ltd., Barnes & Noble Books, NY, 1996.

The Gilgamesh Epic and Old Testament Parallels, University of Chicago, IL 1946

Goetz, Delia and Morley, *Popul Vuh, The Sacred Book of the*

Ancient Quiche Maya, Norman University of Oklahoma Press, OK, 1950.

Halevi, Z'ev ben Shimon, *An Introduction to the Cabala*, Samuel Weiser, Inc., NY, 1972.

Hall, Manly P., *The Secret Teachings of all Ages*, The Philosophical Research Society, CA, 1977.

Hall, Manly P., *The Adepts in the Eastern Esoteric Tradition*, Part IV, The Mystics of Islam, The Philosophical Research Society, CA, 1975.

Hill, Paul R., *Unconventional Flying Objects*, Hampton Roads Publishing Co, Inc., VA, 1995.

Hoagland, Richard C., *The Monuments of Mars: A City on the Edge of Forever*, North Atlantic Books, CA, 1987.

Hurtak, Dr. J. J., *The Keys of Enoch*, The Academy For Future Science, CA, 1977.

James, M. R., *The Apocryphal New Testament*, Oxford University Press, London, England, 1975.

James, William, *The Varieties of Religious Experience*, NAL, Reprint Services Corp., 1902.

Johnson, Paul, *History of Christianity*, Penguin, London, England, 1978.

Josephus, *Brief Historical Summary of the Interval Between the Old and New Testaments*, from the *Book of Maccabees* and *Teachers Edition of the Holy Bible*, Oxford University Press, NY, 1860.

Joyce, Donovan, *The Jesus Scroll*, Angus & Robertson, London, England, 1973.

Keating, *Open Mind, Open Heart*, Continuum, 1994.

Kingsland, William, *Christs, the Religion of the Future*, John M. Watkins, London, England, 1929.

Kolosimo, Peter, *Not of This World*, University Books, NJ, 1971.

Krapf, Philip, *The Contact Has Begun*, Hay House, CA, 1998.

Krajenke, Robert W., *Edgar Cayce's Story of the Old Testament*, Bantam Books, Inc., NY, 1974.

Lambert, W. G., and Millard, A. R., *Atra-Hasis, The Babylonian Story of the Flood*, Oxford Clarendon Press, 1969.

Levi, *The Aquarian Gospel of Jesus the Christ*, DeVorss & Co. Publishers, CA, 1972.

Lewels, Joe, *The God Hypothesis*, Wild Flower Press, NC, 1997.

Lockhart, Douglas, *Jesus the Heretic*, Element, Shaftesbury, 1997.

Marciniak, Barbara, *Bringers of the Dawn: Teachings from the Pleiadians*, Bear & Co., NM, 1992.

Marciniak, Barbara, *Earth: Pleiadian Keys to the Living Library*. Bear & Co., NM, 1995.

Marciniak, Barbara, *Family of Light: Pleiadian Tales and Lessons in Living*. Bear & Co., 1999.

Mayotte, Ricky Alan, *The Complete Jesus*, Steerforth Press, VT, 1997.

Mead, G. R. S., *The Gnostic John the Baptiser*, John M. Watkins, London, England, 1924.

Melchizedek, Drunvalo, *Ancient Secret of the Flower of Life*, Vol. I and II, Light Tech Publications, 2000.

Merrill, Bill, *Messages From Beyond*, messages of Glenn Johnson, Deer Publishing Co., OR, 1993.

Merrill, Bill, *Sir George, the Ghost of Nyack*, messages of Glenn Johnson, Deer Publishing Co., OR, 1995.

Merrill, Bill, *The Creating Intelligence Theory*, messages of Glenn Johnson, The Moses Group, OR, 1999.

Merrill, Bill, *Go To The Light*, messages of Glenn Johnson, The Moses Group, OR, 1999.

Nelson, Ralph, *Popul Vuh*, Houghton, MS, 1976.

Potter, Charles Francis, *The Lost Years of Jesus Revealed*, Fawcett Publications, Inc., CT, 1962.

Prabhupada, Swami, *Srimad Bhagavatam, Seventh Canto*, The Bhaktivedanta Book Trust, NY, 1976.

Prabhavananda, Swami, and Isherwood, Christopher, *The Song of God: Bhagavad Gita*, Phoenix House, London, England, 1953.

Ravenscroft, Trevor, *The Spear of Destiny*, Samuel Weiser, Inc. ME, 1982.

Robinson, James M., *The Nag Hammadi Library*, Harper/Collins, CA, 1990.

Roy, Pratap Chandra, *Mahabharata*. Bharata Press, 1884.

Rushdie, Salman, *The Satanic Verses*, Viking Penguin Inc., NY, 1989.

Rux, Bruce, *Architects of the Underworld*, Frog, Ltd., Berkeley, CA, 1996.

Sanders, *The Epic of Gilgamesh*, Penguin, MD, 1960.

Schechter, Sylvia Moss, *The Letters of Paul*, Triad Publishing, OR, 1989.

Schellhorn, G. Cope, *Extraterrestrials in Biblical Prophecy*, Horus House Press, Inc. WI, 1990.

Schonfield, Hugh J., *The Essene Odyssey*, Element Books,

Shaftesbury, 1984.

Schure, Edouard, *From Sphinx to Christ*, English translation of *L'Evolution Divine*, by Eva Martin, printed in Great Britain; reprinted by David McKay Company, Philadelphia, PA, 1920

Sendy, Jean, *The Coming of the Gods*, Berkeley,, NY, 1973.

Sendy, Jean, *The Moon: Outpost of the Gods*, Berkeley, NY, 1975.

Sendy, Jean, *Those Gods Who Made Heaven and Earth, Berkeley*, NY, 1972.

Shanks, Hershel, *The Mystery and Meaning of the Dead Sea Scrolls*, Random House, NY, 1998.

Sitchin, Zechariah, *The Twelfth Planet*, Avon Books, NY, 1976.

Sitchin, Zechariah, *Divine Encounters*, Avon, NY, 1996.

Sitchin, Zechariah, *Genesis Revisited*, Avon, NY, 1990.

Sitchin, Zechariah, *The Lost Realms*, Avon, NY, 1990.

Sitchin, Zechariah, *The Stairway to Heaven*, Avon Books, Inc., NY, 1980.

Sitchin, Zechariah, *The Wars of Gods and Men*, Bear & Co., NM, 1992.

Sitchin, Zechariah, *When Time Began*, Avon, NY, 1999.

Smith, Joseph, *Times and Seasons*, a newspaper in Nauvoo, IL, 1842; *History of the Church of Jesus Christ of Latter-day Saints*, Vol. 1, chapters 1 to 6, IL, 1839-1846.

Smith, Morton, *The Secret Gospel*, The Dawn Horse Press, CA, 1960.

Sora, Steven, *The Lost Treasure of the Knight Templar*, Destiny Books, VT, 1999.

Spence, Lewis, *The History of Atlantis*, 1926.

Stacy-Judd, Robert B., *Atlantis Mother of Empires*, Adventures Unlimited Press, IL, 1999.

Starr, Jelaila, *We Are the Nibiruans*, Granite Publishing, NC, 1999.

Steiner, Rudolf, *Lucifer and Ahriman*, Steiner Book Center, Inc., England, 1976.

Steiner, Rudolf, *Mystic Seals and Columns*, Health Research, CA, 1969.

Steiner, Rudolf, *Christ in Relation to Lucifer and Ahriman*, 1915, reprinted by Anthrosophical Press, NY, 1975.

Steiner, Rudolf, *The Ahrimanic Deception*, 1917, reprinted by Anthrosophical Press, NY, 1985.

Steiner, Rudolf, *An Occult Outline of Science*, Anthrosophical Press, NY, 1972.

Temple, Robert, *The Sirius Mystery*, Destiny Books, VT, 1976.

Thompson, R. C., *The Epic of Gilgamesh*, London, Luzac, 1928.

Tomas, Andrew, *We Are Not the First,* G. P. Putnam's Sons, NY, 1971

The Urantia Book, The Urantia Foundation, IL, 1955..

Van Nelsing, Jan, *Secret Societies and Their Power in the Twentieth Century*, Ewertverlag, Spain, 1995.

Vermes, Geza, *The Dead Sea Scrolls in English*, Pelican, Harmondsworth, England, 1987.

Villars, Abbe N. De Montfaucon De, *Comte De Gabalis*, The Brothers, London, 1670.

Von Daniken, Erich, *Arrival of the Gods*, Penguin Putnam, NY, 1998.

Von Daniken, Erich, *Chariots of the Gods*, Berkeley, CA, 1999.

Von Daniken, Erich, *Odyssey of the Gods*, Penguin Putnam, NY, 2000.

Von Daniken, Erich, *The Return of the Gods*, Penguin Putnam, NY, 1997.

Wallace-Murphy, Tim and Hopkins, Marilyn, *Rosslyn*, Element, MA, 2000.

Walter, Benjamin, *Gnosticism*, Aquarian Press, Wellingborough, England, 1983.

Whishaw, E. M., *Atlantis in Spain,* Rider & Co., London, 1928.

Puranic and Vedic Texts
Mahabharata
Ramayana
Samaragansutradhara
Atri-Hasis
Dronaparua
Bhagavad Gita
Book of Dzyan
Zend Avesta
Catholic Holy Bible
Dead Sea Scrolls
Gospel of Love
Gospel of Peace
Secret Gospel of Mark
Emerald Tablets
Holy Bible, King James version.
Kabala
Koran
Kerygmata Petrou
Nag Hammadi Codices

Popul Vuh
Septuagint
Talmud.
The Babylonian Epic of Creation
The Sumerian Texts
The Lost Books of the Bible
The Forgotten Books of Eden

K

Karma/Karmic Board - 13, 88, 195, 208.
Kumaras (also see Sanat Kumara) - 7.
Kundalini, serpent force (also see Holy Spirit and serpent/knowledge) - 19, 26.

L

Languages/ancient writings - v, 161-163, 165, 235.
Ley lines - v.
Liberty/Libertine Movement - 193, 208, 212, 216, 220-221.
Light:
    Children of - 53, 193, 207, 232.
    City of - 30, 44, 82, 90-91.
    Sons of - 7, 43.
    Wall of -276.
Love:
    Cosmos of Love - 239-40.
    Power of - viii, 52, 59, 87, 90, 211, 218, 238-241, 275-276, 278, 282.
    To be restored on Earth - ii, 282.
Lucifer/ Satan/Devil/Prince of Air/Adversary/tempter/Anti-Christ (also see Ahriman) - ii, vii, 5-6, 12, 27-28, 31-32, 44, 51-52, 174, 191, 233.

M

Magic - 15, 96-97, 122, 141, 234, 240.
Maitreya (also see Jesus, overshadowed by)- 78, 194.
Mana/divine connecting threads - 18.
Manna - 2, 53, 108, 113, 131, 136, 145, 204-206
Mary Magdalene (also see reincarnation of Bathsheba) - 223-234.
Marduk, Sumerian god - 29-32, 167.
Meditation: 18, 197, 200-201, 212, 239, 264.
    Bliss/Samadhi/Nirvana - 18, 181.
    Fourth Dimensional -18.
    Silence - 91, 198, 282.
    Yogic/Zen - 18, 213.
Melchizedek/Order of (also see Jesus) - vi, 36-37, 92, 95, 140, 156, 167, 172, 192, 216.
Merkabah Vehicle (also see Mothership) - 7, 52, 78, 92, 188.
Miracles/technological - 3, 78, 154, 156, 159, 191, 233-234.
Mohammed - 51, 159, 173, 236-237, 245-247, 271.
    Allah same as Jehovah - 245-251.
    Archangel Gabriel visited - 245-246.
    Some Bible prophecies refer to him - 249.
    Visited Seven Heavens (also see spacecraft) - 246-247.
Moses abducted by reptilian god - 14, 142.
Mother Earth - 19, 209-211, 277.
Mother God/Divine
Mother/Goddess/"She"/Wisdom (also see Holy Spirit) - 19, 21, 26, 54, 92, 160, 181, 194, 224, 237.

Mothership (also see Spacecraft, Etheric Temple, Merkabah Vehicle, New Jerusalem, Illiyum, Seraphic Transport, and Zion) - vii, 2, 7, 17, 72, 81-84, 87-90, 124, 172, 175, 177, 246, 266, 270.
Music used to move massive stones (also see sound waves) - iv.
Mysteries (secret/esoteric/occult) guarded (also see Wisdom Teachings) - 38-39, 87, 95, 112, 114, 122, 169, 181, 190, 196-199, 213, 214, 216, 218, 221, 223, 233, 235-236, 238, 255, 257, 270, 275, 282.
Mystery schools/School of Prophets - 28-29, 39, 95, 115, 163, 190, 197, 213, 216, 237, 245, 255.
Mystical marriage - 19, 92, 230.
Mystical union/mind born/mysticism (also see meditation) - i, 9, 18-19, 21, 34, 38, 91-91, 142, 181, 199, 215, 219, 221-222, 229, 231, 238, 240, 270, 274-275, 282.

N

Nefilim/Nephilim/"giants" - ii, 3, 12, 28-31, 47, 88.
New Age (see Age)
New Jerusalem - 17, 90.

O

Oneness - 196-197, 200, 207-210, 212, 274.
Oracles (see Communication Devices and Chambers)
Other gods (also see Jehovah, only one god among many) - 1-2, 35-36, 40-41, 51, 58, 85, 103, 136-137, 140, 146, 150-151, 160-161, 164, 167, 168, 171-173, 249, 251.

P

Paul - 18, 32, 34, 38-39, 44, 51, 59, 78, 84, 87, 89-90, 96, 122, 139, 187, 190-191, 199-200, 204, 209, 212, 217-223, 228-231, 238.
Peace:
    Age of - viii, 19, 30, 89, 209, 237, 274.
    Covenant of - 139.
    "Peace that passeth understanding" - 17
    Salem means/Jerusalem means foundation of - 37, 148.
Peter - 38, 191, 218-223, 227-230.
Peter/Paul controversy - 218-223.
Philosophies/traditions - i, 26, 60, 86, 140, 152, 165, 167, 186, 189, 192, 202-203, 206, 208-209, 214-216, 222, 234, 239, 245, 247, 256, 274-275, 277.
Priests/Priesthoods:
    Aaron and sons - 115.
    Ate remnants of sacrifices - 56, 100, 127.
    By-pass to go directly to God - 9, 78, 167, 194, 230, 232, 270.
    Catholic - 2, 233-234
    Conduct rituals/sacrifices.give
readings/transported ark and tabernacle - 55, 118, 120-122, 124, 128, 137, 145, 148, 150, 152, 164-165, 177, 185, 193-194, 203, 206.

Egyptian performed magic - 97.
Garments for - 105, 116, 118, 137.
Greeks were against - 167.
Had to be Levite - 152.
Jehovistic/patriarchal - 9, 19.
Jesus against priesthoods - 9, 187, 214.
Jesus not of priestly line - 178.
Joseph Smith/Aaronic Priesthood - 270.
Martin Luther rebelled against - 237.
Odin, Druid priest - 168.
Order of Melchizedek, higher than Levitical and
Aaronic - 9, 37.
Overpowered by Pharisees, Scribes and Lawyers
- 187.
Polluted/corrupted - i, 9, 160, 165, 181, 186,
217, 232, 255.
Prepared food for Jehovah - 108.
Raised Samuel - 152.
Sethite, higher order - 37, 164.
Zadok, higher order/Ezra/Ezekiel/Jeshua - 158,
172, 174, 178-180, 192.
Prometheus (see Enlil, Enki) - 4, 6, 10, 29.
Pyramid:
Aligned to Orion - iii, v, 163.
Built around 10,500 BC - iii, 20, 163, 165,
227.
Initiation chamber - iv, 91, 112, 197.
Texts - iv.
Wars - iv, 31.

Q

Quickening - iv, 19, 91, 197.

R

Reincarnation - vi, 7, 12, 36-37, 47, 86, 99,
158, 172, 178, 189, 191-194, 197, 213, 219,
230, 237.
Reincarnation of Bathsheba as Mary Magdalene-
149, 223.
Reincarnation of David - vi, 208, 219, 225.
Reincarnations of Jesus - vi, 7, 10, 36-37, 156,
172, 178, 189, 192-193, 198, 207-208, 215,
219, 223, 225, 229, 237.
Reincarnation of John, the Baptist - 128, 156,
193-194.
Reincarnation of John, the Beloved - 229.
Reincarnation of Moses - 99.
Reincarnation of Paul - 219, 223.
Reincarnation of Peter - 219.
Religion/binding/based on dogma/Luciferic
fanaticism - i, vii, 5-6.
Four Jehovistic religions - 271-272.
Renunciation - iv.

S

Sacrifices (also see Jehovah and Priests):
Beamed up - 55
Used to feed Jehovah, ETs and Levites - vii, 1,
53-54.
Saints/Watchers/Warners/mediators of wisdom -
ii, vii, 19, 85-89, 124, 165, 237, 248.
Sanat Kumara;"Lord of the World"/"Ancient of

Days" - 7.
Science/philosophy/spirit blend - iv, 1, 5, 79,
217, 234, 240.
Self Realization - 11, 197, 231.
Seraphic Transport - iii, 51, 79, 92, 215.
Serpent/knowledge (see Brotherhood of the Snake,
Enki, Prometheus, and Kundalini) - 4, 6, 10, 26-
28, 122.
Lower serpentine energy - 10, 209, 215.
Technological/intellectual knowledge - 209.
Smith, Joseph - 32, 261-263, 270-271.
Sound waves - iv, 112.
Spacecraft: (also see Mothership)
Abode of gods - 81-85.
Abductions - 14, 16, 77, 85, 142, 154, 160,
262, 266..
Ancients thought craft was a being - 69-71, 75.
Brass - 82.
Capsule - 4, 29.
Chariots - ii, 3, 64-65, 68-69, 75, 80-82, 94,
99, 154, 164.
Circle of fire - ii, 3, 269.
Clouds - ii, iii, 63-64, 72, 81.
Comets - 256.
Doors/windows/portholes - ii, 65, 72, 87, 99,
177.
Eagles - 18, 75.
Effect on humans and Earth - 66, 68, 75-77,
81, 175, 268.
Evidence of - iii, iv, v.
Fiery/"consuming, devouring fire" - ii-iii, 45,
48, 55, 63, 66-69, 72-75, 79, 95, 98-99, 108,
123, 128, 132, 154, 174-176, 195, 207-208,
236, 247, 252-253, 256, 266, 269.
Flying boats - 165.
Forcefield around - 1, 63, 108, 262, 269.
For the gods, not man - 49-50.
Landings and takeoffs - 30.
Landing legs - 51, 70.
Laser beams - ii, iv, 4, 73, 76, 122, 133, 164.
Legion ship - 72.
Lift off/"rapture" - 16, 87, 91, 187.
Mass landing predicted - ii, vii, 17-18
Modern museums and airports for - 77.
Multi-storied - 104.
Nuclear-like explosions from - 73-74.
Pillars - ii, 72, 75, 98-99.
Radiation from - 45, 102, 107.
Rockets/missiles/thunderbolts - ii, 49, 73, 164.
Seven Heavens - 71, 85, 160-161, 246-248.
Several spaceships - 54.
Shield shaped - ii, 82.
Shuttle Craft - 72, 81, 84, 124, 175, 246.
Skipped/bowed-down - 66-68.
Some from Nibiru - 30.
Sound of - ii, 64-65, 103, 164, 174, 199.
Star of Bethlehem - 51, 188.
Teleportation - 51, 87, 262, 265.
"Beamed up" - 14, 51, 58, 65, 80-82, 86, 91-
92, 96, 123-124, 177, 253, 270.
Thunderbirds - 18, 63, 65, 72-73, 82, 105-

ABOUT THE AUTHOR

Dorothy Leon was born in a log cabin in the Missouri Ozarks in 1935. Arriving with a black "cap" atop her head, the local psychic said she had to be named Dorothy, meaning "gift of God", because she had a spiritual job to do. Throughout her life she felt as though she had a mystical connection.

She was transplanted to Oregon when her parents moved there after World War II, and it has been her home ever since. She majored in Journalism and counseling at Rogue Valley and Clackamas County Colleges, and later studied with Walter Russell's "University of Philosophy and Science" in Virginia. She studied with a Kahuna Priest in Hawaii in 1971, and began training for the Ministry at the "Cosmic Star Temple" in Roseburg, Oregon in 1973. She was ordained and also received a "Healing Practitioners License" in 1977. During this time she was also busy being a wife and mother.

She has written five other books: *Triangle From Mountains* (ley lines and energy vortexes), *The Clock With Thirteen Numbers* (thirteen steps of Ascension), *The Mystical Quest For Democracy* (the Ascended Masters' quest for freedom from Atlantean times onward), *The Three R's Series* (Reality of the Light, Reincarnation Reviewed and Revelation Revealed), and a humorous book *Tell Me About the Ozarks, Grandpa*. She has also written articles and poems for various magazines. She produced two videos: *Group Merkaba Vehicle* and *Reality of the Light*, and is also the founder of three spiritual organizations: the "Violet Flame Center", the "New Age Center" and the "Anchor of Golden Light Retreat". Over the years she has been active teaching, lecturing, writing and serving on the Board of Directors for three other spiritual organizations.

In addition to all this activity she pursues hobbies of music, gardening, hiking, bird watching and rock-hounding. Now living on a twenty-acre wilderness she says she has never experienced the meaning of the word "boring". "To me life is a daily adventure, both physically and mentally. There is so much yet to be discovered!"

You may communicate with Dorothy Leon by writing to:

Dorothy Leon
P.O. Box 724
Merlin, OR 97532

Please enclose a self-addressed, stamped envelope for reply.